Death and Culture

Series Editors: **Ruth Penfold-Mounce**, University of York, UK, **Kate Woodthorpe**, University of Bath, UK and **Erica Borgstrom**, The Open University, UK

Mortality is a research theme in evidence across multiple disciplines, but one that is not always explicitly acknowledged. This series provides an outlet for a social science and cross-disciplinary exploration of all aspects of mortality. The aim of the series is to create a forum for the publication of sociologically relevant research that approaches death from a cultural perspective, supported by evidence and framed by theoretical engagement. The series advances cross-disciplinary, international and social discussions about death and culture.

This series was previously published by Emerald Publishing as *Emerald Studies in Death and Culture*.

Forthcoming in the series

Dissection Photography
Cadavers, Abjection, and the Formation of Identity
By **Brandon Zimmerman**

Find out more

bristoluniversitypress.co.uk/
death-and-culture

Death and Culture

Series Editors: **Ruth Penfold-Mounce**, University of York, UK,
Kate Woodthorpe, University of Bath, UK and
Erica Borgstrom, The Open University, UK

International advisory board

Jacque Lynn Foltyn, National University, US
Margaret Gibson, Griffith Centre for Cultural Research, Australia
Hannah Gould, University of Melbourne, Australia
Tsepang Leuta, University of the Witwatersrand, South Africa
Lisa McCormick, University of Edinburgh, UK
Montse Morcate, University of Barcelona, Spain
Ben Poore, University of York, UK
Melissa Schrift, East Tennessee State University, US
Johanna Sumiala, University of Helsinki, Finland

Find out more

bristoluniversitypress.co.uk/
death-and-culture

DEATH'S SOCIAL AND MATERIAL MEANING BEYOND THE HUMAN

Edited by
Jesse D. Peterson, Natashe Lemos Dekker
and Philip R. Olson

First published in Great Britain in 2024 by

Bristol University Press
University of Bristol
1–9 Old Park Hill
Bristol
BS2 8BB
UK
t: +44 (0)117 374 6645
e: bup-info@bristol.ac.uk

Details of international sales and distribution partners are available at bristoluniversitypress.co.uk

© Bristol University Press 2024

British Library Cataloguing in Publication Data
A catalogue record for this book is available from the British Library

ISBN 978-1-5292-3014-7 hardcover
ISBN 978-1-5292-3015-4 ePub
ISBN 978-1-5292-3016-1 ePdf

The right of Jesse D. Peterson, Natashe Lemos Dekker and Philip R. Olson to be identified as editors of this work has been asserted by them in accordance with the Copyright, Designs and Patents Act 1988.

All rights reserved: no part of this publication may be reproduced, stored in a retrieval system, or transmitted in any form or by any means, electronic, mechanical, photocopying, recording, or otherwise without the prior permission of Bristol University Press.

Every reasonable effort has been made to obtain permission to reproduce copyrighted material. If, however, anyone knows of an oversight, please contact the publisher.

The statements and opinions contained within this publication are solely those of the editors and contributors and not of the University of Bristol or Bristol University Press. The University of Bristol and Bristol University Press disclaim responsibility for any injury to persons or property resulting from any material published in this publication.

Bristol University Press works to counter discrimination on grounds of gender, race, disability, age and sexuality.

Cover design: Liam Roberts Design
Front cover image: Oscar Bluemner, *Death*, 1926, Smithsonian American Art Museum, Bequest of Helen Hayes Smith
Bristol University Press uses environmentally responsible print partners.
Printed and bound in Great Britain by CPI Group (UK) Ltd, Croydon, CR0 4YY

Contents

List of Figures		vii
Note on the Figures		viii
Notes on Contributors		ix
Acknowledgements		xiii
Series Editors' Preface		xv

Introduction   1
Jesse D. Peterson, Natashe Lemos Dekker and Philip R. Olson

Part I   Ontologies and Epistemologies

1   'Seeing for Real': Forensic Pathologists Testing the Demonstrative Power of Postmortem Imaging   13
Céline Schnegg, Séverine Rey and Alejandro Dominguez

2   Death at a Planetary Scale: Mortality's Moral Materiality in the Context of the Anthropocene   27
Philip R. Olson

3   Death in the Fields: Microbial 'Destruction' in Polluted Soils   42
Serena Zanzu

4   Can the Baltic Sea Die? An Environmental Imaginary of a Dying Sea   54
Jesse D. Peterson

Part II   Care and Remembrance

5   Viral Flows and Immunological Gestures: Contagious and Dead Bodies in Mexico and Ecuador during COVID-19   71
Rosa Inés Padilla Yépez and Anne W. Johnson

6   Advertising the Ancestors: Ghanaian Funeral Banners as Image Objects   83
Isabel Bredenbröker

7   Dying Apart, Buried Together: COVID-19, Cemeteries and Fears of Collective Burial   100
Samuel Holleran

8	Spirit Mediums at the Margins: Materiality, Death and Dying in Northern Zimbabwe *Olga Sicilia*	114

Part III Troubling Agencies

9	Rehabilitate or Euthanize? Biopolitics and Care in Seal Conservation *Doortje Hoerst*	131
10	Troubling Entanglements: Death, Loss and the Dead in and on Television *Bethan Michael-Fox*	143
11	Material Entanglements of the Corpse *Marc Trabsky and Jacinthe Flore*	156
12	The Dead Who Would Be Trees and Mushrooms *Hannah Gould, Tamara Kohn, Michael Arnold and Martin Gibbs*	168
13	Beyond the Norms *Jesse D. Peterson, Natashe Lemos Dekker and Philip R. Olson*	180

Index 187

List of Figures

1.1	Radiological equipment	16
1.2	Autopsy room	17
1.3	Radiological and autopsy images of a cardiac death	18
2.1	Screenshots of Vimeo video created by Columbia University Graduate School of Architecture, Planning and Preservation, DeathLAB	30
2.2	Human composting system design developed by the Urban Death Project	33
2.3	Human composting system design developed by Recompose	34
4.1	Depiction of 'How water bodies change: Oligotrophic conditions versus eutrophic conditions'	58
4.2	Oxygen ratio effects on benthic fauna in the Kattegat	59
6.1	Obituary banners as welcome committee at the entrance to the town of Peki, Ghana, in November 2016	84
6.2	Obituary banner placed next to a stall selling cocoyam	86
6.3	Mixing of Christian and traditional imagery in obituary banners	88
6.4	Examples of good and bad death represented on obituary banners	89
6.5	Funeral poster and banner for Bright Akosua Brempong	92
6.6	Cleaning of George's funeral banner during dancing at the evening of the lying-in-state	93
6.7	Banner of Bobi worn by participant during the picking up of his body from the Peki morgue in 2017	94
6.8	Banner used as temporary headstone in the Peki-Avetile cemetery in 2016	95
6.9	Banner left on the roadside as trash	96
6.10	Funeral banner placed in the company of presidential election campaign advertisement	97

Note on the Figures

Some figures in this book have been published in a smaller size than our house style. To see full-sized versions of these figures, please visit https://bristoluniversitypress.co.uk/deaths-social-and-material-meaning-beyond-the-human

Notes on Contributors

Michael Arnold is Professor in the History and Philosophy of Science and a Science and Technology Studies scholar at the University of Melbourne. Arnold's ongoing research activities lie at the intersection of contemporary technologies and daily life; for example, studies of digital technologies in the domestic context, online memorials and other technologies associated with death, social networking, community informatics, and ethical and normative assessments of technologies.

Isabel Bredenbröker is a social and cultural anthropologist whose work focuses on material, sonic and visual culture, specifically the anthropology of death, afterlives of colonialism, synthetic materials, art and museums, queer theory and intersectionality. As Deutsche Forschungsgemeinschaft Walter Benjamin Postdoctoral Researcher, they work between the Centre for Anthropological Research on Museums and Heritage and the Hermann von Helmholtz-Zentrum für Kulturtechnik at Humboldt University Berlin.

Natashe Lemos Dekker is Postdoctoral Researcher at the Institute of Cultural Anthropology and Development Sociology at Leiden University. Her work focuses on death and dying, palliative care and ageing, both in the Netherlands and Brazil. She was awarded her PhD from the University of Amsterdam, in which she studied time and value at the end of life with dementia in the Netherlands. Her work has been published in the *Journal of the Royal Anthropological Institute*, *Death Studies* and *Culture, Medicine and Psychiatry*, among others. She was a visiting scholar at the University of California Los Angeles and the Université de Montréal and is a board member of the Medical Anthropology Europe Network.

Alejandro Dominguez is a forensic radiographer and Senior Lecturer at the School of Health Sciences (Haute Ecole de Santé Vaud [HESAV], University of Applied Sciences and Arts Western Switzerland). He has been technical manager for the last 15 years, until 2022, at the University Center of Legal Medicine – postmortem forensic and anthropology imaging unit. His research interests are linked with the employment of diagnostic techniques, including the use of computed tomography and postmortem angiography (contrast injections). He is in charge of the bachelor postmortem radiography courses.

Jacinthe Flore is Lecturer in Science and Technology Studies in the discipline of History and Philosophy of Science, School of Historical and Philosophical Studies at the University of Melbourne. She is an interdisciplinary researcher focused on the history of psychiatry, and the social implications of advanced technologies in mental health. She has published *A genealogy of appetite in the sexual sciences* (Palgrave Macmillan, 2020) and *The artefacts of digital mental health* (Palgrave Macmillan, 2023).

Martin Gibbs is Professor in the School of Computing and Information Systems at the University of Melbourne. His research interests include how people use interactive technologies (video games, community networks, mobile phones, and so on) for convivial and sociable purposes; the social dynamics of digital and board games; digital commemoration and the use of interactive technologies at end-of-life, including the future cemetery.

Hannah Gould is a sociocultural anthropologist working in the areas of death/discarding, religion and material culture. Her research is focused on how the deceased are memorialized and materialized in everyday life, with a regional focus on Northeast Asia. She is currently Melbourne Postdoctoral Fellow in the School of Social and Political Sciences at the University of Melbourne. Her first book, *When death falls apart*, was published by the University of Chicago Press in 2023.

Doortje Hoerst recently graduated from the Research Master Social Sciences at the University of Amsterdam. Her research focused on seal rehabilitation centres in the Netherlands and investigated care and multispecies entanglements in a framework of STS anthropology. She is now doing a PhD on women in sailing at the University of Queensland. Her research continues to engage with technologies and multispecies interactions, studying gender in practices of coastal leisure.

Samuel Holleran is PhD Candidate in the School of Culture and Communication at the University of Melbourne. His work focuses on urbanism and tools for public participation in the built environment; he is currently examining the reimagination of Melbourne's cemeteries. Previously, he was a researcher and educator at the Center for Urban Pedagogy in New York City and the Chair for Architecture & Urban Design at ETH-Zürich.

Anne W. Johnson is Professor of Anthropology in the Department of Social and Political Sciences at the Universidad Iberoamericana in Mexico City.

Her research engages with performance studies, historical memory, future imaginaries, science and technology, material culture, and the ethnography of Guerrero.

Tamara Kohn is Professor of Socio-cultural Anthropology in the School of Social and Political Sciences, the University of Melbourne. Kohn's current research focuses on creative practice, death studies, mobility and leisure, methods and ethics, and the anthropology of the body and senses, based on fieldwork in the United States, Japan and Australia.

Bethan Michael-Fox, SFHEA, FRSA teaches at The Open University on a range of English literature and language courses as well as interdisciplinary modules. She also works as Assistant Editor for the academic journal *Mortality* and is co-host of the *Death Studies Podcast*. Her research and publications focus on popular and unpopular cultural representations, in particular of death and the dead. You can find out more at www.drbethanmichaelfox.com

Philip R. Olson is a technology ethicist and Associate Professor in the Department of Science, Technology and Society at Virginia Tech. His work focuses on technologies of the human body (especially the dead body), and on gender, labour, expertise and technology. Born into a four-generations old funeral family, Phil has worked and lived with the dead and their caretakers all his life.

Rosa Inés Padilla Yépez is an anthropologist currently working at the College of Communication and Contemporary Arts at Universidad San Francisco de Quito. She holds a PhD in Social Anthropology from the Universidad Iberoamericana in Mexico City, and a Master's degree in Visual Anthropology from the Latin American Faculty of Social Sciences in Ecuador. Her research focuses on photography, representations of death, funerary spaces and rituals.

Jesse D. Peterson is Lecturer with the Radical Humanities Laboratory and School of Human Environment (Geography) at University College Cork. His research explores the relationships between life and environmental sciences, technology, and the arts in order to better understand how humans ascribe and derive meaning, purpose and value to and from nonhuman lives and phenomena. He researches more-than-human relations, environmental change, and science and technology (with a specific focus on biodiversity loss and environmental degradation) so that people can better resolve environmental challenges and achieve more just and mutually beneficial societies.

Séverine Rey is a socio-anthropologist and Senior Lecturer at the School of Health Sciences (Haute Ecole de Santé Vaud [HESAV], University of Applied Sciences and Arts Western Switzerland). She conducts research in two main fields: gender studies (particularly in relation to training and occupational integration) and anthropology of techniques (medical imaging and professional practice, clinical simulation in health professions training).

Céline Schnegg is a sociologist and Research Fellow at the School of Health Sciences (Haute Ecole de Santé Vaud [HESAV], University of Applied Sciences and Arts Western Switzerland). After a PhD thesis on prenatal alcohol exposure, she conducted a post-doctoral research on postmortem imaging in the forensic device. Her research interests focus on the articulation between care, diagnosis, technologies and ontology, in a pragmatic sociology perspective.

Olga Sicilia is an anthropologist based at the University of Vienna. Her research interests focus on ritual, memory work, phenomenological perspectives on spirit mediumship and the politics of ancestors in Northern Zimbabwe, and materiality and death. She is currently working on a prospective ethnographic monograph.

Marc Trabsky is Associate Professor and Australian Research Council Discovery Early Career Researcher Award Fellow at La Trobe Law School, La Trobe University. He writes on the intersections of law, dying and death. He has published *Law and the dead: Technology, relations and institutions* (Routledge, 2019) and *Death: New trajectories in law* (Routledge, 2023). He is also co-editing the *Routledge handbook of law and death* (Routledge, forthcoming 2024).

Serena Zanzu recently completed her PhD in the Department of Sociology at the University of Warwick. Her thesis examines the constitution of the soil microbiome across interconnected fields of expertise and practices in the UK. She holds an MA in Sociology and a BSc in Social Sciences.

Acknowledgements

In the five years that this book has been in the works, we have benefited from the intellectual, personal and professional support of many. This project began with support from the Department of History of Science, Technology and Environment at Kungliga Tekniska Högskolan (KTH) Royal Institute of Technology, who approved the workshop that initially brought us all together in the beautiful city of Stockholm in September 2019. The workshop, titled 'Dying at the margins: A critical exploration of material-discursive perspectives to death and dying', was supported through the Environmental Humanities for a Concerned Europe, with funding from the European Union's Horizon 2020 research and innovation programme under the Marie Sklodowska-Curie grant agreement No 642935. We are grateful to all the scholars and practitioners who shared their fascinating research during the KTH workshop and for encouraging us to pursue this project beyond the workshop. Thanks especially to Marietta Radomska, whose keynote address calling for a queering of death studies set the tone for challenging and productive conversations throughout our second day in Stockholm. Inspired by the success of the KTH workshop, we organized a follow-up open panel session at the 2020 Society for Social Studies of Science (4S) annual conference, which was held virtually (due to the COVID-19 pandemic) in Prague. Our gratitude goes out to all those who participated in the panel and to the 4S attendees whose interest in our project first prompted us to think about putting together an edited volume. Additionally, we are very grateful to the contributors to this volume for producing exciting research and letting us print it in this publication. We are grateful to all of those who shared their work with us and inspired us to move forward with this project over the years!

We are indebted to Ruth Penfold-Mounce, Julie Rugg and Jack Denham of the *Death and Culture* series for encouraging us to submit our book proposal to Bristol University Press and to Bristol University Press staff for their care, patience and advice throughout the publication process: Inga Boardman, Laura Vickers-Rendall, Jay Allen, Emily Ross, Amber Lanfranchi and Anna Richardson have each provided invaluable help and advice at various stages of the publication process. Thank you all!

Phil would like to thank his dear life partner and intellectual companion, Emily Satterwhite, for innumerable conversations about death, dying and disposal and for precious emotional and spiritual support through all phases of work and life. His thanks also extend to the Science and Technology Studies community at Virginia Tech – especially those who find themselves somewhat enlivened by thinking about death. Jesse also thanks the many supporters of this project at the four(!) institutions he has been a part of since this project began: Sabine Höhler and Marco Armiero at KTH, René Van Der Wal at Swedish University of Agricultural Sciences, Cecilia Åsberg and Marietta Radomska at Linköping University, and his research fellows with the Radical Humanities Laboratory at University College Cork, Ireland. Finally, Jesse thanks Claire for the numerous personal sacrifices she has made which have opened up opportunities for him, such as this book, and for her willingness to listen and empathize with him throughout this project. Natashe would like to extend her gratitude to Kristine Krause for her support at the University of Amsterdam and Annemarie Samuels at Leiden University. Finally, she would like to thank Arvid for thinking with throughout this project and for his support and care.

Series Editors' Preface

Erica Borgstrom, Ruth Penfold-Mounce and Kate Woodthorpe

About the series

Studying death can tell us an incredible amount about life. More specifically, it can illuminate a seemingly endless evolving relationship between humans and mortality. From sense-making and rituals around dying to how deceased persons are disposed of and even interwoven within human/nonhuman grief as ecologies shift, studying deaths not only deepens our understandings about loss and endings, but also of societies and culture. By attending to these matters, this book series seeks to shine a light on the cultural and social dimensions of death, exploring the wider contexts in which it is experienced, (re)presented and understood.

At a time when recognising the differences inherent in these broader sociocultural contexts has never been more important, the series adopts a broad use of the term 'culture' to enable us to bring together a rich multidisciplinary set of monographs and edited collections. We appreciate that the concept of culture has long been debated in several disciplines, most notably within anthropology, as well as contested in terms of how to optimally study 'culture'. While this series will acknowledge this, we do not seek to replicate some of these wider theoretical and epistemological debates. Rather, we want to open out 'culture' to include anthropological, sociological, historical and philosophical perspectives as well as drawing on media and culture studies, art and literature. By adopting such an open position to what culture is and how it can be known, we welcome both the sharing of new empirical work within the series as well as theorising about how engagements with death (re)shape understandings of what culture is, how it operates and what the future of culture(s) may be.

As social scientists spanning anthropology, sociology, criminology and cultural studies, and supported by an international editorial board that includes experts in death, dying and the dead our default position when thinking about death is typically two-fold. First, that death and dying are inherently social; that is, they are not only about biological or material processes and endings. Second, by attending to and foregrounding 'the social' when it comes to death, issues of culture and cultural practices necessarily organically come to the fore. Such is the importance of culture to death, that the topic does not 'fit' neatly into one discipline over another. It is a truly interdisciplinary issue that affects everyone who has lived, is living, or will live in the future; all life on the planet; and Earth itself.

This series launched in 2018 with Emerald Publishing, but relocated in 2021 to Bristol University Press. The series represents a commitment to empirically building our collective understandings about death and culture across time and places, in monographs and edited collections. As editors, we want to take this moment to thank existing and previous editors and authors, the presses we work with, and the wider academic and professional communities that facilitate the flourishing of studies of death and culture. It is only through this collective endeavour that books like this can be made, read and built upon, and we are excited to see the series grow. We welcome enquiries about future volumes, and hope that you enjoy reading this book.

About the book

Death's Social and Material Meaning Beyond the Human is an edited collection by Jesse D. Peterson, Natashe Lemos Dekker and Philip R. Olson with nearly 20 international contributors. Central to this collection is an in-depth handling, and detailed accounts of the entangling, of social meanings and materialities of dying and death. And importantly, this is 'beyond the human' – the limits are not the physical body that dies and how people make sense of this in finite terms. But across the volume readers learn to think about wider ecologies, technologies, politics and ethics. As outlined in the Introduction by the editors, across the 13 chapters they have provided material to enable us to see and discuss 'new forms of deathly concern'. Specifically, recognizing death as something that affects the entirety of the earth system and requires a more-than-human interdisciplinary dialogue to fully appreciate and act within these new forms.

This is a timely contribution to the *Death and Culture* series. Not a month goes by without news reporting about global warming and the ecological emergency that looms large: potential of mass death projected on the now and future. And yet, societally and internationally we are still learning how to think about this beyond questions of climate-friendly action. There is a desperate need to find new ways of being within and part of the earth system than what we currently inhabit, and as this collection shows, how we die within it. These new ways must be pluralistic, inclusive and draw on multiple forms of knowledge. The detailed and careful articulations in the chapters of this book illustrate how we may begin to do this as well as why this is important.

From considering dying seas to COVID-19 to transforming the waste of corpses into trees, each section within the book shows what is at stake. Cleverly, the editors and authors do not assume that what is at stake is a given or universally appreciated, nor is it situated purely around a nature/culture binary. Instead, they expertly unfold how the objects of their study matter and the ways in which they are understood by people. Culture here is not a monolithic external factor. Within some chapters, culture is something that is made visible through practices and values, a collective that is both regularly repeated by individuals and changed over time. In other chapters, authors talk about 'deathcare cultures' that represent dominate modes, discourses and professions that exert power over what it means to be human and the importance of death in certain contexts. Across these, by taking a more-than-human approach, the entanglements between culture and nature are made apparent.

For those more familiar with more-than-human approaches to academic study, the mighty and humble fungi will not be an unexpected companion in this text. If at this point an eyebrow is raised querying what is meant by that last sentence, dear reader you are in for a treat that spans dinner plates to forest floors and afterlives.

Introduction

Jesse D. Peterson, Natashe Lemos Dekker and Philip R. Olson

The third and final plate of mushroom risotto arrived. We were seated together at a Stockholm restaurant on the eve of a workshop on death and dying titled 'Dying at the margins: A critical exploration of material-discursive perspectives to death and dying', organized by Natashe Lemos Dekker and Jesse D. Peterson, with funding provided by the KTH Environmental Humanities Laboratory as part of the Environmental Humanities for a Concerned Europe innovative training network. The multidisciplinary workshop would bring together 16 scholars from nine different countries to connect scholars around research exploring how dying 'bodies' – broadly understood to include humans, animals, plants, things and places – challenge natural and normative notions of a 'good' death. Joining Natashe and Jesse at dinner was Phil Olson, who would give the next morning's keynote address. It seemed fitting that each of us would settle on fungus to nourish our minds and bodies during our first in-person meeting. After all, fungi are a symbol of decay, dissolution and putrefaction, fruiting harbingers that, by confronting their observers with the transformation of death back into life, challenge the definitions of the living, dying, alive, dead, not-alive, undead, and more. Reflecting on this moment, we can say that it was this very challenge that brought us together.

Though the three of us operate in different fields – Jesse in environmental humanities, Phil in science and technology studies, and Natashe in anthropology – we confirmed over the course of the next two days of workshop activities that we and the rest of the workshop participants were asking similar questions about how materialities, practices and stories challenge and complicate standard human conceptions of death and dying. Such questions are deeply important, as death's social and cultural meanings in society underscore practices ranging from efforts to defer death to preparations for funeral and burial rites; from practices of grief and mourning to forensic efforts to understand the causes of death; and from intervening in the processes of death and decomposition to interrogating the agentic dynamics of death and decomposition.

Enthused by a successful workshop, we three organized a 2020 4S/EASST (virtual) conference panel on the same theme but with all new contributors, some of whom have contributed to this volume. At this conference, entanglements between human and nonhuman death emerged, again, as a central theme. The growing COVID-19 pandemic inflected much of the conversation at the conference, but presenters on our panel shed light on the ways in which individuals, governments and other interest groups negotiate with non-pandemic forms of dying, including the disappearance of loved ones, the loss of a child before birth, the inability to care for oneself due to dementia, the planned eradication of an invasive plant, the successive extinction of multiple species, and the death of a river or lake. While we all must face our own inevitable deaths, we also encounter the countless deaths of others throughout our lives. By meeting the messiness of death and dying, we, as scholars, hope to stay with the complexity of loss, grief, relief, struggle and release that attend our many encounters with the demise and cessation of all lives.

After a successful 4S conference we were approached by a publisher other than Bristol University Press about possibly creating an edited volume around the topics explored in our panel. Having enjoyed working together, and feeling now some optimistic momentum, we were keen to explore the possibility of editing a volume together. Our call for proposals was met by over 50(!) submissions, indicating considerable interest in the subject matter of our call. We deliberated collectively about which press we should approach with a book proposal, and settled on Bristol University Press, to which the 'Death and Culture' series had recently moved.

Framing this book

This book explores the social meanings and materialities of death and dying by attending to death as a state, an event, a process, and as a site for political, scientific, medical, environmental and ethical negotiations regarding the significance of mortality. But across all these investments, the book underscores the relationality of death, for the primary motivation behind this project is to articulate (both in the sense of stating and in the sense or establishing connections between) new forms of deathly concern that affect not only humans but the entire earth system and that necessitate new thinking and interdisciplinary exchange for situating death, and human relationships to it, in more-than-human terms.

Death studies typically take the death of the human subject as its object of study, thereby overlooking the wider networks of relations involved in social and natural processes surrounding death. Yet, as the COVID-19 pandemic and the climate crisis have shown, human death intermingles with microorganisms, environmental conditions, developments in science and medicine, and more. Additionally, as a result of anthropogenic changes to the planet Earth, humans must also deal with the nonhuman deaths we cause and the complicated material, emotional and practical consequences that the loss of nonhuman creatures and entities may entail. While death as a more-than-human affair – as a category built upon human emotions and knowledge, as well as human relationships with technologies, more-than-human beings and socio-ecological environments – has existed at the margins of death studies research, we see more scholarly attention devoted to the ecological, material and queer aspects of death and dying. For instance, the recent emergence of queer death studies challenges the primacy of human death as the only kind of death of interest as well as focuses on the 'necropolitics' surrounding the dead (Mbembé, 2003; Radomska et al, 2019: 5). Scholars working in this arena explore 'queer' bonds between the living and dead as well as 'queer' this relationship (Radomska et al, 2019: 6). They point to the epistemological and symbolic violence that marks some deaths as more valuable than others (Radomska et al, 2020). Additionally, scholars working in extinction studies look beyond the death of the individual human to explore how species extinctions – driven by humans – complicate and transform understandings of death, time and generations (Heise, 2016; Rose et al, 2017). While others working on environmental issues continue to explore the degradation of environments (Tsing et al, 2017; Lidström et al, 2022), the poisonous toxicities and wastes that infiltrate human and other creatures' bodies (Alaimo, 2010; Armiero et al, 2019; Muller and Nielsen, 2022), and the political, social and cultural moves which make some lives 'killable' (Haraway, 2008: 77–82; Beisel, 2010; Mehrabi, 2020). In the natural sciences, additional philosophical and conceptual conversations that define life as ecosystemic rather than organismic (Fiscus, 2001) or as flows of energy masses (Wei et al, 2022) also present unique formulations for application by scholars researching dying and death. Each of these various strands of research dealing with the death of people, places and other beings offers fruitful ground for extending human knowledge and practices surrounding the dying and the dead.

This collection brings these marginal matters into focus, centring discussion of the death of nonhuman others, the relational materiality of the human corpse, new narratives about the work of death caretakers, and newly emerging deathcare practices and technologies. The transdisciplinary and transnational character of this collection reveals how deeply human death is intertwined with the lives and deaths of nonhuman things, objects, places and discourses. By shedding light on deaths and dyings that exist in many unlooked-for places, this collection challenges death studies' focus on human death, as well as the norms that govern standard approaches to studying human death. Thus, this volume addresses urgent questions facing death research, including:

- What boundary work takes place to construct and maintain the categories of alive, not-alive, dead, dying and undead for places, objects and beings?
- How do modes of existing between life and death affect normative categorizations of the living, the non-living and the dead?
- What are the implications of reconfiguring understandings of death to a more ecological frame that accommodates more-than-human lives and deaths?
- How do such challenges alter ethical approaches and values attached to dying and death?

The contents of this book

This volume draws together diverse material-discursive perspectives on socio-ecological networks of the dying and dead. In addition to gathering a wide range of international perspectives – contributors hail from North America, Europe, Asia, Africa and Oceania – this collection showcases a range of theoretical and methodological approaches to the study of death and dying from scholars doing cutting-edge research in death studies, feminist and queer studies, new materialism and waste studies, plant and animal studies, and non-Western or indigenous studies. In so doing, this volume broadens the scope of conventional research on death and dying, and focuses the discussion towards death as a more-than-human affair. Thinking and writing along the themes of mediation, care and power, the collection further challenges normative understandings and categories of life and death.

The organization of edited volumes always involves choices about how best to draw out certain contents by grouping specific chapters in distinct parts, and in particular orders. Recognizing that these choices always take place among a field of possible alternative arrangements, we have organized the book's chapters into three parts, which, respectively, highlight the themes of (I) ontologies and epistemologies of death and dying, (II) care and remembrance, and (III) troubling agencies.

Part I explores how scientific, technological and discursive practices mediate ontologies and epistemologies of death in human bodies, microbial soil communities, waterbodies, and at large scales. These chapters challenge normative understandings of death by exposing the complexity of material and creaturely forms of death and dying, and by critically examining relationships between individual and collective death. The chapters collected in this section also highlight new perspectives occasioned by new medical and funerary technologies, growing concerns about the harmful effects of anthropogenic climate change, and the interests of nonhuman organisms.

Grounded in fieldwork conducted in a Swiss forensic medicine department that is on the cutting-edge of new postmortem imaging technologies, Céline Schnegg, Séverine Rey and Alejandro Dominguez explore ontological and epistemological negotiations between conventional autopsy techniques (*in situ*) and emerging radiological technologies (including MRI and CT scans). Their opening chapter reveals how new imaging technologies are taken up by radiologists and pathologists who are generating and responding to new forms of evidence – even new, onto-epistemic 'realities' of the dead body – as well as new forms of expertise in the morally and legally charged field of forensic investigation. While some postmortem imaging enthusiasts have proposed that new imaging techniques could one day replace conventional autopsy practices, Schnegg et al point out that, in practice, postmortem imaging tends to serve as a compliment to *in situ* examination, which, for the time being, retains its ascendancy in forensic investigation. In Chapter 2, Philip Olson, too, examines how the development and use of new technologies has challenged normative practices, and how those norms have pushed back against technology-backed challenges. Using discourse analysis to examine long-standing proscriptions against the 'commingling' of human remains, Olson argues that thinking about and designing for death at large scales has provoked a moral dialectic that moves between individual and collective death, and between anthropocentric and ecocentric perspectives on death's meaning and materiality. Reconciliation across constructed scales of death and disposition calls for an alignment of human purposes and natural processes, Olson argues; and achieving this alignment, he concludes, may require explicit attention to collective deathcare policy. Collective death emerges as a point of interest in Serena Zanzu's Chapter 3 as well. Interrogating the exploitative instrumentalism that has dominated human–microbe relations in bioremediation practices, Zanzu evokes the 'microbial turn' as a means by which to 'problematize the human understanding of individuated death', and to make space for appreciating the (sometimes engineered) death of whole microbial communities. In bioremediation practices, the termination of invisible, microbial life is understood as 'destruction', but not 'authentic death', because microbes are reduced to tools or potential threats. Zanzu concludes that a microbiopolitcs of the invisible may generate new narratives of life and death that enrich microbial being with non-instrumental value. In Chapter 4, Jesse Peterson rounds out Part I of the volume by drawing explicit attention to the question of what sorts of beings or entities can live or die. Provoked by characterizations of the Baltic Sea as 'dead' or 'dying', Peterson illustrates how cultural and scientific representations of the sea contribute to an environmental imaginary of a dying Baltic Sea. Valuations of specific characteristics of the sea's water shape ideas about the sea's 'natural' state, and about 'unnatural' threats to those valued characteristics. Guided by an onto-epistemic pluralism that resonates with Schnegg et al's Chapter 1, Peterson notes that a dying Baltic Sea is one among many possible Baltic Seas, each of which consists of a different set of value-laden claims about its water, and each of which could 'die' if that definitive set of characteristics undergoes substantial changes.

Part II (care and remembrance) focuses on the sociality of caring for, and disposing of deceased bodies, and the prominence of the body in processes of grief and remembrance. From banners that materialize the deceased in absence of the body (Bredenbröker, Chapter 6) and ambiguous relations between spirit and body (Sicilia, Chapter 8), to COVID-19 protocols for treatment of 'contagious' bodies (Yépez and Johnson, Chapter 5) and fears of mass burial (Holleran, Chapter 7), the chapters in this section provide insight into the cultural significance of deceased bodies. They show how the discursive and physical spaces occupied by the dead may transform relationships with the dead and among the living, in so doing probing into issues of affect, memory and responsibility. In different ways, all of the chapters deal with questions of containment and separation of dead bodies. Moreover, the chapters consider what happens when ethical obligations towards the dead cannot be fulfilled due to cultural, biological, institutional or temporal constraints. This exposes some of the values and expectations that underpin memorialization and notions of a good death, as expressed in funerary practices and postmortem care relations.

In Chapter 5, Rosa Inés Padilla Yépez and Anne W. Johnson reflect on the experiences of family members of people who died of COVID-19 infections in Mexico and Ecuador. Family members were in many cases prohibited from accompanying the dying person and from practising funerary rituals, which has had a detrimental effect on the mourning process. Yépez and Johnson relate this experience to the sanitary protocols that were enforced in funerary and healthcare institutions, and which were based on a logic of containment and separation. They argue that such protocols are a way in which states exercise power over the lives and deaths of citizens – a form of power that also faces resistance in the families' creative practices. Isabel Bredenbröker explores in Chapter 6 the cultural significance of obituary banners in Ghana. Based on fieldwork, they suggest that these funeral banners, which depict the deceased person and are placed centrally in the community, materialize the important position of the dead in social life. Their analysis of the changes in mortuary practices from colonization through to the present, reveals that the banners enable a good death for the deceased by blending indigenous and Christian ways of responding to death, which involves both separation from the body of the deceased and their continued presence in the community. Returning to COVID-19 in Chapter 7, Samuel Holleran traces contemporary fears of mass burial through an historical analysis of images of death and large-scale burials that proliferated in the media during the pandemic. Holleran juxtaposes these images and the fears they represent with emerging death technologies, such as *hakatomo* and human composting. Such alternative modes of disposition, he suggests, might be understood as shifting the cultural perception of collective burial, although public reception and social and religious customs may hold their acceptance in check. Continuing in the theme of culturally problematized funerary practices, in Chapter 8, Olga Sicilia draws on fieldwork in Zimbabwe to describe the funerary protocols and practices for deceased spirit mediums. Sicilia shows that, as the deceased body is considered to incorporate both the person and a spirit ancestor, deceased spirit mediums are treated in a distinct way and separated from relatives. As in Yépez and Johnson's chapter, this separation and absence of the body means relatives struggle to mourn their relatives. Moreover, she relates this to the complexities and cultural (in)appropriateness of disgust in relation to the decaying body.

Part III brings together research on the human and nonhuman agencies that 'trouble' the world of the living. Ranging from seal population management, those who refuse to stay buried, legal definitions of human cadavers, and the promise for an ecological afterlife, chapters in this section raise critical questions regarding what objects and discourses influence dying and death and what benefits and consequences arise therefrom. They evidence how nonhuman agencies enacted by lungworms, television series, legal definitions and burial continuously interrupt and trouble our conceptions of death, who deserves to die, and what to do about the dead.

In Chapter 9, Doortje Hoerst looks at how lungworms enact biopolitical relationships in collaboration with scientists, veterinarians and the general public. Using a material semiotics approach, Hoerst focuses on the multispecies entanglements between seals, lungworm parasites and the Dutch rehabilitation scientists who are studying infected seals. In the matter of the life and death of these seals, Hoerst displays how the pragmatics of policy and the ethics of care place hold on how these veterinarians respond to seals dying from lungworm infection. Based on her anthropological data, she challenges an exclusive attribution of biopolitical power to human actors by revealing that lungworms, too, enact biopolitical power in ways that impact conservation care practices. In Chapter 10, Bethan Michael-Fox provides a look into how materialities of television apparatus and narrative function as a space where 'morbid' relationalities get enacted through an analysis of the French supernatural television drama series, *Les Revenants* (2012–2015). Drawing on feminist theory to provide a diffractive analysis, she points to how such relationalities issue practical and theoretical challenges to the dichotomies of 'alive/dead' and 'then/now'. That is, she shows us how the dead who return in this series upset notions of death as a final state and time as a linear construct and explains that these once/now dead characters draw attention to the diminished power and agency of the self in the face of the prospect of planetary extinction.

In Chapter 11, Marc Trabsky and Jacinthe Flore illustrate how the human corpse and the lucrative necro-waste extracted from it trouble the legal frameworks that legislate the dead body. They illustrate how understanding the corpse through feminist new materialism breaks down and challenges the corpse as both person and thing. Instead, they argue, corpses ought to be considered as 'emergent material-discursive' phenomena and suggest that 'this re-conceptualization potentially can animate an improved regulation of the global trade in cadaveric tissue'. In Chapter 12, Hannah Gould and her co-authors explore the imaginaries of ecological afterlives, highlighting different burial practices that promise to convert the dead into trees or mushrooms. Thinking seriously with these beings, they highlight the differences in arboreal versus mycelial afterlives and point out how imagining the dead as angels is becoming more grounded and earth-bound. Doing so, they argue that vernacular values are caught up in and vivified by the biological forms and symbolic values proffered by these and other organisms that can have an ecological relationship with the deceased.

In Chapter 13, the book's concluding discussion, we summarize core findings across all sections of the book, suggesting future trajectories for transdisciplinary death scholarship. Focusing in particular on the various new relationalities explored in this volume, we articulate a number of the ecological, social and philosophical implications of the contributors' research. We hope the rich, interdisciplinary work contained in this volume will inspire deeper conversations about the complex socio-ecological dynamics of death, dying and deathcare that await the attention of scholars, practitioners and artists working across a variety of fields.

References

Alaimo, S. (2010) *Bodily natures: Science, environment, and the material self.* Bloomington: Indiana University Press.

Armiero, M., Andritsos, T., Barca, S., Brás, R., Ruiz Cauyela, S., Dedeoğlu, Ç. et al (2019) Toxic bios: Toxic autobiographies – A public environmental humanities project. *Environmental Justice*, 12(1): 7–11.

Beisel, U. (2010) Jumping hurdles with mosquitoes? *Environment and Planning D: Society and Space*, 28(1): 46–49.

Fiscus, D. (2001) The ecosystemic life hypothesis I: Introduction and definitions. *Bulletin of the Ecological Society of America*, 82(4): 248–250.

Haraway, D. (2008) *When species meet.* Minneapolis: University of Minnesota Press.

Heise, U.K. (2016) *Imagining extinction.* Chicago: University of Chicago Press.

Lidström, S., Meyer, T. and Peterson, J.D. (2022) The metaphor of ocean 'health' is problematic: 'The ocean we want' is a better term. *Frontiers in Marine Science*, 9: 1–4.

Mbembé, J.-A. (2003) Necropolitics. Translated by L. Meintjes. *Public Culture* 15(1): 11–40.

Mehrabi, T. (2020) Queer ecologies of death in the lab: Rethinking waste, decomposition and death through a queerfeminist lens. *Australian Feminist Studies*, 35(104): 138–154.

Muller, S. and Nielsen, M.O. (2022) *Toxic timescapes: Examining toxicity across time and space*. Athens: Ohio University Press.

Radomska, M., Mehrabi, T. and Lykke, N. (2019) Queer death studies: Coming to terms with death, dying and mourning differently. An introduction. *Women, Gender and Research*, (3–4): 3–11.

Radomska, M., Mehrabi, T. and Lykke, N. (2020) Queer death studies: Death, dying and mourning from a queerfeminist perspective. *Australian Feminist Studies*, 35(104): 81–100.

Rose, D.B., van Dooren, T. and Chrulew, M. (2017) *Extinction studies: Stories of time, death, and generations*. New York: Columbia University Press.

Tsing, A.L., Bubandt, N., Gan, E. and Swanson, H.A. (eds) (2017) *Arts of living on a damaged planet: Ghosts and monsters of the Anthropocene*. Minneapolis: University of Minnesota Press.

Wei, Y., Yang, Y., Zhang, Y., Mu, Z. and Bu, F. (2022) A frame theory of energetic life: A twisting energy solidified on the holographic fractal structure. *Applied Sciences*, 12(21): 10930.

PART I

Ontologies and Epistemologies

1

'Seeing for Real': Forensic Pathologists Testing the Demonstrative Power of Postmortem Imaging

Céline Schnegg, Séverine Rey and Alejandro Dominguez

In cases of homicides or suspicious deaths, corpses undergo a series of technical and scientific tests during examination to make them 'talk' and to establish the cause of death. Nowadays, modern postmortem imaging is increasingly being used to complement conventional autopsy (Grabherr et al, 2017). Specific features characterize each imaging technique. For example, postmortem computed tomography (PMCT) provides a view of the whole body in just a few minutes and allows excellent visualization of the skeleton (trauma cases), gases, fluids and foreign materials (such as projectiles) (Grabherr et al, 2017). PMCT angiography artificially re-establishes blood circulation by means of a perfusion system, enabling the full investigation of the vascular system; most importantly, it can detect the exact source of bleeding, for example, in a case of aneurysm or haemorrhage (Grabherr et al, 2018). Postmortem magnetic resonance imaging (MRI) is the only radiological technique that provides good visualization of soft tissues and organs; however, its use is still limited to paediatric cases due to the duration of the examinations and the lack of scientific research supporting its diagnostic power in postmortem cases (Magnin et al, 2020). Postmortem imaging is a unique visualization tool that allows visual examination of the inside of a body before opening it. Thus, forensic pathologists would know in advance the lesions they will find during the autopsy, enabling them to efficiently prepare their instruments and conduct an accurate examination. These techniques also make it possible to observe lesions that are difficult to detect through autopsy, such as multiple fractures in the case of polytrauma or even the source of haemorrhage. In this way, autopsy and imaging are considered complementary techniques in the scientific literature, which argues that their combined use improves the sensitivity and quality of postmortem examinations (Grabherr et al, 2018; Michaud et al, 2019).

However, the challenge of integrating postmortem imaging techniques into the forensic investigation process cannot be limited to simply adding further techniques to the chain of investigations on a body. During our ethnographical fieldwork in a forensic medicine department that uses and develops postmortem imaging, we were confronted on several occasions with debates between forensic doctors and imaging specialists discussing discrepancies between radiological interpretations and direct observations of the body. How could they explain that a vertebral fracture, clearly visible at autopsy, could not be seen on the computerized tomography (CT) images? How is it that the forensic pathologist, holding the spleen and its peripheral vessels in her hands, is unable to discern the origin of a leakage in the splenic vein described by the radiologist? Why are the coronary arteries clean on dissection of the heart when postmortem angiography suggests stenosis? This lack of overlap between lesions seen in situ and on CT scans can be explained by the different sensitivities of autopsy and radiological techniques, each providing specific insights into the interior of the body.

From a sociological perspective, we postulate that those situations of discordance are moments of friction concerning the reality of the lesions, and reflect on the practical and ontological transformations (Cussins, 1996; Mol, 2002; Woolgar and Lezaun, 2013) associated with the integration of postmortem imaging techniques into the 'dispositif' (Dodier and Barbot, 2021) of forensic investigations.[1] The addition of this radiological sequence has important organizational, practical and reflexive consequences and requires adjustments on the part of forensic pathologists. By offering a new view of the inside of the body, imaging techniques have transformed the entire investigation process. For example, radiological images can now be used as autopsy guides. Yet, the mobilization of these two types of exams – autopsy and radiological imaging – generates ontological tensions involving the distinction between inert bodies and life simulation, real organs and their virtual reconstructions, natural organisms and artificial perfusion of vessels, and visualization through the screen and direct attestation in the autopsy room. More precisely, we argue that these two techniques *enact* two 'realities' of the body and its lesions that are not necessarily congruent (Berg and Mol, 1998; Law and Mol, 2002; Mol, 2002). Thus, when radiology and scalpels do not tell the same truth, forensic pathologists work to test and reconcile these two 'versions' of the body. During their ontological inquiry, they make a distinction between the 'real' elements and the 'artefactual' ones, discussing the respective demonstrative power of radiological techniques and autopsy. In the same movement, pathologists attribute different degrees of reality to lesions or pathologies, thus untangling the 'true' from the 'wrong' in the determination of the cause of death. In contrast to the clinical field, where radiological images have diagnostic power due to their visual evidence (Burri, 2012), their demonstrative value has generated further debates in the postmortem domain, where imaging results can and must be compared with in situ examination of organs and cavities. Therefore, postmortem imaging raises specific questions insofar as the radiologists' field of action overlaps with that of forensic pathologists and direct attestation through autopsy.

Following other ethnographic studies on forensic practices (Timmermans, 2006; Juston, 2020), we develop a pragmatic analysis of expertise and judgment (Bowen et al, 2021; Tavory and Timmermans, 2013).[2] Here, we conceive the passage of the body in forensic medicine as a series of tests (Chateauraynaud, 2004; Dodier and Barbot, 2021) enabling forensic pathologists, mandated by the court, to determine the causes of death. The body is subjected to various examinations (scene investigation, external examination, radiological exams, autopsy, laboratory analyses) that depend on specific techniques and instruments (scalpel, ruler, voice recorder, camera, CT scan, MRI). Submitted to these different types of tests, a corpse undergoes more or less reversible transformations as well as successive translations and reductions (Latour, 1986; Reed et al, 2016) to demonstrate tangibility (Chateauraynaud, 2004). Thus, the nature of the body and its lesions change according to their engagement in the different sequences of the investigative dispositif, especially during the imaging and autopsy phases; hence, the body becomes alternatively talkative, mute, opaque, transparent, docile, versatile or resistant to the manipulations of forensic pathologists, radiologists and radiographers (Schnegg and Rey, 2017). However, it is also the 'reality' of the lesions that fluctuates, implying the work of coordination (Mol, 2002; Moreira, 2006) and reconciliation among the different versions of the body by the forensic doctors. This work is imperative because both the reputations of forensic pathologists and the quality of the exam are always at stake. Furthermore, the presence of discrepancies in the medico-legal report could lead to the challenging of its conclusions in court.

In our study, we conducted a long-term ethnography[3] in a Swiss forensic medicine centre, which has a CT scanner, a Virtangio®[4] and an MRI. The imaging unit consists of a radiologist, several radiographers and forensic pathologists specializing in imaging, all of whom work in close collaboration with the forensic medicine unit, which includes forensic pathologists and autopsy assistants. During our fieldwork, we observed the performance of the various examinations and the ways in which the staff handled the instruments and radiological equipment (Figure 1.1). We focused on the gestures of the professionals handling the bodies, especially the ways in which they observe, touch, feel, cut and mobilize the bodies or their parts (organs and samples). We also paid attention to the more or less

Figure 1.1: Radiological equipment. From right to left: mobile X-ray equipment, CT scanner and Virtangio®

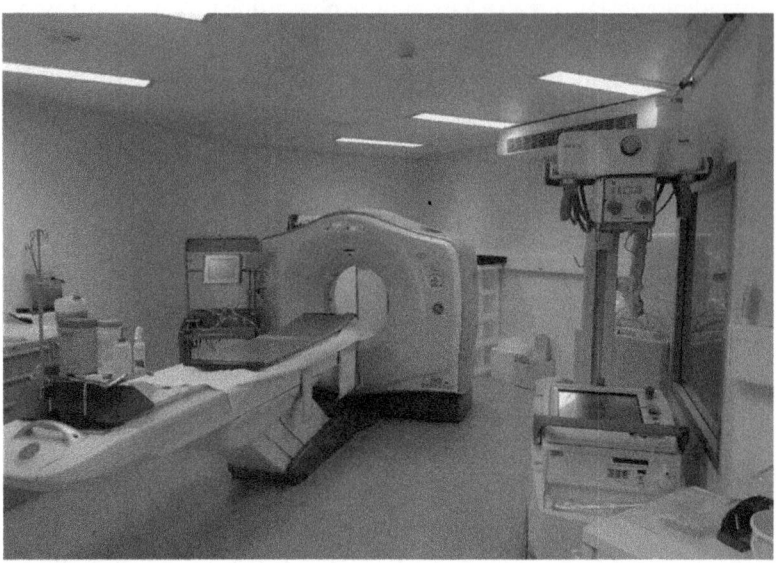

institutionalized moments of discussion (morning meetings and briefings following autopsies), in which senior and resident pathologists[5] debated about the work organization, indications and results of the various examinations, particularly the radiological ones.

The centre has developed its own protocol for examining bodies. First, all bodies are scanned before undergoing an external examination and/or autopsy (Figure 1.2), depending on the prosecutor's mandate. Additional radiological exams are discussed on a case-by-case basis. Their performance depends on arbitrations made by pathologists and radiologists in relation to forensic requests, the circumstances of the death, the nature of the body to be examined and the sensitivity of each technique, which may or may not inform the judgement of the forensic experts in charge of the case. For a woman who died in front of her home a few hours after an angioplasty, forensic doctors recommended an angiography to check the permeability of the vessels and to exclude any vascular injuries related to the procedure. In the case of a man who was stabbed several times, angiography was supposed to help identify fatal trajectories and lesions. In cases of sudden paediatric death, MRI was mainly used to visualize fractures and infiltrations of soft tissues, all of which are signs of possible child abuse.

How do pathologists confront radiological interpretations and direct observation of organs, vessels and the skeleton? How do they work with these two versions, which can be discordant, and try to reconcile

Figure 1.2: Autopsy room. From right to left: autopsy table, dissection board with instruments (scalpel, ruler, surgical scissors), scales for weighing organs, cupboard containing equipment (gloves, masks, gowns, glasses, jars, scalpels)

them? We will now focus on four cases and the different configurations, as well as the strategies of confrontation or combination of techniques and views. We will analyse the moments of debate as central places of reconciliation of the radiological and autopsy versions of the body or, on the contrary, of the disqualification of one version in favour of the other, all while questioning the respective probative force and sensitivity of each technique used.

Guiding the pathologist's view

In most cases, radiological images are used as the first version of the internal composition of a body – one that guides and frames the forensic pathologists' investigations. Several pathologists explain that imaging makes it possible to 'open up a path', 'define a plan of action' and 'visualize the autopsy', mainly because it provides a first map of lesions and pathologies that are necessarily indicative and transitory until the direct confrontation with bodily organs (Figure 1.3). Following this logic, radiological images are interpreted before an autopsy, and the most relevant results of this initial radiological scanning are transmitted to the team. The following case highlights the use of imaging as a tool to guide the autopsy.

Figure 1.3: Radiological and autopsy images of a cardiac death: a 30-year-old man complaining for some weeks of pain in the left arm and found dead at home. The PMCT did not show calcification or occlusion (circled in the image [a]). The angiography (images not available here) allowed the visualization of a severe nearly completely occluding stenosis. The autopsy presented a macroscopic view of a thrombosis in an artery (b)

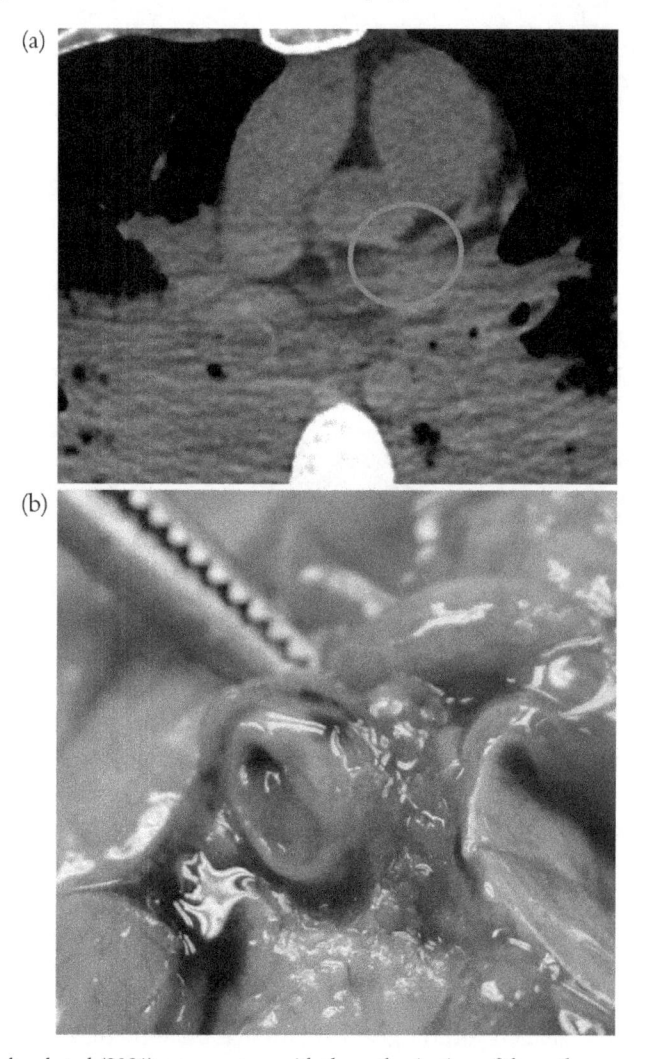

(a)

(b)

Source: Michaud et al (2021), open access, with the authorization of the authors.

> Dr Moser [resident pathologist] presents the case during the morning meeting. A man in his 50s collapsed while picking mushrooms with his partner who explained that he collapsed after intercourse. The team postulates an intoxication linked to picking. The body first undergoes a CT scan. On the images, the radiologist sees a large meningeal haemorrhage and proposes an angiography. Dr Moser agrees because she says angiography can help determine the origin of the ruptured aneurysm (which can be very difficult to find during autopsy). She can also temporarily put aside the intoxication hypothesis and focus the autopsy on the cerebral haemorrhage. During the autopsy, before opening the skull, she tells the autopsy assistant to be careful because there will be some blood and a haematoma. (Observation notes, reformulated extracts, Case 1, 2018)

The addition of this radiological sequence makes it possible to 'know before opening' the body, so to speak. The autopsy follows a standard protocol, with a systematic examination of all organs in a precise order. The forensic pathologists in the autopsy room can also anticipate a ruptured aneurysm and the presence of a haematoma when opening the skull cap. The eyes of the forensic pathologists confirm and validate what is seen on the screen (that is, a haematoma), the origin of which will be confirmed by the neuropathological examination. In this case, the autopsy version of the body supports and confirms its radiological version. These two versions of the body are consistent, while the radiological interpretation remains indicative, aiming to guide the physicians' view.

The same applies to cardiac cases, where angiographic images indicate to the pathologists the presence or location of a coronary stenosis, which is confirmed (or not) by the systematic examination and cutting of the heart. In this procedure, the coronary arteries are opened 'in slices' to determine whether there is thrombotic material that effectively obstructs the passage of the lumen. If, in these cases, the imaging guides the examination of organs and cavities, then both autopsy and the forensic eye attest lesions: only the autopsy test can provide evidence.

Seen but not attestable

The interpretation of radiological images performed as an initial sequence may, in certain situations, trouble the judgement of forensic pathologists. This happens when the two versions of the body, generated by the radiological and autopsy tests, are discordant, as in the following case.

A woman in her 60s with a known history of heart disease collapsed while shovelling snow. As it happened in front of witnesses and her death seemed natural, the prosecutor only asked for an external examination. During the morning meeting, the pathologists assume a cardiac death. The body undergoes a CT scan. Dr Jaccot [resident pathologist] carries out the external examination, during which he describes in detail the surface of the body and palpates the limbs and chest to determine whether any fractures can be found. He doesn't notice suspicious clues that would suggest third-party intervention (for example traumatic lesions). However, when Dr Müller [resident pathologist, imaging unit] looks at the CT images,[6] she notices that the intubation tube, used by paramedics for resuscitation, went instead to the oesophagus (and not the trachea) and that resuscitation attempt had been ineffective. She then calls Dr Kohler [senior pathologist] to relay this observation. I can hear Dr Kohler asking Dr Müller why she has looked at the images and then abruptly hanging up. (Observation notes, reformulated extracts, Case 5, 2019)

In this case, Dr Müller saw something she should not have seen, and that created confusion. The prosecutor only asked for an external examination and limited the possible attestation of the doctors; however, the radiological images gave her access to the inside of the body, in which the intubation defect was observed. The team of pathologists must consider what to do with this information. The first option would be to consider it relevant and invite the prosecutor to investigate further; in other words, an autopsy could be suggested to determine whether the woman would have survived with proper resuscitation. This option involves questioning whether the emergency services team's response was responsible for her death. The second option, finally chosen by Dr Kohler after discussion, is to reduce the significance of this discrepant information by reporting that an external examination does not allow for a judgement on the cause of death: 'The radiological examination by CT scan showed the presence of anterior fractures of several ribs, as well as the intubation cannula placed in the esophagus. No major traumatic injury was found to explain death. The cause of death was not established based on the external examination' (extract from the autopsy report). The discrepancy between the body seen by the pathologists and the body represented by the radiological images is resolved by simply mentioning the intubation defect that, following the prosecutor's mandate, would have remained unseen. Insofar as the objective of the examination was achieved (that is, to exclude major traumatic injuries by examining only the surface of the body), the mention of this intubation defect becomes secondary, as it is not the cause of death. With only the sequence of external examination, the forensic pathologists do not have access to the body's interior and cannot document it. Even if the CT scan is performed, the radiological body, following the pathologists' argument, has no explanatory power because it cannot be confirmed by the autopsy test.

The body contradicts images

Tensions also emerge in cases where imaging and autopsy do not overlap. For example, lesions found during an autopsy may be missed or invisible on imaging. These situations often involve vertebral fractures that may be difficult to discern on CT images, particularly in cases of compression fractures. They induce transitory trouble on the pathologists' judgement as they confront the body's inside.

A 75-year-old man, obese and polyvascular, was found unconscious in the alley next to his home and finally died in the hospital. Dr Moser [resident pathologist] and Dr Rüegg [senior pathologist], who are in charge of the case, start on the cardiac track. The angiography shows nothing special, apart from bypasses and permeable stents. The autopsy reveals multiple cardiopathies and pleural effusions. As the autopsy nears completion (the chest and abdomen are empty), Dr Rüegg examines the spine from the inside and finds a fracture of D8 that has not been described on the CT scan. She wonders how it happened: "Is it a compression fracture? There is nothing visible in the back [on external examination], and it raises questions", she says, lifting the body to check again. Both doctors wonder whether this fracture is an artefact of the autopsy that should be disregarded and ask the autopsy assistant if the body has been handled roughly. She answers "No", so the hypothesis of autopsy artefact is ruled out. Dr Rüegg and Dr Moser think that this fracture is visible on the CT scan and that it should be checked. Finally, part of the spine is removed for examination after fixation. At the next day's meeting, hearing about this fractured vertebra, a senior doctor asks both doctors to re-examine the body and dissect the back and limbs to rule out a fall or shock by identifying any haemorrhagic suffusions. (Observation notes, reformulated extracts, Case 6, 2019)

In this example, the discrepancy between the radiological and autopsy views raises questions and destabilizes the judgement of the doctors examining the body: as the CT scan has excellent sensitivity at the bone level, Dr Rüegg and Dr Moser expect the fracture to be visible on the images. The two pathologists then start an inquiry into the ontological nature of the lesion by successively disqualifying its autopsy version, hypothesizing that the fracture is an artefact linked to abrupt handling of the body, and its radiological version, postulating a reading error of the images. This discordance reduction strategy fails because of the medico-legal importance of such a lesion in the sense that it may indeed suggest a fall or that someone pushed the old man. Therefore, it must be documented by additional examinations (incisions of the back and limbs and inspection of the vertebrae once fixed in formalin) and a re-reading of the CT images. In doing so, this fracture will finally be qualified as a compression fracture, implying that it was not caused by an impact. Moreover, despite the CT scan sensitivity, this type of lesion is difficult to see on the images or even invisible. This qualification thus makes it possible to reconcile the autopsy and radiological versions of the body. The discordance, a lesion identified during autopsy but not on the images, temporarily troubled the judgement of the two pathologists in the autopsy room, but it did not weaken the quality of expertise in the final report: the autopsied body, which was opened and whose lesions were attestable through the senses of the forensic pathologists, remained the most reliable version.

Contesting the power of images

When a lesion described on radiological images cannot be attested during an autopsy, forensic pathologists tend to disqualify the demonstrative power of radiological interpretation, even in vascular cases. While they have anticipated an autopsy with these lesions in mind and expect to find them, direct confrontation with the organs and vessels causes them to revise their judgement and question their existence altogether. As we will see in the next case, pathologists do not question their own view and capacity to visualize the body.

During the morning meeting, Dr Moser [resident pathologist] presents the case of a young woman, a Jehovah's Witness, who died in a hospital where she had been admitted because of severe abdominal pain. The ultrasound showed blood in the abdomen, but the parents refused any transfusion. The young woman died shortly afterwards. Dr Moser says she suspects an ectopic pregnancy. Her hypothesis is quickly refuted by the CT scan, which shows a normal uterus. However, according to Dr Vogel [radiologist], the spleen is large (splenomegaly); thus, Dr Moser postulates mononucleosis. The external examination shows signs of medical interventions, but little else. To find the source of abdominal bleeding, Dr Vogel suggests performing an angiography,[7] which later shows a lot of fluid around the spleen with a blood leak at the lower pole and the splenic vein.

During the autopsy, Dr Moser and Dr Rüegg [senior pathologist] take special care to examine the spleen, describing it in situ and noting a rupture of the spleen. They then open the thorax so that they can remove it without damaging it and keep its anatomical relationships intact. They place it on the board, photograph it and examine it at length. Dr Rüegg takes it in her hands, turns it over, introduces a rod into the splenic vein and notes its integrity. She repeats several times that she does not understand, seems annoyed ("I can't see anything, there's nothing!" she repeats), and asks whether the radiologist has indeed mentioned the splenic vein. During the briefing following the autopsy, Dr Moser and Dr Rüegg offer the view that abdominal haemorrhage is the cause of death (signs of exsanguination with very pale organs) and inform Dr Vogel that they could not confirm her interpretation. Dr Vogel says she is surprised because she is sure of herself. (Observation notes, reformulated extracts, Case 35, 2019)

In the case of this abdominal haemorrhage, the origin of the leak, although described on imaging, is not confirmed through autopsy, leading to great tension in the autopsy room. Generally, an angiography is the best test to locate vascular lesions as vessels are perfused. Yet the impossibility for the two forensic pathologists to visualize the leak in the splenic vein leads them to dispute its existence not only in the body but also on the images, calling into question the radiological interpretation. From their perspective, the reality of a lesion visible on the screen depends on its attestation in the autopsy room. However, as the lesion is invisible to the naked eye and resists the autopsy test, Dr Rüegg concludes that there is nothing on the splenic vein and says so to Dr Vogel, the radiologist, during the briefing. Finally, while Dr Vogel seemed affirmative when reading the images, when writing her report, she had to adapt her interpretation in a way that did not contradict the forensic pathologists' observations. For the sake of consistency, she qualifies her conclusions to make them compatible with the expertise of the pathologists: instead of providing a diagnostic interpretation, mentioning a leak in the splenic vein, she produces a more descriptive one, only indicating 'perisplenic contrast agent leaks and massive haemoperitoneum in all four quadrants'. She thus makes it possible to produce a truth about the body and the cause of death: that it is the result of a massive abdominal haemorrhage originating from a ruptured spleen. In other words, the reconciliation of the radiological and autopsy versions of the body requires the adaptation of the radiological interpretation to the pathologists' ability to attest.

Conclusion: truth is in the body

Our ethnography of forensic investigations in an institute specializing in postmortem imaging reveals the issues linked to the combined use of autopsy and radiological techniques, as well as the reconciliation work necessary for these kinds of examinations to produce a tangible cause of death. Radiology and autopsy, which enact two realities of the body, can be interpreted as two specific 'practices of seeing' (Goodwin, 2000). Postmortem imaging involves working with images on screen and is a form of mediated gaze inside the body. Autopsy, for its part, entails a direct proximity relationship, which involves not only the forensic pathologists' sight but also their sense of smell, touch and hearing. Behind these debates around the practices of seeing, the introduction of postmortem images raises the question of reality and evidence. Forensic pathologists restrict reality to direct observation of bodies, expressing a strong attachment to flesh and dead bodies as they are – sometimes bleeding, smelling or putrefied. From the pathologists' point of view, attestation must go through a multisensorial experience in proximity to bodies and organs. Although imaging techniques make it possible to see lesions that autopsy alone could not reveal, particularly vascular lesions, the fact remains that the lesions visualized on the screen must be confirmed by a forensic pathologist's view of the body, with the only exception being multiple fractures in cases of polytrauma. Our observations highlight the strong dependence of imaging on autopsy from the point of view of its probative force. Thus, radiological images have a lower degree of reality within forensic expertise. In other words, they must be confirmed by the senses of the forensic pathologist during autopsy, which remains the 'gold standard' and the ultimate visualization technique.

In an informal discussion, a forensic pathologist commented that imaging could help bypass the destructive and barbaric process of autopsy. He then interrupted and added, pointing to the dissection board, "But I want to see cardiac pathology for real!" This doctor's statement illustrates what seeing means in forensic medicine. In particular, it shows the importance of direct observation and attestation through the senses in the 'professional vision' (Goodwin, 1994) of forensic doctors. Furthermore, the logic of attestation requires the copresence of the forensic pathologist and the body as an obligatory step in the expertise process. It also implies being able to say in front of the court, "I have seen and I can testify". In this sense, there is no equivalence between the autopsy and radiological ways of seeing. Some versions of the body are definitely more valuable, powerful and real than others.

Notes

[1] The notion of 'dispositif' is used 'to refer to any stipulated series of sequences intended to qualify or transform a state of affairs through an arrangement of material and language elements' (Dodier and Barbot, 2021: 60).

[2] The pragmatic approach, as defined by French authors, is inspired by pragmatic philosophers Charles S. Pierce, John Dewey, William James and George H. Mead, but not exclusively. It is resolutely empirical and proposes to analyse the practices of actors by 'taking them seriously', from the point of view of their reflexivity, their resources and their limits. See Barthe et al (2013).

[3] This involved 120 days of observations, including 70 autopsies combined with radiological examinations, analysis of 45 autopsy reports and interviews with the 22 members of the forensic medicine and imaging section (research supported by the Swiss National Science Foundation).

[4] Virtangio® is a perfusion device that allows the complete filling of the vessels (cannulation of femoral artery and vein) with a specific oily contrast agent, Angiofil®, developed by the institute in partnership with the industry during the 2000s (Grabherr et al, 2017).

5   In Switzerland, forensic medicine is a medical specialty. Thus, young medical graduates work as residents and are trained for several years by senior pathologists before obtaining their diploma as forensic pathologists.
6   In the case of an external examination, the protocol is that radiological images are interpretated without a radiological report being drawn up. The resident tells us that the aim of this reading is to identify the 'big things' (for example, a projectile in the case of a train accident).
7   PMCT angiography is performed after the external examination of a body.

References

Barthe, Y., de Blic, D., Heurtin, J.-P., Lagneau, E., Lemieux, C., Linhardt, D. et al (2013) Pragmatic sociology: A user's guide. *Politix*, 103(3): 175–204.

Berg, M. and Mol, A. (eds) (1998) *Differences in medicine: Unraveling practices, techniques, and bodies*. Durham, NC: Duke University Press.

Bowen, J.R., Dodier, N., Duyvendak, J.W. and Hardon, A. (eds) (2021) *Pragmatic inquiry: Critical concepts for social sciences*. London: Routledge.

Burri, R.V. (2012) Visual rationalities: Towards a sociology of images. *Current Sociology*, 60(1): 45–60.

Chateauraynaud, F. (2004) L'épreuve du tangible: Expériences de l'enquête et surgissements de la preuve. In B. Karsenti and L. Quéré (eds) *La croyance et l'enquête. Aux sources du pragmatisme*. Paris: EHESS, pp 167–194.

Cussins, C. (1996) Ontological choreography: Agency through objectification in infertility clinics. *Social Studies of Science*, 26(3): 575–610.

Dodier, N. and Barbot, J. (2021) Dispositif. In J.R. Bowen, N. Dodier, J.W. Duyvendak and A. Hardon (eds) *Pragmatic inquiry: Critical concepts for social sciences*. London: Routledge, pp 55–67.

Goodwin, C. (1994) Professional vision. *American Anthropologist*, 96(3): 606–633.

Goodwin, C. (2000) Practices of seeing. Visual analysis: An ethnomethodological approach. In T. van Leeuwen and C. Jewitt (eds) *Handbook of visual analysis*. London: SAGE, pp 157–182.

Grabherr, S., Egger, C., Vilarino, R., Campana, L., Jotterand, M. and Dedouit, F. (2017) Modern postmortem imaging: An update on recent developments. *Forensic Sciences Research*, 2(2): 52–64.

Grabherr, S., Heinemann, A., Vogel, H., Rutty, G., Morgan, B., Wozniak, K. et al (2018) Postmortem CT angiography compared with autopsy: A forensic multicenter study. *Radiology*, 288(1): 270–276.

Juston, R. (2020) *Médecins légistes. Une enquête sociologique*. Paris: Les Presses de Sciences Po.

Latour, B. (1986) Visualization and cognition: Thinking with eyes and hands. In E. Long and H. Kuklick (eds) *Knowledge and society: Studies in the sociology of culture past and present*. London: Jai Press, vol 6, pp 1–40.

Law, J. and Mol, A. (eds) (2002) *Complexities: Social studies of knowledge practices*. Durham, NC: Duke University Press.

Magnin, V., Grabherr, S. and Michaud, K. (2020) The Lausanne forensic pathology approach to postmortem imaging for natural and non-natural deaths. *Diagnostic Histopathology*, 26(8): 350–357.

Michaud, K., Genet, P., Sabatasso, S. and Grabherr, S. (2019) Postmortem imaging as a complementary tool for the investigation of cardiac death. *Forensic Sciences Research*, 4(3): 211–222.

Michaud, K., Magnin, V., Faouzi, M., Fracasso, T., Aguiar, D., Dedouit, F. et al (2021) Postmortem coronary artery calcium score in cases of myocardial infarction. *International Journal of Legal Medicine*, 135(5): 1829–1836.

Mol, A. (2002) *The body multiple: Ontology in medical practice*. Durham, NC: Duke University Press.

Moreira, T. (2006) Heterogeneity and coordination of blood pressure in neurosurgery. *Social Studies of Science*, 36(1): 69–97.

Reed, K., Kochetkova, I. and Molyneux-Hodgson, S. (2016) 'You're looking for different parts in a jigsaw': Foetal MRI (magnetic resonance imaging) as an emerging technology in professional practice. *Sociology of Health and Illness*, 38(5): 736–752.

Schnegg, C. and Rey, S. (2017) Quand les morts passent un scanner. *Anthropologie et Santé*, 15. https://doi.org/10.4000/anthropologiesante.2698

Tavory, I. and Timmermans, S. (2013) A pragmatist approach to causality in ethnography. *American Journal of Sociology*, 119(3): 682–714.

Timmermans, S. (2006) *Postmortem: How medical examiners explain suspicious deaths*. Chicago: University of Chicago Press.

Woolgar, S. and Lezaun, J. (2013) The wrong bin bag: A turn to ontology in science and technology studies? *Social Studies of Science*, 43(3): 321–340.

2

Death at a Planetary Scale: Mortality's Moral Materiality in the Context of the Anthropocene

Philip R. Olson

Attunement

In the United States, which serves as the primary site for this chapter's study, the early part of the 21st century has witnessed several disruptions to nearly one hundred years of relative stability in deathcare. Since the turn of the century, cremation has surpassed burial as the preferred form of final disposition in the United States; multiple new, environmentally conscientious disposition technologies (including alkaline hydrolysis, green burial and natural organic reduction) have emerged as legally and commercially viable options; and home funeral guides (Olson, 2016) and end-of-life doulas (Krawczyk and Rush, 2020) are developing 'counterprofessional' (Goldensher, 2020) practices and social roles in deathcare. Meanwhile, a global pandemic has forced individuals, communities and institutions to confront mortality and retool deathways with unwelcome rapidity, urgency and intensity. These recent developments in deathcare coincide with, and are often attuned to, increasing awareness of the abiding perils of global, anthropogenic climate change and environmental degradation. Indeed, deathcare practices – and discourse about death and deathcare – are being shaped by concerns about 'the climate and ecological emergency' (Walter, 2022: 1) in ways that draw attention to death *at large scales*.

In *How to die in the Anthropocene*, Roy Scranton declares that we human beings must now learn 'how to die not as individuals, but as a civilization' (2015: 21):

In the epoch of the Anthropocene, the question of individual mortality — 'What does my life mean in the face of death?' — is universalized and framed in *scales* [my emphasis] that boggle the imagination. What does human existence mean against 100,000 years of climate change? What does one life mean in the face of species death or the collapse of global civilization? How do we make meaningful choices in the shadow of our inevitable end? (Scranton, 2015: 20)

Death studies scholar Tony Walter, too, has argued that 'climate and ecological emergency discourse entails a (new) death *mentalité*' (2022: 2), one that 're-focuses attention from the death of personally known individuals to the climate-induced collective deaths of millions, perhaps billions, of humans in coming decades, along with species extinctions on a *scale* [my emphasis] hitherto unknown during *homo sapiens*' time on Earth' (2022: 13). Scranton and Walter fix their attention on collective death, death in very large numbers. They actively shift focus away from the individual deaths and dispositions of the billions of individual humans inhabiting the planet. Yet thinking about and planning for death at civilizational or species-level scales necessarily entails managing the material remainders of so much death. Thus, communications scholar Joshua Barnett recommends, '[a]s we learn to dwell on Earth in the Anthropocene ... we would do well to incorporate dying, death, decay, decomposition and "deathcare" into our critical lexicon' (2018: 23). Doing so, Barnett argues, 'offers us an opportunity to resist some of anthropocentrism's unquestioned assumptions about our bodies and the worldly relationships they enroll us in — and, therefore, an opportunity to live more ecocentric lives' (2018: 27). Indeed, Barnett views some new, environmentally conscientious disposition technologies — natural organic reduction in particular — as possibly 'propelling our bodies into more ecocentric relationships with(in) the teeming more-than-human world' (2018: 23).

Science and Technology Studies scholar Jon Agar points out that technologies 'perhaps essentially, intervene between scales' (2020: 381). An excavator amplifies human-sized muscle power and range of motion. The dials and knobs of an electron microscope translate relatively enormous finger motions into minuscule adjustments. Yet the scales over which technologies intervene are not *given*; they are produced, constructed, enacted. As geographer Philip Kelly puts it, 'the *production of scale*' is 'the creation of a level of resolution at which phenomena are deemed understandable' (2000: 10, emphasis added). To this constructivist approach to understanding scale, Bruno Latour contributes the observation that moving between different scales entails moving between different sets of information. 'It cannot be said that the small or the short lie *within* the large or the long, in the sense that the largest or the longest contain them but with "fewer details"';

rather, each scale is 'dealing with different findings', and a reconfiguration of findings is necessary to 'reconcile' the information provided at different scales (Latour, 2014: 121, original emphasis). Thus, when we 'zoom out' to focus on the disposal of human remains at large scales, we should not expect that any norms governing the disposition of individual/personal remains will naturally 'lie *within*' practices devoted to managing remains at a universal/planetary scale.

Herein lies the rub: thinking about and designing for death at a planetary scale boggles the imagination to the point of rattling what Haraway (2016) calls the 'old saws' of 'human exceptionalism and bounded individualism'. Yet these old saws have long shaped the normative contours of Western deathcare practices, and, as we shall see, their bite remains sharp. It is not easy to reconcile the vital patterns and rhythms of thought, action and care that fund individual lives (and deaths) with meaning, on the one hand, and, on the other hand, the vast horizons of epochal, planetary time and transformation within which *all* bio-geological assemblages are transient. It is difficult to find moral footing in the 'gap' between the individual/personal and the universal/planetary. For students and advocates of environmentally conscientious disposition technologies and deathcare practices, learning how to die in the Anthropocene means coming to grips with a profound waste management problem (Olson, 2016), one that emerges when collective death and disposition are viewed as *sources* of environmental degradation (rather than as *outcomes* of the climate and ecological emergency). Yet it also means coming to terms with the profound importance of continuing to acknowledge the meaning and value of individual/personal lives and deaths.

In the present chapter I provide an initial analysis of the moral discourse (including images, designs, descriptions and theorizations) regarding environmentally conscientious disposition technologies. Specifically, I examine how these technologies have challenged long-standing, moral proscriptions against the '*commingling*' of human remains, and how these normative proscriptions have pushed back against the techno-environmental discourse that would propel our bodies into a collective heap of hot compost (Haraway, 2016). Instead of focusing on any singular disposition technology, this chapter tracks a technologically mediated, moral dialectic that is developing across multiple disposition technologies: a dialectic between the individual/personal and the universal/planetary, which has emerged as a feature of thinking explicitly about death and disposition at a planetary scale. My aim is not to resolve this emerging, moral tension. Nor am I able to diagnose the nature or causes of this tension. My primary aim is, instead, to draw attention to a particular moral tension that is emerging in contemporary techno-environmental discourse of death and disposition, and to lay bare (to some extent) the difficulty of finding a fitting moral frame of reference from which to approach death at a planetary scale.

Figure 2.1: Screenshots of Vimeo video created by Columbia University Graduate School of Architecture, Planning and Preservation, DeathLAB

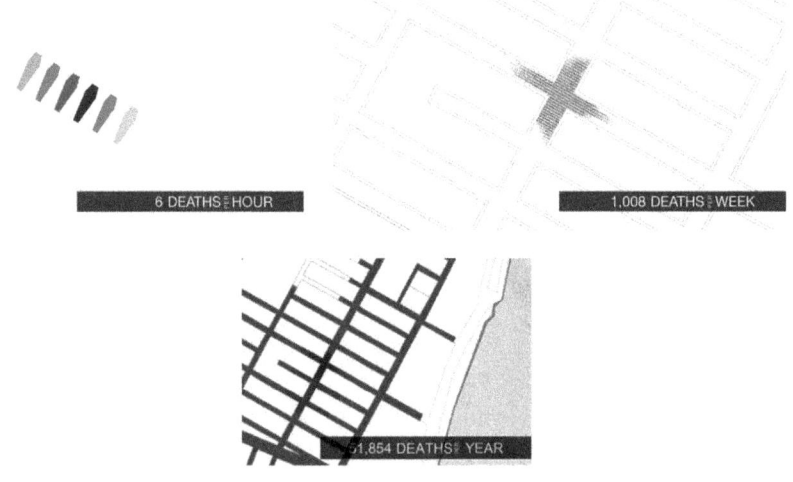

Source: http://deathlab.org/@gsappDeathLAB

Zooming out, scaling up and commingling

Figure 2.1 comprises screenshots taken from a video[1] produced by Columbia University Graduate School of Architecture, Planning and Preservation's DeathLAB, 'a trans-disciplinary research and design initiative focused on reconceiving how we live with death in the city'.[2] In the video, successive images convey the spatial and temporal scales of accumulating corpse production in New York City in order to contextualize and motivate the work of DeathLAB, which involves 'engag[ing] with the complex challenges of our *individual* and *collective* mortality [my emphasis]', particularly as 'the need for environmentally friendly funerary processes increases'.[3] DeathLAB approaches mass death not as a product of social and environmental harms, but as a *source* of social and environmental harms, citing both 'diminishing burial space' and cremation's emission of 'harmful toxins into already polluted air' as problems we must face as more and more corpses produced by '[t]he growing [human] population continues to stress the natural environment'.[4] The first image depicts six coffins located at the intersection of Avenue C and 6th Street, Manhattan: one hour's worth of New York City deaths. As the video 'zooms' out to depict deaths per day, per week and per month, the number of individual caskets depicted increases exponentially.

By the fifth image, when the scale reaches a year's time and roughly one square mile in area, individual coffins are no longer represented. Instead, at this 'level of resolution' we see only solid, gray lines indicating the total, collective space taken up by the dead. The individual 'bodies' of the dead – as represented by distinct coffin pixels – become graphically 'commingled'. To paraphrase Latour, it cannot be said that the individual coffins are contained *within* the solid gray lines, in the sense that the solid lines contain the individual coffins but with fewer details; rather, the solid lines are 'dealing with different findings', and reconfiguration of findings is necessary to 'reconcile' the solid lines with the coffins containing individual bodies. Reconciling these different scales requires a recalibration of not just the material, technical, legal and infrastructural aspects of human disposition, but also of the social and moral norms that have stabilized around conventional burial and cremation.

DeathLAB's images of coffins lined up in neat rows on Manhattan streets bear some resemblance to images of casketed bodies lying in long, narrow trenches on Hart Island, a mass grave site in the Bronx, New York, which, since 1869, has received the bodies of over one million people[5] – people whom Hart Island cemetery chaplain Justin von Bujdoss describes as 'people who live on the margins – the homeless, the sickly, the neglected, the forgotten and overworked' (Hennigan, 2020). Globally, mass graves evoke associations with violence, injustice, disaster, neglect and dehumanization: evidence of a grave undervaluation of human dignity at wholesale, if not an outright failure to acknowledge the dignity of human persons. Mass graves discovered in the aftermath of armed conflict are frequently identified and investigated as evidence of war crimes, crimes against humanity or genocide.[6] At the peaks of multiple waves of the COVID-19 pandemic, countless media reports described bodies as 'piling up' in hospitals, nursing homes, mortuaries, crematoria and even unrefrigerated U-Haul trucks (Dienst et al, 2020) that were 'overflowing' with corpses. Even as I write this, the bodies of people who are dying during the Russian siege of Mariupol, Ukraine are 'piling up' and being hurriedly buried together in an 80-foot 'common burial' trench outside the city (Maloletka, 2022). And in Ethiopia, bodies buried in mass graves are being exhumed and burned, eliminating potential evidence of war crimes (Kassa, 2022). The language and practices surrounding mass burial often convey a sense of moral urgency about restoring dignity and humanity to the dead through re-individuation – if possible, through identification, naming (both the dead and the accountable) and repatriation of remains. And in academic, popular and funeral industry discourses about disposition practices, the commingling of multiple human remains is frequently met with disapprobation that is tied to a perceived failure to acknowledge and respect the dignity of individual human lives.

Concerns about the commingling of multiple human remains are not confined to burial. Commingling has long anguished cremation providers and cremation customers alike, frequently leading to civil litigation during which multidisciplinary teams of experts, including forensic anthropologists, are called upon to deploy principled, practised and technically sophisticated methods for detecting commingled remains (Warren and van Deest, 2014). The issue of commingling has arisen as a point of contestation between competing alkaline hydrolysis system competitors (Olson, 2018: 160), and in Catholic deliberations about the relative moral merits of flame cremation and alkaline hydrolysis (Mirkes, 2008: 687–688).

Even if, as Walter argues, the climate and ecological emergency is spurring a new death *mentalité*, according to which death awareness has expanded to include collective death, the cultural, legal and moral norms governing human disposition technologies and practices continue to harbour powerful proscriptions against the commingling of multiple human remains. The challenge we face is not a matter of having to overcome the old saw of 'western individualism' (Walter, 2022: 11), but rather a matter of reconciling emerging concerns about dealing with death and disposition at large scales, on the one hand, with, on the other hand, persistent interests in acknowledging the importance of personal/individual life, death, loss and grief, and deathcare practices that fund personal/individual death with meaning.

Of vats, vessels and commingling

The moral dialectic between the individual/personal and the universal/planetary is evident in the evolution of the design of natural organic reduction technologies – specifically the history of the design of Seattle-based Recompose (formerly the Urban Death Project [UDP])'s natural organic reduction system. Emphasizing mass death as a *source* of environmental harm (rather than a product of environmental harm) the UDP sought to develop a practicable alternative to both cremation and earth burial, proposing a system for composting human remains into nutrient-rich soil. Like DeathLAB, UDP was initially conceived as a way to dispose of human remains in an environmentally sustainable way in dense urban environments, and the resulting compost was to provide residents and municipalities with a resource for private or community gardens and green spaces (Tradii, nd). In a 2016 interview, UDP founder Katrina Spade promotes human composting as not only 'part of the climate drawdown puzzle' (Monnier 2019), but also as 'an opportunity to let go of Americans' obsession with individualism' (Ross, 2016).

The initial designs for UDP's human composting system included a multiple-storeys tall, central vat (or 'core') surrounded by a spiralling rampway extending from the base to the top of the core. Human bodies were to be placed in the top of the core, which would contain carbon-rich composting materials and, of course, other dead human bodies. Figure 2.2 depicts multiple bodies commingling over time, with fresher remains retaining sharper individuality at the top of the core, while the boundaries of older remains progressively dissolve as they travel towards the bottom of the core,

Figure 2.2: Human composting system design developed by the Urban Death Project

Source: Reprinted with permission of Katrina Spade, Recompose

where an auger moves a collectively composted and fully commingled soil towards a collection area. Subsequent UDP designs also depicted a common core in which multiple human remains would be commingled.[7]

Yet UDP's vision for a disposition technology that challenges the old saw of bounded individualism has found those teeth still to be sharp – at least in the domain of deathcare. In a 2019 post to the conservative news website *WorldNetDaily*, Patty Ann Malley asks, 'Since when is wanting dignity in death an obsession with individualism?' Malley continues:

> I'm not sure about you, but the idea of being composted in bulk smacks of a mass grave. ... Same goes for ... claim[ing] 'some' of the resulting dirt. ... [T]hat new soil could be anybody. ... Families could be toting home a complete stranger, or a combination thereof. ... Burying one's dead en masse with strangers has never been ideal. (Malley, 2019)

Malley gives voice to widely held concerns about the commingling of human remains – concerns that are occasionally revived by news reports of funeral service or cremation providers who, through honest error, carelessness or misconduct, present next of kin with the wrong person's remains. My aim is not to diagnose this concern, but rather to trace a moral dialectic that has emerged with respect to thinking about death and disposition a large scales – a dialectic in which the commingling of human remains plays a central role.

In 2018, the non-profit UDP was dissolved but reconstituted as a for-profit, 'benefit corporation' named Recompose, which has successfully lobbied for the legalization of 'natural organic reduction'[8] in seven states: Washington, Colorado, Oregon, Vermont, New York, California and Nevada. The rebranding of Spade's company was accompanied by a redesign of the

Figure 2.3: Human composting system design developed by Recompose

Source: Reprinted with permission of Katrina Spade, Recompose

composting system. According to the Recompose website's account of the company's history, Spade's early idea of 'placing bodies in a collective core where human composting takes place' gave way, in 2017, to a design that involves 'placing each body in an individual vessel'.[9] In the new design (Figure 2.3), individual bodies are composted separately in distinct, steel vessels. The moral dialectic manifests materially in the design history of Recompose's natural organic reduction technology. Moreover, all other natural organic reduction providers have adopted individual vessel designs. None have developed common vat designs in which multiple human remains are collectively reduced.[10]

According to Recompose, the shift from a collective 'core' design to a multiple 'vessel' design 'allowed for an easier path to legalization'.[11] The law of human remains in Washington state (the first state to legalize natural organic reduction) allows for the commingling of multiple human remains during disposition – provided those with authority over disposition give written informed consent – but this allowance is explicitly articulated as an 'exception' to 'individual final disposition', and inapplicable 'when equipment, techniques, or devices are employed that keep human remains separate and distinct before, during, and after the final disposition process' (Revised Code of Washington 2022). Moreover, the Washington 'exception' is accompanied by a note stating the legislature's affirmation that some deathcare practices, 'which have never been acceptable', 'violate common notions of decency and generally held expectations' or even 'principles of human dignity' (Revised Code of Washington 2022). Similarly, in California the law presumptively forbids the commingling of human remains during and after the natural organic reduction process in the absence of 'express written permission of the person entitled to control the disposition of the reduced human remains' (California Health and Safety Code 2023). The path to legalizing human composting turns out to be smoother than the path towards cultural, legal and moral acceptance of commingling multiple human remains.

Learning to care for the dead during the Anthropocene has provoked conscious probing of the moral underpinnings of contemporary deathcare norms and practices. In particular, designing for the disposition of human remains at a large scale has initiated a material and discursive dialectic between individual and collective death that has drawn critical attention to the persistent power of individualism as a moral force in US deathcare culture. The *composting* of human remains is gaining traction in the United States, but the *commingling* of multiple human remains lies beyond the pale – for now.

Commingling the human and nonhuman

Learning how to die in the Anthropocene has challenged not only moral proscriptions against the commingling of multiple human remains, but also moral proscriptions against the commingling of the human and the nonhuman, thereby challenging that 'old saw' of human exceptionalism. Natural organic reduction, green burial grounds and alkaline hydrolysis have emerged as viable means by which to reimagine and rematerialize human remains in ways that address popular concerns about the environmental impacts of flame cremation and conventional earth burial. Almost invariably, these new technologies seem to enrol our dead bodies 'into more ecocentric relationships with(in) the teeming more-than-human world' (Barnett, 2018: 23).

Western deathcare culture has long been invested in a form of human exceptionalism, according to which humans are understood as the consummatory end point of all of nature's provisions: unusable users; uneatable eaters; ends, not means. Hence ecofeminist Val Plumwood's observation that contemporary mortuary practice 'prevents the decaying body from nourishing other forms of life' (2008: 325). In his 1973 article 'Attitudes toward the newly dead', philosopher William May cites Erich Neumann's *The origins of history and consciousness* (1954) to illustrate what May takes to be human beings' *natural* horror at the thought of being eaten. Neumann points out that in ancient mythologies and current death tropes alike, death is represented as an eater and devourer. 'Eating, devouring, hunger, death, and maw go together', Neumann writes, 'and, we still speak ... of "death's maw", a "devouring war", a "consuming disease"', noting that medieval paintings of hell and the devil often include images of people '[b]eing swallowed and eaten' (May, 1973: 28). Moreover, writes May, 'the corpse, which is hidden in the earth, is thereby *swallowed up* and absorbed; the flesh, which is *devoured* by the scavenger, at the same time disappears' (1973: 6, my emphasis). And in Colorado, the legalization of 'natural reduction' explicitly prohibits 'using the [natural reduction] soil to grow food for human consumption'.[12] Concerns not only about being eaten, but also about eating or drinking other humans often enter into public conversations about the fate of human remains – as is evident (and unsurprising) in countless references to the dystopic film *Soylent Green* (1974)[13] in media reports and social media comments about alkaline hydrolysis, natural organic reduction and green burial. The concern expressed in these reports is not only about perceived violations of boundaries between the bodies of individual persons, but also about the development of attitudes towards the dead body that are too utilitarian. Executive Director of the California Catholic Conference Kathleen Domingo's worry that natural organic reduction 'reduces the human body to simply a disposable commodity' (Molina, 2022) finds a secular expression in the idea that the 'nutritive' corpse may be an extension of 'our #riseandgrind capitalistic mentality to the grave' (Cummins, 2020).

Thinking about and designing for human disposition at large scales has, however, challenged the exceptionality of human materiality. Recompose's description of a 'Carbon Cycle Ceremony' – a liturgy written by Recompose employee Morgan Yarborough to accompany the 'laying-in' of a body into a 'recomposition' vessel – references the National Oceanic and Atmospheric Association's (NOAA) 'Ocean Facts' webpage, 'What is the carbon cycle?'. The NOAA site notes that '[t]he carbon cycle is nature's way of reusing carbon atoms, which travel from the atmosphere into organisms in the Earth and then back into the atmosphere over and over again', pointing out that this perspective 'helps remind us of our place in that cycle and the transition of our person [that is, the dead human body] from their human form to a part of the natural collective'.[14] Likewise, among its publicly available outreach tools, the Green Burial Council (an international, non-profit organization that recommends standards for a variety of green burial practices) includes an infographic titled 'Your body after death', which positions the human body in relation to the 13+ billion-year history of the universe. 'The carbon and oxygen [atoms in your body] were forged in the stars between 7 and 12 billion years ago' and '[w]hen you die, the work begins of returning your atoms to the universe'.[15] This vast, universal work is accomplished at a much more familiar level of resolution by '[l]acy, infinite webs of mycelium ... [t]he diptera order [flies] ... [a]nd the coleoptera [beetles]'.[16] Descriptions of 'green' disposition technologies reference a variety of inhuman creatures, including microbes, fungi, insects and plants (but rarely animals), all of which receive credit for their aid in breaking down the corpse and returning its elemental, nutritive load to the universal pool of nourishment from which new life may draw (see Chapter 12, this volume). In this way, the construction of death at scale brings the vast/universal into relation with the minute/atomic – a relation that is enacted, in part, by the work of nonhuman actors. There are 'multispecies collaborations' (see Chapter 9, this volume) happening here.

Developers and providers of ecologically conscientious disposition technologies seek alignment between human *purposes* and natural *processes*, while also embracing a fluidity between the human and the nonhuman that does not position human beings as the consummatory end point of all of nature's provisions. Recompose describes the process of natural organic reduction as one that 'takes guidance from nature', 'emulat[ing] nature's cycles and regenerative design', and which 'uses nature's principles to return our bodies to the earth' in order to 'give back to the earth that supports us all our lives' by 'gently converting human remains into soil, so that we can nourish new life after we die'.[17] Promessa describes its freeze-drying technology as a process that 'prepares your body for a burial that mimics nature's way of decomposition' by 'enabling you to bring your precious carbon back into the earth, [which] helps reduce climate change'.[18] Providers of alkaline hydrolysis like Minnesota-based Bradshaw funeral services describe their technology as a '*gentle*, eco-friendly alternative to flame-based cremation and casket burials'. Through this process, the funeral firm states, 'the body is recycled without harm to the environment. With Green Cremation [the firm's branding of alkaline hydrolysis] we return to the earth through a cycle of life, helping to promote new life as nature intended it to occur'.[19] And designers involved in the *Capsula Mundi* burial pod project, too, state that death

> is not the end, but the beginning of a way back to nature. ... The biological life cycle and its transformations are the same for every living being. It is time for humans to realize our integrated part in nature. *Capsula Mundi* wants to emphasize that we are a part of Nature's cycle of transformation.[20]

However, the human often reasserts itself. We are talking, here, not only about technologies of disposal, but also technologies of recognition, remembrance, memorialization. For example, the landing page for *Capsula Mundi* – an Italian company that hopes to sell biodegradable, egg-shaped urns and large, egg-shaped burial pods designed to hold a human body that 'feed' a tree as the body decomposes – cycles through three images of mature trees, which are identified as particular individuals. Bearing the caption, 'I love you Grandma!', one image depicts a tree trunk being hugged by a bare-armed man. A second image depicts a hand touching the bark of tree with the caption, 'Hi, Dad!'. A third image gazes up the trunk and into the high canopy of a pine tree: 'John, how you've grown!'. Reincarnated in new, arboreal forms (see Chapter 12, this volume), 'Dad', 'Grandma' and 'John' have not entirely lost their individual identities. *They* live again – or continue to live – in the form of these particular trees. *These* trees demand a kind of care and attention that other trees might not demand. John's story continues as 'he' grows – and this story surely includes the birds that make a home in 'his' canopy, and any mushrooms that grow around the base of 'his' trunk.

Conclusion

In *The work of the dead: A cultural history of mortal remains*, historian Thomas Laqueur claims that caring for the bodies of the dead 'is *a*, if not *the*, sign of our [species'] emergence from the order of nature into culture' (2015: 8, original emphasis), and that caring for the dead is – Laqueur quotes Gadamer here – 'the immutable anthropological background for all the human and social changes, past or present' (Gadamer, 1981: 75). If caring for dead human bodies possesses the significance that Gadamer and Laqueur suggest it does, then we should view contemporary reimaginings and rematerializations of death and dead bodies as articulations of new cultural forms of deathcare that aim to align human purposes with natural processes at large scales.

Rethinking death and disposal at large scales has exposed and challenged commitments to both individualism and human exceptionalism, but it has not rendered those norms '[s]eriously unthinkable: not available to think with' (Haraway, 2016) in the realm of deathcare science and technology. Even while reimagining and rematerializing human disposition in ways that acknowledge 'ongoing multispecies stories and practices of becoming-with' (Haraway, 2016), environmentally conscientious disposition practices do not relinquish the desire for human-centred control over the decomposition of dead bodies. Natural organic reduction, alkaline hydrolysis, green burial grounds and other newly emerging disposition technologies involve carefully controlled processes. Indeed, the unexpected is not entirely welcome when disposition practices are state-regulated and privately insured commercial investments and endeavours. In the United States, state deathcare laws and regulations both shape and are shaped by persistent, popular moral proscriptions against the commingling of multiple human remains, and human-centred control over human/nonhuman transactions. The moral dialectic emerging around environmentally conscientious disposition technologies demonstrates an abiding commitment to the specialness of human remains and a recognition of the importance of acknowledging, remembering and memorializing the *personal/individual* importance of the dead. Perhaps, instead of trying to leave human exceptionalism and bounded individualism behind we should instead carry them into the compost heap with us, where they can work and be worked upon in collective efforts to reduce the environmental harms caused by now-dominant disposition and burial practices. Moreover, the shift towards thinking about collective death and disposition at scale may serve as one motivation for rethinking and retooling collective deathcare *policies*. Instead of continuing to relegate deathcare to the private sector, where environmentally conscientious disposition methods are presented as mere options among a growing set of deathcare products and services from which *individual deathcare consumers* may choose, it may be time to think more collectively about deathcare practices as matters of broad public policy. While a shift from private to public management certainly would be costly and challenging, it could also provide a means for hastening acceptance and availability of environmentally conscientious disposition technologies *at scale*, while promoting a sense of collective solidarity in death and deathcare.

Notes

[1] https://vimeo.com/80307370 (accessed 9 March 2022).
[2] http://deathlab.org/ (accessed 9 March 2022).
[3] http://deathlab.org/ (accessed 9 March 2022).
[4] http://deathlab.org/ (accessed 9 March 2022).
[5] https://council.nyc.gov/data/hart-island/ (accessed 10 March 2022).
[6] https://phr.org/issues/investigating-deaths-and-mass-atrocities/investigating-mass-crimes-for-prosecutions/ (accessed 14 March 2022).
[7] Illustrations are available online: https://www.wired.com/2016/10/inside-machine-will-turn-corpse-compost/ and https://www.seattletimes.com/life/from-corpse-to-compost-the-urban-death-projects-modest-proposal/ (accessed 30 October 2022).
[8] See Washington SB 5001, https://app.leg.wa.gov/billsummary?BillNumber=5001&Year=2019&Initiative=false (accessed 19 March 2022).
[9] https://recompose.life/who-we-are/#history (accessed 21 March 2022).
[10] Providers include The Natural Funeral (Colorado), Earth Funeral Group (Washington and Oregon), Herland Forest Natural Burial Cemetery (Washington) and Return Home (Washington).
[11] https://recompose.life/who-we-are/#history (accessed 21 March 2022).
[12] https://leg.colorado.gov/bills/hb20-1060 (accessed 19 April 2022).
[13] *Soylent Green* is a dystopic, 1974 film starring Charlton Heston, in which dead bodies are processed into food for the unknowing but starving population of an overcrowded earth.
[14] See NOAA website, https://oceanservice.noaa.gov/facts/carbon-cycle.htm. See also Recompose, https://recompose.life/education/about-the-laying-in/ (accessed 17 April 2022).
[15] See https://www.greenburialcouncil.org/outreach-tools.html (accessed 7 April 2022).
[16] https://www.greenburialcouncil.org/outreach-tools.html (accessed 7 April 2022).
[17] https://www.recompose.life/ (accessed 18 September 2019).
[18] http://www.promessa.se/ (accessed 18 September 2019).
[19] https://www.bradshawfuneral.com/BMV/what-is-green-cremation and https://www.bradshawfuneral.com/BMV/why-green-cremation (accessed 18 September 2019).
[20] https://www.capsulamundi.it/en/project/ (accessed 18 September 2019).

References

Agar, J. (2020) What is technology? *Annals of Science*, 77(3): 377–382.

Barnett, J.T. (2018) On dying ecologically in the Anthropocene. *Ecological Citizen*, 2(1): 23–29.

California Health and Safety Code, 7054.9 (2023) https://casetext.com/statute/california-codes/california-health-and-safety-code/division-7-dead-bodies/part-1-general-provisions/chapter-2-general-provisions/section-70549-operative-112027-prohibited-acts-violation-a-misdemeanor (accessed 3 July 2023).

Cummins, E. (2020) Why millennials are the 'death positive' generation. *Vox*, 22 January. https://www.vox.com/the-highlight/2020/1/15/21059189/death-millennials-funeral-planning-cremation-green-positive (accessed 8 November 2022).

Dienst, J., Siegal, I. and Shea, T. (2020) Dozens of bodies found in U-Haul trucks outside Brooklyn funeral home. *NBCNewYork.com*, 30 April. https://www.nbcnewyork.com/news/local/dozens-of-bodies-found-in-u-haul-trucks-outside-brooklyn-funeral-home/2395703/ (accessed 13 December 2022).

Gadamer, H.-G. (1981) *Reason in the age of science.* Translated by F. Lawrence. Cambridge, MA: MIT Press.

Goldensher, L. (2020) Homebirth politics: Feminists, conservatives, and the struggle over expert knowledge. Unpublished dissertation. Princeton University.

Haraway, D. (2016) Tentacular thinking: Anthropocene, Capitalocene, Chthulucene. *E-Flux*, 75. https://www.e-flux.com/journal/75/67125/tentacular-thinking-anthropocene-capitalocene-chthulucene/ (accessed 4 March 2022).

Hennigan, W.J. (2020) Lost in the pandemic: Inside New York City's mass graveyard on Hart Island. *Time*, 18 November. https://time.com/5913151/hart-island-covid/ (accessed 10 March 2022).

Kassa, L. (2022) Ethiopian war: Evidence of mass killing being burned – witnesses. *BBC News*, 7 May. https://apnews.com/article/russia-ukraine-war-mariupol-mass-graves-286b84d5d795ef91fb8c9ee48ed26612 (accessed 11 March 2022).

Kelly, P. (2000) *Landscapes of globalization: Human geographies of economic change in the Philippines.* New York: Routledge.

Krawczyk, M. and Rush, M. (2020) Describing the end-of-life doula role and practices of care: Perspectives from four countries. *Palliative Care & Social Practice*, 14: 1–15.

Laqueur, T. (2015). *The work of the dead: A cultural history of mortal remains.* Princeton: Princeton University Press.

Latour, B. (2014) Anti-Zoom. In Studio Olafur Eliasson (ed) *Contact* (exhibition catalogue). Paris: Flammarion, pp 121–124.

Malley, P.A. (2019) Have 'green' burials gone too far? *WND.com*, 1 January. https://www.wnd.com/2019/01/have-green-burials-gone-too-far/#IDDHPQfB1FZ6fKgk.99 (accessed 23 March 2022).

Maloletka, E. (2022) Amid heavy shelling, Ukraine's Mariupol city uses mass grave. *AP News*, 10 March. https://apnews.com/article/russia-ukraine-war-mariupol-mass-graves-286b84d5d795ef91fb8c9ee48ed26612 (accessed 11 March 2022).

May, W. (1973) Attitudes toward the newly dead. *The Hastings Center Studies*, 1(1): 3–13.

Mirkes Sr, R. (2008) The mortuary science of alkaline hydrolysis. *National Catholic Bioethics Quarterly*, 8(4): 683–695.

Molina, A. (2022) California legalizes human composting bill against Catholic bishops' opposition. *AmericaMagazine.org*, 22 September. https://www.americamagazine.org/politics-society/2022/09/22/california-human-composting-243830 (accessed 8 November 2022).

Monnier, J. (2019) How to die in the Anthropocene. *Anthropocene Magazine*. https://www.anthropocenemagazine.org/2019/06/how-to-die-in-the-anthropocene/ (accessed 3 July 2023).

Neumann, E. (1954) *The origins and history of consciousness*. Princeton: Princeton University Press.

Olson, P.R. (2016) Domesticating deathcare: The women of the U.S. natural deathcare movement. *Journal of Medical Humanities*, 39(2): 195–215.

Olson, P.R. (2018) Basic cremation. *Wake Forest Journal of Law & Policy*, 8(1): 149–171.

Plumwood, V. (2008) Tasteless: Towards a food-based approach to death. *Environmental Values*, 17(3): 323–330.

Revised Code of Washington, 68.50.185 (2022) https://app.leg.wa.gov/RCW/default.aspx?cite=68.50.185 (accessed 3 July 2023).

Ross, R. (2016) Inside the machine that will turn your corpse into compost. *Wired*. https://www.wired.com/2016/10/inside-machine-will-turn-corpse-compost/ (accessed 3 July 2023).

Scranton, R. (2015) *Learning to die in the Anthropocene: Reflections on the end of a civilization*. San Francisco: City Lights Books.

Tradii, L. (nd) Death, technology, and the 'return to nature'. *Dilettante Army*. https://dilettantearmy.com/articles/death-technology-return-nature (accessed 30 October 2022).

Walter, T. (2022) 'Heading for extinction': How the climate and ecological emergency reframes mortality. *Mortality*, 1–19. https://doi.org/10.1080/13576275.2022.2072718.

Warren, M.W. and Van Deest, T.L. (2014) Human cremation: Commingling and questioned identity. In B.J. Adams and J.E. Byrd (eds) *Commingled human remains*. Amsterdam: Academic Press, pp 239–255.

3

Death in the Fields: Microbial 'Destruction' in Polluted Soils

Serena Zanzu

The introduction and persistence of industrial pollutants in soil is recognized as an increasingly urgent environmental concern. Soil pollution can occur via a number of sources like volcanic eruptions or mineral percolation, but it mainly originates from anthropogenic endeavours such as agricultural practices, waste management, and the metallurgical and smelting industry. These and other human activities generate and disperse heavy metals such as copper, lead, nickel, zinc, cadmium, platinum, chromium and arsenic. It is widely acknowledged that the presence of heavy metals in soil has a negative impact on the ecological surroundings. Industrial waste and residues can accumulate and persist in soil in the long term, with damaging effects on the ecosystem and on human health. Specifically, the environmental pollution of soil can lead to serious imbalances in the abundant microbial communities living underground (Lenart-Boroń and Boroń, 2013). Among their many activities, microbes assist plants in finding nutrients and they contribute to the formation and structure of soil. Some naturally occurring metals with metabolic or cell enhancing properties can be sustained by the ecosystem and turn useful for microbial life and development, whereas high concentrations of metals with no biological functions can become harmful, disruptive and toxic. Among the damaging effects, these chemicals can lead to a decreased abundance and destruction – death – of the soil *microbiome*, a term indicating the complex community of microorganisms inhabiting a specific environment or host, such as oceans, animals and plants (Microbiology Society, 2017). The health of soil microbial communities in turn has an impact on the wider soil ecosystem.

Removing heavy metals entirely from the environment is a problematic undertaking. While prevention is recognized as most effective in avoiding heavy metal pollution, in many sites this is no longer feasible. Solutions adopted so far include the relocation of the contaminated soil to landfill or incineration of the pollutants, but these have proved to be expensive and potentially hazardous practices (Vidali, 2001). What is emerging as scientifically interesting however is the high tolerance to heavy metals shown by strains of microbes like *Firmicutes*, bacteria capable of enduring heavy metals such as lead and zinc (Fajardo et al, 2019). Bacteria tolerant to heavy metals also include *Cupriavidus metallidurans, Pseudomonas maltophilia* and *Pseudomonas aeruginosa* (Lenart-Boroń and Boroń, 2013). When exposed to toxic pollutants, these microbes show resistance and survival. Moreover, through complex chemical and metabolic activities including methylation, a biological process involving DNA modification (Singal and Ginder, 1999), certain microbes are able to break down, transform or bioabsorb heavy metals, reducing their toxicity. Microbes such as *Alcaligenes* and *Sphingomonas*, for instance, employ the pollutants as their energy source, converting them through metabolic processes and enzymatic activity (Vidali, 2001).

The scientific field studying the potential of microbial communities to decontaminate polluted soil is referred to as *bioremediation* and it traverses diverse areas of research including molecular biology, ecology, environmental biotechnology, microbiology, synthetic biology, biochemistry and engineering. Arguments for microbial bioremediation focus on the reduced cost of these techniques that require lower amounts of resources compared to other tools. Microbial bioremediation is currently employed worldwide and particularly in the United States and Europe (Vidali, 2001).

The study of bioremediation involves multiple tests and attempts to identify the resistant microbial strains and the 'qualities' and specific properties that allow them to survive the chemicals. The understanding of microbial responses to pollutants emerges as instrumental in the selection of microbes for bioremediation purposes. To investigate microbes' reaction to heavy metals exposure, scientists employ a number of recent and evolving technologies including molecular approaches, bioinformatics analysis, ecotoxicological tests and metagenomics, the study of the entire microbial DNA taken from the environment (Debarati et al, 2005; Thompson et al, 2005; Fajardo et al, 2019). Microbial decline, vulnerability to pollutants and subsequent death become relevant in the identification of the specific communities who are most impacted, thus 'sensitive' to contaminants, and those who are usefully resistant, hence capable of withstanding and adapting to toxic substances. Microbes able to tolerate and transform heavy metals can be inoculated in polluted soils to assist in decontamination interventions. The inoculated microbes consist of either isolated strains or 'microbial consortia', groups of diverse microorganisms identified as capable of degrading heavy metals (Adams et al, 2015: 31). These can be both aides to the already present microbial populations as well as potentially in competition with the indigenous communities (2015).

In order to examine the ways in which microbial life and death emerge in decontamination practices, this chapter draws on a variety of documents and published scientific literature addressing bioremediation technologies and processes. These include peer-reviewed articles, texts and documents aimed at the public. The material presented reflects the diverse range of disciplines that intersect to form this scientific field. In exploring this data, the chapter specifically focuses on the ways in which microbial death is conceptualized and defined in bioremediation literature.

The chapter begins with a brief analysis of the field, documenting the central role microbes are assigned in bioremediation practices. The chapter then considers the ways in which alongside microbial life, death itself emerges as significant at different stages of the bioremediation. This knowledge field constitutes microbial death as critical to the success of the intervention. The chapter then claims that a depersonalizing language used in the literature contributes to the formation of a detached and unimportant conceptualization of death in soil microbial populations. The current recognition of microorganisms as increasingly relevant in biology and wider social relations is defined by anthropologists Heather Paxson and Stefan Helmreich as a 'microbial turn' (2014: 166). In considering this shift, the chapter argues that bioremediation literature locates microorganisms in an ambivalent position between friendly and harmful characterizations. The 'remedial microbe' emerges as a technoscientific intervention that resonates with narratives of exploitation of life and death to address anthropogenic crises. By considering the specific role of microbial death in the successful implementation of bioremediation, the chapter attempts to unsettle anthropocentric conceptualizations of death that obfuscate the worthiness of microorganisms. In doing so, the chapter problematizes the human understanding of individuated death to begin appreciating the death of communities, suggesting that dead organisms can be recognized regardless of their multitude and seeming lack of individuality. What kind of materiality of the invisible can emerge when stories of microbial death are allowed to be told? What concerns around their decline may be raised?

Microbial bioremediation in toxic fields

'We can help nature clean up nature faster, naturally', proposes Dr Shaily Mahendra, a professor of civil and environmental engineering at the University of California, Los Angeles, at a TED talk held in Manhattan in 2019 (Mahendra, 2019). In her speech, Mahendra argues that 'nature-inspired' biotechnologies offer a critical opportunity to remove toxic chemicals from the environment. The technologies she is referring to are microbial-based. Microbes 'are awesome', she offers, for their roles in so many processes and as providers of specific services, hence 'we need to switch our thinking about microbes' (2019). The environmental engineer explains that 'mother nature' has been practising bioremediation for millennia. Equating the invisible work that microbes carry out underground with the technological intervention proposed as bioremediation, she presents the process of recruiting microbes to decontaminate soils, so-called 'nature-inspired biotechnologies', as a technique implemented entirely in harmony with nature. This analogy resonates with a narrative proposing 'nature-based solutions' present in conservation and policy debates, that recommend the employment of sustainable interventions, including ecological technologies and engineering, to address urgent environmental crises (Eggermont et al, 2015).

A document aimed at the public, issued by the United States Environmental Protection Agency (EPA), illustrates the processes and numerous stages of intervention involved in the implementation of bioremediation (EPA, 2012). The leaflet addresses the practice of bioremediation both 'in situ', without the need to remove the soil, and 'ex situ', when the soil is collected and processed elsewhere. Because microbes need specific favourable conditions to effectively decontaminate soil, bioremediation often involves the addition of amendments such as vegetable oil. When processed in situ, to provide the right conditions for microbes to perform their task, amendments may be 'pumped underground through wells' (EPA, 2012: 1), through an intervention that requires drilling and disturbance of the soil. Microbes are then added to the soil in need of decontamination. When it comes to the removal of soil and the processing at a different site, the operation involves digging the soil and treating it above ground. Bioremediation requires therefore the 'operation of pumps, mixers, and other construction equipment' (EPA, 2012: 2). The practice is carried out through a number of diverse steps and it appears more complex and disruptive than the narrative of 'nature-based' solutions proposed. The image of technological machinery deviates quite starkly from a depiction of bioremediation as an intervention in harmony with nature.

The EPA document also addresses issues of safety, reassuring the reader that microbes employed for bioremediation live naturally in soil and are harmless. Besides, the microorganisms typically die after the bioremediation is carried out. Once microbes are augmented through amendments and employed to solve the anthropogenic pollution of soil, they are left to die 'naturally'. This, however, does not always occur. To improve the microbial ability to decontaminate, it is possible to genetically modify microorganisms, but the resulting 'biocatalysts' may introduce the risk of 'uncontrolled proliferation' (Debarati et al, 2005: 139). The genetically engineered organisms, where certain enzymes are modified to enhance specific degradation qualities, can pose a hazard of unrestrained growth and evolution. If microbes persist after having remedied the soil by 'escaping this environment' (2005: 139), they can become a safety preoccupation. As I will now consider, the safety and effectiveness of the process become entangled with microbial death at different stages of the intervention.

Temporalities of death

A solution to possible issues of microbial proliferation occurring post-remediation involves enforcing the programmed death of the microorganisms immediately after the remediation is performed (Debarati et al, 2005; Gunjan et al, 2005). In the event they refuse to succumb naturally, microbes are modified so that they are effectively forced to kill themselves through gene manipulation. Forced death can be implemented by introducing a 'killer' gene that only switches on when the contaminants decrease, thus when the microbes have performed their work. Part of the bioremediation knowledge field is therefore concerned with programmed cell death. This typically occurs when microbes are exposed to certain environmental stressors such as acetic acid, a compound that in microbes causes DNA fragmentation, damage and death (Gomaa, 2012). The process is said to be effective in discarding microbial cells after use.

The operation is scientifically defined in a mechanical, quantifiable and unreflexive language, through descriptions such as 'bacterial containment systems' that 'restrict the survival' of the organisms, 'killed by the induction of a controlled "suicide" system' (Debarati et al, 2005: 139). This detached terminology denies and excludes the possibility for a discussion on how death is inflicted and what constitutes a proper death. It also illustrates the ambivalence of a scientific field that proposes itself as able to reconcile the dichotomy human/nature, while at the same time conducting disruptive processes with possibly unwanted and unknown consequences.

If bioremediation involves the deliberate killing of the surviving microbes once the decontamination is carried out, microbes also die in the process of identification of the useful organisms through exposure to toxic chemicals. The scientific experiments themselves entail the death of those microbes unable to tolerate the heavy metals. Unlike the final steps of the remedial process that entail forced suicide, at the experimental stage the desired result is non-death, an outcome that allows for the employment of microbes in clearing the soil. Death at this stage represents an unwanted outcome; it means that a particular group in a specific condition and environment is unable to cope with the toxicity. In scientific papers on the impact of heavy metals on the soil microbiome, a distant terminology also contributes to the obfuscation of microbial death, described as 'cell abundance' being 'impacted', or 'organismal survival' and 'parameters' being 'significantly affected' (Fajardo et al, 2019: 58). Microbes studied and killed in the process of bioremediation undergo a form of death described as 'destruction' (Lenart-Boroń and Boroń, 2013: 760), disruption, disturbance, impact or decrease, in a sterilized language only hinting at their actual death. Microbial death becomes invisible not only because of the inability for humans to sensorially detect microorganisms, but because of the scientific attempt to sanitize the process of microbial demise, reducing it to a mechanical process of reduced abundance.

These discursive techniques act as boundary work, keeping microbial death distinct from other deaths and reinforcing a characterization of microbes as not fully alive. As suggested by anthropologist Noémie Merleau-Ponty (2019) in her ethnography on developmental biology laboratories studying cells, embryos and mice, biologists perform a distinction between being alive and living a life. This hierarchical difference plays a role in the ways death can be inflicted without attention upon those who are constructed as merely alive but not living a life. Because of this distinction, microbes in bioremediation too can be 'destroyed' without being recognized as undergoing an authentic death. Invisible deaths – invisible lives – are constituted and told as lacking an embodied experience. The collateral death in the search for environmental solutions is not acknowledged because the embodied life of microbes is also not recognized.

It is therefore important to interrogate the fate of those microbes not considered beneficial. What are the implications for the microorganisms unable to tolerate heavy metals, such as the bacteria *Nitrospirae* when exposed to chromium, lead and zinc (Li et al, 2020)? Sensitive microbial communities forced to face toxic metals both in experiments and in the fields, may risk loss and extinction. Social scientists Céline Granjou and Catherine Phillips (2018) suggest addressing the question of loss in the context of the promised improvement of agricultural soils through metagenomics. They argue that an enthusiasm for seemingly unlimited opportunities for discovery can have the effect of neglecting the decrease and loss of microbial life. The conceptualization of microbial life as one that refutes the idea of extinction and even death, and a sense that the microbial ecosystem has no finitude, in supposedly unlimited boundaries, can create an absence in concern. In bioremediation literature, the notion of infinite numbers of microorganisms promotes a perspective that lacks a sense of individuation, where the single, individual microbe does not matter and effectively ceases to exist.

The death of sensitive microbial communities in the process of research is only considered problematic for the resulting absence of decontamination services that dying microbes are unable to provide and therefore for the persistence of metals in soil. The suffering and loss of microbial life does not emerge as an issue in itself, but merely as a practical obstacle to remediation, a sacrifice for the higher purpose of the scientific enterprise.

Vulnerable microbes become fruitless actors in the bioremediation effort to rid the soil of human produced poisons. Dying is connected to being futile, death representing the weak response, the inability to help, the lack of resistance and flexibility. But it can also be seen as a microbial rebellion to augmentation, inoculation and forced death. This points to a force operating within death itself, a possible agency of the dead microbe, an element also found in Chapter 1 of this volume when dead human bodies seem to be willing to cooperate or refuse to assist in postmortem examinations. In bioremediation, if surviving is cooperating with the human enterprise, perishing is the unwillingness to assist in the ongoing interventionist attitude to environmental destruction.

Microbial death emerges therefore in this knowledge field as concerning in multiple ways and entangled with specific temporalities, assuming different meanings according to the stage of intervention. Before the remedial work, death entails lack of microbial services that are not provided. After the decontamination, lack of death itself becomes a public health risk. Death is a necessary step and a solution to possible harm caused by surviving microbes. Microbial communities at this stage *need* to die. Unwanted before the decontamination, death is a requirement that ensures safety once the remediation is accomplished, with forced suicide being the price microbes pay to become involved in the anthropogenic polluting enterprise. Death in toxic fields appears and disappears when most suitable, the act of dying being in turn prevented, accepted or enforced in line with the point of intervention.

Emerging 'remedial microbe'

So far, this chapter has proposed that microbial life and death in toxic fields emerge entangled with diverse temporalities of intervention, raising the question of a life form turning instrumental in human and social life. This proposition is in line with the recent coming to matter of microbes in the biological sciences across different fields and knowledge spaces like the study of oceans (Helmreich, 2009), soils (Granjou and Phillips, 2018) and human health (Hodgetts et al, 2018). This event is recognized by social science scholars from diverse disciplines such as anthropology, sociology and geography (Greenhough et al, 2020). Noticing the 'microbial turn' (Paxson and Helmreich, 2014: 166), a multilayered occurrence where microbes become the focus of social conceptualizations of life and of the human itself, it is possible to examine the reconfiguration of a life form that now assumes a critical role and significance as collaborator in diverse human undertakings. From harmful characterizations of microbial life, this shift entails a refashioning of microorganisms as human allies in endeavours as diverse as artisan cheese making (Paxson, 2008) and agriculture (Granjou and Phillips, 2018). Paxson proposes that microbial regulations in place in the United States to ensure food safety coexist alongside conceptualizations of microbes focused on their assistance in creating added nutritional value to artisanal cheese (Paxson, 2008). Her concept of *microbiopolitics* as the recognition of the emergence of the microbial category as an entity that involves agency can assist in thinking about how shifting human relations with invisible agents are discerned and managed (Paxson, 2008).

In the context of bioremediation, microorganisms living underground are constituted as critical in the effort to sanitize polluted soils, emerging as central aides capable of performing the task of decontamination. But as discussed in the previous section, they also retain an image of hazard and possible harm, where death assumes the meaning of a safe outcome around a life form that may be useful but still poses some risks, especially in the public perception. There is therefore a tension between issues of safety, management and exploitation ingrained in bioremediation and elements of respect and appreciation of microbial life. Bioremediation microbiopolitics, alongside agricultural 'soil microbiopolitics' (Granjou and Phillips, 2018: 397), does not embrace a clear-cut distinction between the good and the bad microbe, but still retains conceptualizations of microorganisms as both helpful and harmful. This is partly because it is the 'good' microbe itself that can turn potentially dangerous if surviving after the decontamination process. The ambivalence rests on the framing of an entity that according to the stage of intervention mutates from assistant to threat. The emerging 'remedial microbe' therefore comes to matter as an entity whose reliability, ever presence and specialized competence coexist with hazardous and unpredictable traits requiring strict regulation. The remedial microbe is admired and defined in terms of 'competencies' (Thompson et al, 2005: 911) and 'attractive skills' (Marques, 2018: 2), and yet in need of careful supervision and control, in an ambivalent balance between respect for its abilities and willingness to harness, manipulate and exploit it.

Similar to the focus on microbial collectivity and functionality Granjou and Phillips identify in the field of soil metagenomics for agricultural improvement (2018), the soil microbiome studied for bioremediation is often described as providing particular functionalities critical to human benefit and the balance and health of wider ecosystems. Because of their complexity, diversity and constant changeability, soil microorganisms are studied as 'a functioning soil microbial community' (Fajardo et al, 2019: 56), rather than for their species characteristics. What matters is not merely the isolation of specific microbes, nor their individuality, but the functions carried out by the community.

The logic characterizing soil microbes for their function and employability emerges for instance when microbial communities are defined an 'invisible workforce' (Philp, 2015), 'bioremediation tiny factories' or 'microfactories' (Marques, 2018: 2) that can be exploited to perform bioremediation. In the context of the emerging acknowledgement of soil as living, 'words matter' (Puig de la Bellacasa, 2014: 35). Celebrating soil microorganisms for their work results in the reaffirmation of a capitalist logic of exploitation (2014). While positioning microorganisms alongside, if not beyond, 'pathogen histories and characterizations', a focus on microbes as workers does not allow for the consideration of a 'microontology' advocated by sociologist Myra Hird, a microbial ethics that recognizes microbial agency and relationalities (2009: 1).

Soil may now be scientifically recognized and celebrated for its diversity, yet microbes become incorporated by a promissory hope of improvement (Granjou and Phillips, 2018). The focus on functions allows for microbial life itself to be reduced and turned into a tool, assigned an instrumental value and become a technology for the purpose of human benefit. The abundant and everlasting microbial communities are seen as offering endless material capital for biotechnological solutions aimed at continuing practices of production and trade, thus becoming capitalized through biotechnology. The study, augmentation and genetic enhancement of microbial populations are at the service of human-centred problems and solutions. The remedial microbe is presented as a technofix that promises salvation from pollution, dealing with the symptoms of soil contamination and not with its root causes. The deeper, wider and systemic dynamic of toxic production and pollution, the commercial and productivist interests that lead to its origin, are left untouched, thus allowing for the continuation of business as usual. The remedial microbe materializes as a mutated tool for sustainable technoscience, its meaningful status confined to the possibility of exploitation, as a commodity to augment, feed, exploit and dispose of safely. This becomes possible through the constitution of a life form as the experiment itself, 'an ordinary commodity in the exchange circuits of transnational capital' and the taking of someone's life so that others can live (Haraway, 1997: 79). The emerging tale is one of exploitation and anticipation. Selected soil microbes resistant to heavy metals provide the promise of ever-increasing remediations, as well as supplies to the decontamination industry, while microbial death is reduced to a safe and instrumental outcome. The knowledge produced in this field assumes the form of an intervention, because the soil microbiome is not studied for the mere purpose of identification, but for the specific aim to genetically exploit a life form that becomes a material to work with, effectively a 'biological capital' (Granjou and Phillips, 2018: 408) or 'microbiocapital' (Granjou and Phillips, 2018: 410) to harness and improve. Bioremediation joins other promissory sciences providing solutions to old and new problems, often created by other interventions guided by the possibility of patenting, intellectual property and the commercialization of research for a supposed higher good. This practice contains a promise and justification through the employment and transformation of ever more hopeful political and situated categories of materials such as genes, molecules and laboratory cells (Haraway, 1997). The remedial microbe has now joined the entities technoscience operates with.

It is therefore important to scrutinize forms of knowledge making that assert themselves as the way forward for present and future solutions. An awareness of the remedial microbe celebrated for its microbiocapital worth in scientific practice and beyond does not require a position of antiscience but instead a critical standpoint that proposes itself as a 'molecular politics' (Haraway, 1997: 95). This politics of the invisible identifies the neglect and loss as the result of situated boundary practices in need of attention for novel stories of life and death to be told. This requires an attempt to reconsider death and dying beyond a functional logic of exploitation, instead altering, embracing and valuing other forms, experiences and tales of death that involve the unseen and the collective, across ecologies, domains and taxonomies.

Conclusion

In the current era characterized by environmental crisis and climate breakdown, urgent attention is called upon the extinction and devastation of diverse forms of nonhuman life. To date, the death and loss of silent communities living underground have not received due consideration in scientific debates. Research on bioremediation is instead focused on the employment, manipulation and exploitation of microbial life for human benefit. Microbial communities capable of transforming heavy metals into harmless compounds come to matter for the innovative and sustainable solution they provide to the anthropogenic toxicity leaching underground. This chapter has made a case for the need to examine how the remedial microbe emerges as an ambivalent entity worthy of respect and yet in need of strict management practices culminating in forced death. Along with the problematic commercialization of life invading all areas of biological enquiry, at stake is the reaffirmation coming from this knowledge field of a hierarchical order of death, with microbial entities being positioned outside the boundaries of individuated death. The microbiopolitical harnessing of the remedial microbe highlights a reconfiguration of the categories of life and death in terms of the instrumental function of the collective, where discursive strategies are set to depersonalize microorganisms in their experience of death and to demarcate, safeguard and delimit what constitutes an authentic death. Unlimited communities with endless potential are constituted as lives in between, at the edge between life and nonlife. Against the backdrop of the microbial turn, to question the assumptions around whose death is worth paying attention to, the inanimation of life, the absence of death, the loss and displacement, all require attention.

References

Adams, G.O., Fufeyin, P.T., Okoro, S.E. and Ehinomen, I. (2015) Bioremediation, biostimulation and bioaugmention: A review. *International Journal of Environmental Bioremediation & Biodegradation*, 3(1): 28–39.

Debarati, P., Gunjan, P., Janmejay, P. and Rakesh, K.J. (2005) Accessing microbial diversity for bioremediation and environmental restoration. *Trends in Biotechnology*, 23(3): 135–142.

Eggermont, H., Balian, E., Azevedo, J.M.N., Beumer, V., Brodin, T., Claudet, J. et al (2015) Nature-based solutions: New influence for environmental management and research in Europe. *GAIA – Ecological Perspectives for Science and Society*, 24(4): 243–248.

EPA (Environmental Protection Agency) (2012) *A citizen's guide to bioremediation*. United States Environmental Protection Agency. https://www.epa.gov/sites/default/files/2015-04/documents/a_citizens_guide_to_bioremediation.pdf (accessed 3 October 2022).

Fajardo, C., Costa, G., Nande, M., Botías, P., García-Cantalejo, J. and Martín, M. (2019) Pb, Cd, and Zn soil contamination: Monitoring functional and structural impacts on the microbiome. *Applied Soil Ecology*, 135: 56–64.

Gomaa, O.M. (2012) The involvement of acetic acid in programmed cell death for the elimination of *Bacillus* sp. used in bioremediation. *Journal of Genetic Engineering and Biotechnology*, 10(2): 185–192.

Granjou, C. and Phillips, C. (2018) Living and labouring soils: Metagenomic ecology and a new agricultural revolution? *BioSocieties*, 14: 393–415.

Greenhough, B., Read, C.J., Lorimer, J., Lezaun, J., McLeod, C., Benezra, A. et al (2020) Setting the agenda for social science research on the human microbiome. *Palgrave Communications*, 6: 18. https://doi.org/10.1057/s41599-020-0388-5

Gunjan, P., Debarati, P. and Rakesh, K.J. (2005) Conceptualizing 'suicidal genetically engineered microorganisms' for bioremediation applications. *Biochemical and Biophysical Research Communications*, 327(3): 637–639.

Haraway, D. (1997) *Modest_Witness@ Second_Millennium. FemaleMan©_Meets_OncoMouse™: Feminism and technoscience*. New York: Routledge.

Helmreich, S. (2009) *Alien ocean: Anthropological voyages in microbial seas*. Berkeley: University of California Press.

Hird, M. (2009) *The origins of sociable life: Evolution after science studies*. Basingstoke: Palgrave Macmillan.

Hodgetts, T., Grenyer, R., Greenhough, B., McLeod, C., Dwyer, A. and Lorimer, J. (2018) The microbiome and its publics: A participatory approach for engaging publics with the microbiome and its implications for health and hygiene. *EMBO Reports,* 19(6): e45786: 1–8.

Lenart-Boroń, A. and Boroń, P. (2013) The effect of industrial heavy metal pollution on microbial abundance and diversity in soils: A review. In M.C. Hernandez-Soriano (ed) *Environmental risk assessment of soil contamination*. Rijeka: InTech, pp 759–784.

Li, C., Quan, Q., Gan, Y., Dong, J., Fang, J., Wang, L. and Liu, J. (2020) Effects of heavy metals on microbial communities in sediments and establishment of bioindicators based on microbial taxa and function for environmental monitoring and management. *Science of the Total Environment*, 749: 141555.

Mahendra, S. (2019) Bioremediation: How biology heals the earth naturally. *TED Conferences*, 2 November. https://www.ted.com/talks/shaily_mahendra_bioremediation_how_biology_heals_the_earth_naturally (accessed 3 October 2022).

Marques, C.R. (2018) Extremophilic microfactories: Applications in metal and radionuclide bioremediation. *Frontiers in Microbiology*, 9: 1191.

Merleau-Ponty, N. (2019) A hierarchy of deaths: Stem cells, animals and humans understood by developmental biologists. *Science as Culture*, 28(4): 492–512.

Microbiology Society (2017) *Unlocking the microbiome report*. https://microbiologysociety.org/our-work/the-microbiome/unlocking-the-microbiome-report.html (accessed 3 October 2022).

Paxson, H. (2008) Post-Pasteurian cultures: The microbiopolitics of raw-milk cheese in the United States. *Cultural Anthropology*, 23(1): 15–47.

Paxson, H. and Helmreich, S. (2014) The perils and promises of microbial abundance: Novel natures and model ecosystems, from artisanal cheese to alien seas. *Social Studies of Science*, 44(2): 165–193.

Philp, R. (2015) Bioremediation: The pollution solution? *Microbiology Society*, 8 December. https://microbiologysociety.org/blog/bioremediation-the-pollution-solution.html (accessed 3 October 2022).

Puig de la Bellacasa, M. (2014) Encountering bioinfrastructure: Ecological struggles and the sciences of soil. *Social Epistemology*, 28(1): 26–40.

Singal, R. and Ginder, G.D. (1999) DNA methylation. *Blood*, 93(12): 4059–4070.

Thompson, I.P., van der Gast, C.J., Ciric, L. and Singer, A.C. (2005) Bioaugmentation for bioremediation: The challenge of strain selection. *Environmental Microbiology*, 7(7): 909–915.

Vidali, M. (2001) Bioremediation: An overview. *Pure and Applied Chemistry*, 73(7): 1163–1172.

4

Can the Baltic Sea Die? An Environmental Imaginary of a Dying Sea

Jesse D. Peterson

Death seems to happen to the living; yet, around the world, different communities talk about dead or dying seas, lakes or rivers. From the Dead Sea to the Aral Sea to the Baltic Sea, these waterbodies have been referred to as dying, which lead many to wonder whether these seas (and other waterbodies) can be saved and restored to 'health'. This discourse of dead and dying waterbodies spurs counterarguments that seek to curb, challenge or upset such dystopic characterizations. The group running the Ocean Health Index, for instance, argues that oceans cannot die, making the case that waterbodies are not living organisms (OCH, 2020). Though this debate may never be settled, these conversations of hope and denial, pollution and harm, invite reflection upon what exactly is meant regarding the life or death of waterbodies. It begs the question: can a waterbody die?

The significance and relevance in asking this question stems from taking seriously the societal contention that seas die or do not as well as attempts to redefine life and death as ecological and environmental issues linked to the Anthropocene epoch. Concerns over the magnitude of human impacts upon environmental habitats and physical processes lead scholars to reconsider human relationships to dying, particularly in respect to the effects of industry, colonialism and pollution as well as the bio- and necropolitical control mechanisms exerted over nonhuman animals, such as invasive species and 'unloved others' (Rose and van Dooren, 2011). Nonetheless, inquiry into the lives and deaths of entities typically considered non-living, such as waterbodies, remains absent. This chapter aims to address this silence, in part, because if industrialized societies understood places, objects and processes as literally (rather than metaphorically) being alive or dead (Lidström et al, 2022), profound philosophical, ethical and political consequences would need consideration.

To think with the tensions of those things that cannot die but seem to be in danger of dying anyways, I focus on a discourse of dying waterbodies, using the Baltic Sea as a particular case. Governmental organizations, non-governmental organizations, media and scientists agree, society must 'save' the Baltic Sea and restore its 'health' (*Sveriges Radio*, 2014; Hinton, 2017). As one of the most polluted seas in the world, it suffers from mercury pollution, ecological disturbance caused by heavy transport, parasites and invasive species, munitions and chemical dumping legacies, increasing water temperatures, low salinity, overfishing, cultural eutrophication, harmful algal blooms and extensive dead zones. Yet, as already mentioned, such narratives of degradation invite challenges. For example, one of the objectives of the Baltic Sea Science Center, upon its inauguration in Stockholm during 2019, was to convey that the Baltic Sea was not a dead sea ('det är viktigt att förmedla att Östersjön inte är ett dött hav') (Östersjöcentrum, 2019).

To explore this sea as one that is dying, I present key physical attributes of the Baltic Sea as depicted in scientific accounts with support from mainstream political and cultural concerns related to the impacts of cultural eutrophication on the sea's status. This presentation of physical attributes gets categorized into three main activities that naturalize, value and reify certain characteristics of the sea as those upon which its death depends. This chapter thus shows what are the dominant, normative ways of thinking about the Baltic Sea as dying as well as the specific features and their performance – or values – upon which this understanding rests. Characterizing the Baltic Sea in this manner helps to reveal how different versions of the Baltic Sea come into being. It discloses dominant paradigms that govern the 'life' or 'health' of a waterbody and thereby illustrate how alternatives threaten a waterbody's life. It helps localize for whom a healthy and dying sea benefits. In sum, this chapter seeks to illustrate how the Baltic Sea becomes a dying sea, in part, through claims about its ontological reality. Second, it aims to articulate how a dying Baltic Sea is one simplified version among many other possible seas. Finally, it seeks to know for whom does a dying Baltic Sea serve, offering reflections on both emitters and environmentalists.

The Baltic Sea as 'natural' object

Scientific accounts about the Baltic Sea's state contribute to the 'naturalization' of the sea as ahistorical and independent of people through ontological claims. This 'naturalization' happens through descriptions that paint a picture of what the sea *is*. Accordingly, the main thrust of such accounts constructs an imaginary of a dynamic sea, one of extreme ontological variability. Being the fifth characterization of water conditions in this locale – described in its multiple iterations as the Baltic Ice Lake, Yoldia Sea, Ancylus Lake and the Littorina Sea – the Baltic Sea's legacy displays significant morphological changes over the centuries. Early in its history, the water in this geographic region was largely covered with ice; whereas, today, the Baltic Sea generally freezes only in some areas during the winter months (Rydén et al, 2003). Such variation points out how waters in the sea can undergo all possible phase changes between solid, liquid and gaseous states. In its previous states, the water oscillated between a lake and a sea, and – due to its 'exceedingly low salinity' and 'almost land-locked basin' with a small outlet to the North Sea through the Kattegat and Skagerrak straits – it has been and may continue to be thought of and treated like a lake (Leclerc, 1797: 4; Björck, 1995).

This 'lake', however, is not really a lake as a result of the variability and concentration of salts within it. Sometimes portions of the Baltic Sea, such as the Gulfs of Finland and Bothnia, have been characterized as having lacustrine, or lake-like, conditions instead of the Baltic in its entirety (Segerstråle, 1969: 169–170). Also, the more saline waters in the Baltic's depths create a 'strong permanent halocline', which 'prevents vertical mixing of the water column' (Zillén et al, 2008: 4). That wave and tidal action in the sea are not as strong as in the open oceans means that these water layers mix less than those in the oceans (Segerstråle, 1969: 170). Moreover, several deep basins lead to 'instability and local variations' in salinity levels throughout this sea (Segerstråle, 1969: 170). Hence, the saltier waters and their (lack of) diffusion in the Baltic Sea complicate the geomorphological imagination of the sea as lake or ocean.

In order to address such confounding saline conditions, the sea's waters have been labelled as 'brackish' water. Such classification simplifies and homogenizes the variable gradient of salt content in the waters, while also making the sea less than ideal for some. In 1858, the British naturalist Edward Forbes argued that the brackish water impoverishes the Baltic as either sea or lake. He suggests that the 'deleterious influence' of brackish water limits biodiversity, allows for intrusion of freshwater species, permits commingling between fresh and saltwater species, and leads to 'overanxious patriots' doing bad science (Forbes, 1859: 84, 87, 89–90). Though the Baltic offers little by way of biodiversity as a 'new' sea and some fauna, such as mussels, do not grow particularly large as a result of the brackish waters, saline conditions and fauna in the Baltic have also varied significantly over the centuries. For instance, conditions varied as a result of saline fluctuations in the 1930s, 1940s and 1950s, when salinity increased in the Baltic Sea as a result of decreases in riverine outflow to the sea as well as meteorological changes. Such changes led to an 'enormously increased abundance of cod' as well as other commercially important fishes but also the 'invasion' of stenohaline animals – organisms that cannot tolerate high fluctuations in salinity levels.

Salinity increases also contributed to stagnating saline bottom waters in the deeper basins, leading to 'practically lifeless deserts' and the accumulation of large amounts of phosphorous (Segerstråle, 1969: 172–175). Variations in salt levels in the Baltic Sea thus figure as an essential condition for determining the sea's value, including its waterbody classification, uses and health.

As far as other qualities are concerned, the Baltic has mediocre to poor visibility. It also gets described as shallow and encompasses about one quarter the size of its drainage basin. It is described as navigable and relatively cold, offering a range of recreational activities, such as sailing and bathing. These features have supported the main ways by which humans have used the Baltic Sea throughout time: from a region of missionary zeal to trade and pilgrimage, to dominion and conquest, to research subject, and to a site for political and cultural redefinitions (North, 2018). They point to concerns related to transportation over the sea, salinity, food sources, recreational opportunities and aesthetic concerns, biological diversity, and water cycling. The Baltic Sea, therefore, means many different things, even ontologically speaking. Ultimately, a broad assessment of the claims about the Baltic Sea's physical attributes through deep time displays 'long-term variability' in geomorphology, temperature and climate, salinity, biodiversity, and hypoxia (Zillén et al, 2008: 5).

Such dynamism contributes to making the sea both resilient but also vulnerable. High degrees of variability ought to make a sea that should offer a great deal of flexibility in terms of challenges to its ontological status as a sea. Nevertheless, the sea often gets described as 'unusually sensitive' (Rydén et al, 2003: 257). Such variability tends to be the point of such characterization, exploring the limits of what constitutes the sea and that which does not. Even so, as in the case of salinity in the Baltic, this variability can lead to certain physical conditions being valued over others. In many respects, therefore, the general tendency of these claims-making activities depicts ontological conditions stripped of value or meaning, albeit a closer look can illustrate subtle forms of valuation. In this way, they imagine the Baltic Sea as a 'natural' object, one that predominantly leans towards depicting it as a dynamic, yet vulnerable sea, one susceptible to change.

Diagnoses as valuing nature

Values about the sea, including those made in ontological claims about it, are further refined through diagnoses that overtly value certain ontological features of the Baltic Sea over others by describing harms. Unlike the preceding ontological claims, diagnoses contribute to an imaginary of what the Baltic Sea *ought to be*, adding to and refining what gets labelled as 'natural' about the sea and, more importantly, demarcate what is 'unnatural' for the sea. Though the Baltic Sea faces various challenges, I focus on nutrient

Figure 4.1: Depiction of 'How water bodies change: Oligotrophic conditions versus eutrophic conditions'

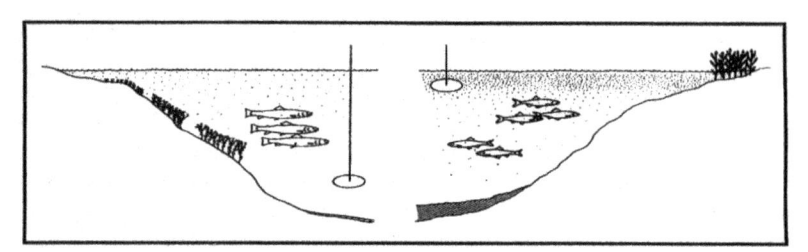

Source: Rydén et al (2003: 269)

pollution impacts, which have become key drivers behind regional policy directed at environmental health, economy, safety and aesthetic value of the Baltic Sea (North, 2015, 2018). Such impacts resemble systemic threats to the Baltic Sea's 'life' as indicated previously. For example, in Figure 4.1, we see oligotrophic (that is, nutrient poor) and eutrophic (that is, nutrient rich) conditions pitted against each other. The image (including its description) reifies eutrophic waters as 'bad' through the separation between the water environments and their arrangement. This separation in the waterbodies implies a mutually exclusive relationship in which eutrophic waters and oligotrophic waters do not mix. They are different seas, in which the transition from one to the other gets represented as a literal 'leap' over a gap. Reading conventions from left to right further frame the oligotrophic status as the default condition and neutral, leading the reader to assume eutrophic waters as less desirable. As such, the image assigns positive and negative values related to oligotrophic and eutrophic conditions, highlighting key values about water bodies that eutrophication 'harms'. These values include visibility, plant growth and location, biological composition, and deposition of sediments and organic matter on the sea floor. Figure 4.2 further expresses deterioration of marine conditions (in the same left to right fashion), highlighting the explicit values placed upon not just species diversity but species of greater taxonomic complexity and the importance of dissolved oxygen. According to such representations, a healthy sea has plants that do not crowd the shoreline or disrupt one's ability to see into the water and supports 'higher' forms of life. These images succinctly capture anxieties over increases in primary production, algal blooms, chlorophyll A concentration, deposition of organic matter on sea bottoms, microbenthic biomass, frequency and severity of oxygen deficiency in bottom waters and decreases in water transparency and depth penetration of bladderwrack, a common seaweed found in the Baltic (Rydén et al, 2003: 269, 277, 274; Andersen and Laamanen, 2009). Setting ecological forms and qualities against others allows for ecological changes to be valued as positive or negative.

Figure 4.2: Oxygen ratio effects on benthic fauna in the Kattegat: 'A: Fish and the benthic macrofauna at normal oxygen levels. B: At 15% oxygen saturation fish and large animals are gone. C: At 5–10% saturation all higher life is gone. (After Baden et al, 1990)'

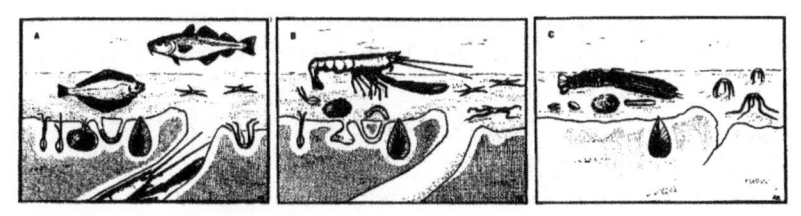

Source: Rydén et al (2003: 277)

Framing oligotrophic conditions as positive and eutrophic conditions as negative defines the limits of acceptability for the variability disclosed through ontological claims. Thus, diagnoses contribute to making some forms and qualities of the Baltic Sea not just undesirable but also 'unnatural'. Algal blooms, for example, exemplify direct challenges to an oligotrophic value system. They cloud visibility and water transparency. They reduce cod breeding grounds while stimulating – but, possibly, also restricting – herring growth. Filamentous algae will also grow on other kinds of algae, like bladderwrack, killing them in the process (Rydén et al, 2003: 272). Some algae release toxins which cause illnesses or kill animals, including people. They deplete oxygen in the seas and convert water into hydrogen sulphide (H2S). Resulting low-oxygen environments may kill benthic animals, change nutrient biogeochemical cycles and further promote algal blooms (Zillén et al, 2008: 4). According to Swedish newspapers as far back as the 1970s, algae bring fisherman to feelings of 'despair' ('förtvivlade') and lead to the sea's death ('havets död' or 'havsdöd') ('Slemmiga grönalger undersökta trivs bara i bukten', 1978; Danielson, 1981; Strömberg, 1984). Diagnoses about algae imply that algae kill the sea by disrupting human use of it, releasing toxins, growing too much, responding positively to human pollution, and also polluting the seas. All these activities contravene what good algae are supposed to do: to get eaten, to medicate, and to get converted into energy. Algae that support what humans desire about them and the sea, therefore, merit protection while the algae that upset these desires do not (Blåstången utrotningsotad, 1982).

Diagnostic claims about the Baltic Sea, thus, construct the possibility for it to die. By constructing normal conditions and abnormal conditions, diagnostic claims do 'boundary work', which excludes and makes algae and other features of the sea aberrations. They suppress and simplify how algae function as agents of ecological change, framing algal presence in the Baltic Sea more a result of indirect human-driven causes than the activities of algae themselves. By framing this ecological activity in terms of a nature/culture separation, algal blooms get understood according to cultural and moral terms, which signify they can be subjected to ethical, political and technocratic responses that are less sensitive to their more-than-human condition. Algae become invaders and pollutants. Diagnostic claims about the Baltic Sea thus police and protect the values set upon certain features and qualities in the sea.

Treatment

In step with those who diagnose the sea as living or dying are those who would do something about it. Efforts to remediate or recreate 'undisturbed' conditions also highlight ways by which the sea can be understood to be dying. Such efforts reify the diagnoses as real. They help give credence to the claims of certain ontological features as unnatural while positing that a natural(ish) sea can be pursued or possibly achieved in the future. Hence, claims about what ought to be done to 'save' the sea paint the most concrete picture regarding which ontological features the sea's life and death depend on.

Most efforts to maintain the Baltic Sea as oligotrophic attempt to reduce nutrient loading through changes in agricultural practices although some efforts have sought to change the sea directly. For instance, multiple geoengineering proposals for resolving hypoxic conditions in the Baltic Sea exist, offering to 'improve' conditions by changing ecological relationships, altering the sea and its waterflows, or by introducing oxygen into the water directly. Reports on the Box project, for instance, described its pumps as 'pacemakers' and noted that its researchers 'literally pumped life into the fjord' ('Forskarna ... har bokstavlingen pumpat liv i fjorden') and that they were 'waking life' in the dead sea bottoms ('det går at väcka liv i döda havsbottnar') (Grill, 2012). Typical of other geoengineering projects, these pumping efforts are also described as enabling control of disturbed ecologies or as possibly being able to heal them using medical metaphors (Luokkanen et al, 2014). Such projects seek to physically alter and reshape the sea to produce an artificial 'naturalness' that supports human use of the sea and all within it. Hence, remediation efforts are similar to research that tries to fix a date and establish 'normal' sea conditions as they appeared before large-scale human impacts. Scientific efforts that invariably depict or seek to recreate environmental conditions and ecological processes that support the use of the Baltic Sea end up informing us about its dying, often as a result of leaving their conclusions up for other actors to politicize. Attempting to stabilize or make controllable certain ontological aspects of the sea, these activities complete the process by which the Baltic Sea can be claimed to die.

The environmental imaginaries of waterbodies

Thus far, I have shown how the life and death of the Baltic Sea presented through the preceding claims depends upon certain features and qualities of the sea. This implies two key insights: first, a living and dying sea are not the only kinds of imaginings that are possible; and, second, the death of the Baltic Sea could rest upon other forms of its ontological qualities, meaning that its death occurs in a particular way. Thus, to help contextualize how the Baltic Sea dies as well as see how other environmental imaginaries of its dying are possible, we need to take a step back and imagine how countless possible other Baltic Seas could come into being.

As this chapter demonstrates, we come to know the sea through various means that build upon each other. We know waterbodies through immediate experience. Second, we come to know waterbodies through ontological claims made about the sea. For example, one may or may not feel water evaporating from the sea's surface, but one cannot bodily sense the claim that the Baltic Sea experiences a net water loss of -185 km3/year due to evaporation (Swedish Meteorological and Hydrological Institute, 2010). That is, both phenomena (that is, being) and onto-epistemological representations of the sea play into its meaning and how it is perceived, interpreted and treated. As science studies scholar Karen Barad argues, we do not know the world without being in the world (2003: 829). We do not know the sea without simultaneously being with the sea. That is, the Baltic Sea can only be ontologically 'true' if society can make it correspond to our own imagination of it (Latour, 1983; Bird, 1987: 259–269). A socio-ecological construction of the sea relies upon conceptual and physical properties that support its continuation as a functional ordering of human–water(body) relationships. Hence, this second layering of 'knowing' the Baltic Sea tends to collapse into the first, leading one to confuse the representation of nature with 'reality'. Yet, not all ontological claims constitute the main value of a waterbody. Thus, certain claims take precedence, simplify the sea, and take shape as an environmental imaginary that functions as a 'hegemonic construction' (Linton, 2010: 9).

That a hegemonic construction of the Baltic Sea comes into being implies that alternate conceptions about the sea can arise. Different conceptions abound when one considers that the various substances, landforms and organisms that contribute in the making of society's version of the Baltic Sea also come into being through *their own* onto-epistemological relationships with humans. Water, animals and landforms, for example – understood as part of the sea but also separate from it – get imagined in their own unique ways. And, any specific conglomeration of some of these conceptual, physical and sensorial experiences of the sea in different times and places combine into the specific set of onto-epistemological relations that govern how humans organize their lives around it. Because such diverse sets of possible seas can be produced – many of which are not compatible – means that the question as to whether or not the Baltic Sea can die could be answered differently in regard to the concepts, forms and qualities that the sea encapsulates and which humans focus upon for their interpretations. For instance, in cultural anthropologist Veronica Strang's *The meaning of water*, dead creatures pollute streams, rivers or lakes while they do not pollute seas or oceans (2004). From this example, something about the volume, or perhaps the freshness rather than saltiness, or even the proximity or uses of the different waterbodies in question plays into perceptions of harm and degradation as well as life, death and not-alive. Hence, a spring might die in a different or similar way to the sea. For instance, different aspects of water might be focal points for asserting a healthy sea, such as its buoyancy or reflectivity rather than oxygen content or clarity. Put differently, if society preferred a eutrophic sea over an oligotrophic sea, then the characteristics upon which the dying Baltic Sea rest would be the main conditions upon which its life depended. Thus, the Baltic Sea could be constructed as different kinds of sea, which highlights how a dying Baltic Sea rests fundamentally upon some but not all its onto-epistemological characteristics.

It should therefore be of no surprise that the Baltic Sea is dying. A dying Baltic Sea illustrates a marked shift in the sensorial experience of the sea as phenomena as well as a disruption of common expectations that have driven its use for centuries. When the onto-epistemological conditions of what makes a waterbody alive start to change, then this waterbody can be interpreted as dying. Or, alternately, when such conditions continue to conform to human expectations (most often by remaining stable), water may be living and alive.[1] Hence, the Baltic Sea is 'dying' because society currently fails in its attempts to recreate the hegemonic environmental imaginary of its value. Put another way, the sea as phenomena defies the imagination of the 'natural' Baltic Sea by accommodating changes that perform the sea in ways that society finds undesirable. These changes – such as those embodied by eutrophic waterbodies – are therefore valued as detrimental and those things which contribute to their existence get labelled as pollutants. Cultural eutrophication and other forms of pollution are what geographer Jamie Linton would call 'hydrosocial hybrids', which arise out of the modern constitution of water as a risk-free resource (Linton, 2010: 190). Like most seas, the Baltic gets treated as a dump site and has been for centuries. Doing so has led pollution to test the limits of major tenets of modern water. Yet, because water and society must be thought of as separate, 'these hybrids are not recognized for what they are' (Linton, 2010: 190). Threats to the seas tend to actually be threats to human use of the seas, as plainly seen in, for instance, this 1974 newspaper headline: 'Tång i Propellern: Ett Nytt Hot till Sjöss' ('Seaweed in the propeller: A new threat for the sea'). In addition, the Baltic's waters become wastewaters because nutrients lose their value immediately after being applied to cropland and then reappear as intrusions within runoff (Thompson, 2017: 232). Hence, the substances that make up Baltic seawater invariably get parcelled into distinct categories: that of seawater and water pollution. Doing so allows for marine pollution to be considered an additive to seawater rather than part of its socio-ecological mix or solution, leading to activities that keep social, political and ontological solutions separate from each other (Linton, 2010: 199). That is, changes to highly valued ontological aquatic features tend to require technoscientific solutions more so than social or political solutions or a combination thereof (Linton, 2010: 195). In this way, water pollution not only threatens human lives but also the lives of waterbodies (Strang, 2004: 79).

Conceived of in this way, life and death happen in relation to onto-epistemological understandings of physical, chemical and biological phenomena in relation to social and cultural particularities. The logical extension of this implies that anything can have a life and a death for humans, and this division comes at the juncture between physical, social and cultural change that disrupts a person's chosen values they attribute to those phenomena. In other words, death occurs when a qualitative relational change takes place, most often when precipitated by physical transformations that no longer can accommodate the as-of-this-moment relational exchanges. These changes are spatio-temporal signs indicating the start of newly forming relationships that are not entirely within human control. Hence, contemporary disruptions to climate, seas, landscapes and soils invite each of us to reconsider dominant modes of thought that propel significant and unintentional physical alterations on and within the vicinity of this planet. According to this model, to be living requires stable, enduring physical forms and qualities that follow predictable patterns and that also satisfy relational – whether human or not – expectations of value as well as managerial schemes and programmes.[2] From this perspective, death and life are both part of the sea's environmental imaginary, and thus, can be made attributable to any phenomena, not just organisms.

For whom the sea dies

Claims made about the sea work together forming a dominant picture of what the Baltic is and does while both providing the grounds for as well as restricting other possible representations of the sea. A Baltic Sea comes into being through claims-making activities regarding: what the sea is; what the sea ought to be; and how to maintain the sea as such. In the case of eutrophication, claims-making activities articulate that the Baltic Sea ought to support higher, more complex life forms in 'appropriate' places; ought to be clear and clean; and ought to be fresher rather than saltier (to its detriment). Freshwater is preferable to saltwater due to the more important value placed upon prevailing environmental conditions (which dovetails with continuing discourse that suggests viewing the sea as a lake). Thus, the sea's main environmental imaginary pins the life and death of the sea upon its water. In this scenario, changes to the Baltic Sea's water that depart from its 'natural' state lead to the death of the sea. This chapter has attempted to show that the Baltic Sea that can die is an environmental imaginary formed, in part, through claims about its onto-epistemological reality. Moreover, it has demonstrated that this construction is one simplified version among many other possible constructions.

For whom, then, does this imagination of the sea serve? Who gains and who loses when a sea lives or dies? Because natural phenomena — such as a sea and its water — come into being through socio-ecological relations, we need to understand the politics of nature, taking time to answer 'the question what water is' as well as which relationships gain primacy (Linton, 2010: 223–224). A sea that can support higher, complex life forms benefits these kinds of organisms, in that they are provided with a liveable habitat. Other forms of organisms potentially lose out. Such conditions favour certain forms of fishing and aquaculture over others, supporting the continued consumption of predatory fish over other aquatic organisms. A sea that is clear and clean supports tourism and recreation. It increases the aesthetic value of the sea for humans. Scuba divers, bathers and beachgoers, and recreational boaters all benefit. If sunlight can pass through its waters, deeper into the sea, certain species of algae and seaweed benefit. It supports coastal dwellings, even if they are a significant source of non-point source pollution. A sea that is fresher rather than saltier supports the local character of the sea. It serves desalination operations and the use of water for irrigating crops or use in husbandry. Fresher water also supports the potential for the seawater's use in industrial operations, such as nuclear energy. Interestingly, as a major contributor to atmospheric deposition of nutrients in the Baltic Sea, shipping neither benefits or loses from such onto-epistemological shifts. In many respects, then, a living Baltic Sea predominantly serves status quo social, cultural and economic relationships to the sea.

Nevertheless, some of these conditions invite conflict. Oligotrophic conditions can perpetuate the exploitation of aquatic goods and services as well as help maintain practices of polluting and disposing waste into the seas. For instance, a clean and clear sea appears capable of handling more trash to be dumped in it while the preferred biocommunity sustains traditional and contemporary fishing practices and management. However, a living sea can also thwart these relationships. The kinds of aquatic organisms desired challenges some forms of polluting activities and pollutants but not others. In addition, environmentalist-oriented non-profits seeking to 'save' the Baltic Sea from pollutants would appear to want a living sea also, albeit perhaps for other reasons. Since a living sea (as well as a dead sea) also benefits those who would exploit the sea, one would expect environmentalists to side with the claim that the sea is dying. From their perspective, it is perhaps better to imagine a polluted sea in order to put pressure on those who would use the sea to externalize costs or exploit its benefits. That is, an environmental imaginary of the Baltic Sea as living or dying prepares the grounds for social and political conflicts around not just what the sea means to different groups but also its ontological status.

Notes

[1] Sterilized water is the abstract ideal of modern water; arguably, it is also perhaps the most dead. This water does not exist but is made. The water is filtered to remove organic compounds and then boiled to stop chemical reactions from taking place within it. Though the water still contains chemicals and other inorganics, meaning that it is not strictly pure, the chemicals and organics remain inert for the most part since their possibility for interaction has been interrupted (informal conversation @Baltic Sea Future 2018). In other words, the production of sterilized water doesn't fully get rid of contaminants, it just creates an environment where they no longer can interact. Inferring from this, death, in terms of both water and the things in it, is the destruction of an environment's capacity to allow those things within it to inter- or intra-act. When it comes to water, in other words, we often confuse sterility for purity. The pursuit for water to embody these characteristics is the pursuit for managing water. Both constitute a particular form of water death. As with animals and plants, we kill our water in order to drink it.

[2] This is why the undying (that is, the horror villain) and zombies induce fear in us. The undying because they ought to die and zombies because they ought to stay dead.

References

Andersen, J.H. and Laamanen, M. (eds) (2009) *Eutrophication in the Baltic Sea: An integrated assessment of the effects of nutrient enrichment in the Baltic Sea region*. Baltic Sea Environment Proceedings 115B. Baltic Marine Environment Protection Commission–Helsinki Commission.

Barad, K. (2003) Posthumanist performativity: Toward an understanding of how matter comes to matter. *Signs*, 28(3): 801–831.

Bird, E.A.R. (1987) The social construction of nature: Theoretical approaches to the history of environmental problems. *Environmental Review*, 11(4): 255–264.

Björck, S. (1995) A review of the history of the Baltic Sea, 13.0–8.0 Ka BP. *Quaternary International*, 27: 19–40.

'Blåstången utrotningsotad'. *Arbetet*, 12 June 1982. SE/GLA/12751/Ö 1 N/1. Landsarkivet I Göteborg.

Danielson, J. (1981) Alger-mat och energi men också havets död. *Aftonbladet*, 1 August. SE/GLA/12751/Ö 1 N/1. Landsarkivet i Göteborg.

Forbes, E. (1859) *The natural history of the European seas*. Edited by R.A.C. Godwin-Austen. London: J. Van Voorst.

Grill, M. (2012) Åter liv i död havsbotten. *SVT Nyheter*, 12 July. https://www.svt.se/nyheter/lokalt/vast/vacker-liv-i-dod-havsbotten [accessed 12 September 2020].

Hinton, S. (2017) The Baltic: A dying sea on the doorstep of industrial giants. *Medium*, 22 February. https://medium.com/@stephenjhinton/the-baltic-a-dying-sea-on-the-doorstep-of-industrial-giants-273341841acf [accessed 12 September 2020].

Latour, B. (1983) Give me a laboratory and I will raise the world. In K. Knorr-Cetina and M. Mulkay (eds) *Science observed: Perspectives on the social study of science*. London: SAGE, pp 141–170.

Leclerc, G.-L. (1797) *Buffon's natural history, containing a theory of the earth, a general history of man, of the brute creation, and of vegetables, mineral, &c. &c.* Translated by James Smith Barr. Vol. 2. 10 vols. London: Printed for the proprietor, and sold by H.D. Symonds.

Lidström, S., Meyer, T. and Peterson, J.D. (2022) The metaphor of ocean 'health' is problematic: 'The ocean we want' is a better term. *Frontiers in Marine Science*, 9: 1–4.

Linton, J. (2010) *What is water? The history of a modern abstraction*. Vancouver: UBC Press.

Luokkanen, M., Huttunen, S. and Hildén, M. (2014) Geoengineering, news media and metaphors: Framing the controversial. *Public Understanding of Science*, 23(8): 966–981.

North, M. (2015) *The Baltic: A history*. Translated by K. Kronenberg. Cambridge, MA: Harvard University Press.

North, M. (2018) The Baltic Sea. In D. Armitage, A. Bashford and S. Sivasundaram (eds) *Oceanic histories*. Cambridge: Cambridge University Press, pp 209–233.

OCH (Ocean Health Index) *Ocean health index*. http://www.oceanhealthindex.org/home [accessed 12 September 2020].

Östersjöcentrum 'Baltic Sea Science Center invigt' (2019) 11 April. https://www.su.se/ostersjocentrum/samverkan/skansen/baltic-sea-science-center-invigt-1.434643 [accessed 12 September 2020].

Rose, D.B. and van Dooren, T. (eds) (2011) 'Unloved others: Death of the disregarded in the time of extinctions'. Special Issue. Vol. 50. *Australian Humanities Review*.

Rydén, L., Migula, P. and Andersson, M. (eds) (2003) *Environmental science: Understanding, protecting, and managing the environment in the Baltic Sea region*. Uppsala: Baltic University Press.

Segerstråle, S.G. (1969) Biological fluctuations in the Baltic Sea. *Progress in Oceanography*, 5: 169–184.

'Slemmiga grönalger undersökta trivs bara i bukten'. *Arbetet*. May 26, 1978. SE/GLA/12751/Ö 1 N/1. Landsarkivet i Göteborg.

Strang, V. (2004) *The meaning of water*. Oxford: Berg.

Strömberg, E. (1984) 'Slemmig alg dödar fjorden', 9 July. SE/GLA/12751/Ö1N/1. Landsarkivet i Göteborg.

Sveriges Radio (2014) Scientists ask just how sick is the Baltic Sea. *Sveriges Radio*. 14 May. https://sverigesradio.se/sida/artikel.aspx?programid=2054&artikel=5862665 [accessed 12 September 2020].

Swedish Meteorological and Hydrological Institute (2010) *The Baltic Sea*. 10 August. https://www.smhi.se/en/theme/the-baltic-sea-1.12289. [accessed 12 September 2020.]

Thompson, M. (2017) *Rubbish theory: The creation and destruction of value*. London: Pluto Press.

Zillén, L., Conley, D., Bonsdorff, E. and Jakobsson, B.-M. (2008) Final report: Hypoxia in the Baltic Sea, 2020 (October).

PART II

Care and Remembrance

5

Viral Flows and Immunological Gestures: Contagious and Dead Bodies in Mexico and Ecuador during COVID-19

Rosa Inés Padilla Yépez and Anne W. Johnson

Introduction

It is never easy to write about death, particularly from the margins, and even less after 2020 and 2021. For us, 'margins' do not only imply a geo-reference – the location of a country and its relation to the centres of power – but also how 'marginal' states and subjects react to emergencies: the very fabric of the health, information and governmental systems. And margins themselves are multiple: within the Latin American contexts we write about, there are margins, and then there are margins. If it is true that a global pandemic necessarily has consequences for the human species, the experience of COVID-19 also has its specificities, depending on, among other things, geography, race, ethnicity and economic class. As one colleague lamented, "We may all be in the same ocean, but we are not in the same boat". Latin America, a region historically characterized by grave inequality and a generalized distrust in public institutions, presents particular challenges.

In Western immunological discourse, the body is seen as a battle site between the individual and a series of foreign invaders, non-selves that threaten the integrity of the self. War is waged through the establishment of protection protocols and the acquisition of appropriate knowledge, actions that function to reaffirm the boundaries between self and non-self (Martin, 1990: 411). But these protocols and other immunological gestures block off precisely the forms of contact that permit care and empathy. Both physically and discursively, these gestures separate selves and others, wrapping them in protective plastic in an attempt to avoid contagion. However, in the context of a pandemic, biological and cultural immune systems are necessarily overwhelmed. Corruption flourishes and rumours flow, like the virus itself. The chaotic movement of information and access to health and other public services contributes to an atmosphere of uncertainty and anxiety around bodies in contact and shared spaces. "No one knows what's going to happen", we are told. And those who have been 'touched' by the pandemic, those who have become sick or lost loved ones, find themselves trapped in their grief; the protocols put into place to protect them restrict their access to the 'normal' rituals that are supposed to help them deal with death and absence. That said, as people try to protect themselves, they also look for ways to maintain contact through creative responses to the pandemic that circumvent immunological gestures.

Because of our own positions and research interests, we focus on Mexico and Ecuador, the countries in which we live and work. Each of these countries administered the pandemic according to its political, economic and technical possibilities. And even within these countries, the pandemic has been experienced in diverse ways. That said, the 'shared' nature of the pandemic is fundamental. Much of the information about the pandemic and possible individual and collective responses to it, including 'official' news, community advice and other information shared through text, video and audio, was circulated without regard to national borders, going 'viral' in record time and in multiple countries at once. This shared information often intensified individuals' sense of vulnerability, mistrust and fear towards the disease and the human body – living, sick or dead. We weave our argument through ethnographic information obtained through observations and interviews with people who have been sick with COVID-19 or have lost loved ones during the worst stages of the pandemic, which were experienced in similar ways in both Mexico and Ecuador.[1]

Fear, uncertainty and the contagious body

In September of 2021, Anne talked to the head of the forensic department of the Secretary of Health in Guerrero, a state in Mexico characterized by high rates of poverty and violence, and low rates of access to health and educational services. When asked about how he perceived the public's reaction to the pandemic, he immediately began to talk about the fear and anxiety experienced by his own employees, especially regarding their encounters with possibly contagious bodies. "There were no protocols", he told her. "No one wanted to pick up the bodies, especially without training, without personal protection equipment. Everything was scarce; everything ran out." "We are working this way, in fear, anxiety and uncertainty. We don't know what's going to happen." Many people are unvaccinated, and there is "much contamination". Not only the bodies of the dead, evaluated as having died by "COVID or probable COVID", but also their families are potentially contagious. And immigrants are still coming into Mexico (many on their way to the United States), he added, alluding to the anxiety caused by a widespread association between immigration and fear of contagion, not just to the physical, but to the social body, as well.[2] He didn't know what the government was really doing, he added, it didn't have a lot of credibility.

'Fear', 'uncertainty' and 'anxiety', he repeated over and over, the affective consequences of potential contagion. His testimony is part of an immunological discourse in which contact between humans is dangerous and must be avoided through strict protective measures, what he referred to as "the protocol". We always try to maintain a "dignified treatment" with respect to the dead and their families, he told her, but the protocols make it more difficult. Normally, the bodies are "dressed, made-up, everything ready for the funeral home". But with COVID-19, "the bodies have to be bagged, sealed, packaged up". Families have the right to say goodbye; it's part of the protocol, although not all the hospitals or clinics respect that part. "Sometimes they just wrap up the bodies in the same sheet that was on the bed." And once the body is sealed, it can't be seen again. As a representative of the government, he got a lot of complaints.

The protocol to which Ben Yehuda repeatedly referred was created by the federal government's Secretary of Health and emphasizes the importance of 'dignified treatment' of the body, solidarity with the dead person's family members, and respect regarding the mourners' personal and cultural attitudes towards death. However, most of the document is devoted to the description of hygienic guidelines for avoiding contagion, rather than suggestions for establishing empathetic relations with mourners. Procedures are described textually and by means of a flow chart, and tables indicate spaces, actions, requirements and the actors responsible for each part of the protocol, according to several possible scenarios. Part of the protocol deals with 'the bag' mentioned by Ben Yehuda, that object which many of our interlocutors decry as an obstacle to proper relations with the dead, a "plastic" – they repeat with disgust – barrier between organic bodies. Other sections consider how to manage the 'probable contagion' of the mourners themselves.

For healthcare workers, this and similar protocols were seen to be protective measures that, when properly implemented, would function as a way of containing the virus through the strict separation of healthy and (potentially) sick subjects. Family members of COVID-19 victims, however, reacted to these institutional protocols with frustration. In many cases, they were prohibited from accompanying their loved ones, either in their final moments or in the funerary rituals that play a fundamental role in the process of mourning, as well as in the constitution of social ties and cultural identity in Latin America.

Álvaro's father died of COVID-19 in a public health clinic in Ecuador. As he told Rosa Inés, "There was no contact. Through a nurse, we could pass him a few things. ... Finally, they had to intubate him. Five days intubated, and he died. There was no way to say goodbye; we couldn't get him a message. He had a heart attack". Also in Ecuador, Isa's grandmother died at home:

> 'It was really hard, because we couldn't bury her, because we didn't know what to do with the body, if we should say it was because of COVID. It was like we had to wait in line because there were so many deaths. When they came for the body, hours later, they were very matter of fact. They just said, "At such and such a time tomorrow you can retrieve the ashes". There was a curfew. My aunt could go out since she's a doctor. She picked up the ashes, she took them to her house, and we cried over Zoom. She wanted her ashes to be scattered in the ocean, but we couldn't do it.' (Isa)

The sense of prolonged melancholy and suspended mourning was a constant in our interviews. 'Later', many told us, they would be able to have a funeral, come together to share memories of the deceased, or dispose of their loved one's ashes according to their wishes. But for now, many are still unable to 'close the cycle' or 'let go' of their grief. Aside from grief, many of our interviewees expressed anger and frustration, not only directed at immunological protocols, but, as we shall discuss later, also at the corrupt institutions and individuals that made pandemic loss even more unbearable.

The immunological discourse that underlies curfews and protocols imposed by state institutions aims to avoid contagion by limiting contact, although, as we will see later, these gestures are unable to fully contain the biological spread of the virus.

Immunological gestures and viral excess

The virus as a public enemy, an invader of the body politic, has been one of the preferred metaphors of medical and governmental institutions, guiding the structuring of public discourse and public policy towards sick and dead bodies.

How do human collectives and institutions comprehend bodies that are, or seem to be, vehicles for contagion? In state discourse in many Latin American countries, the virus is often seen as an invisible foe that doesn't just occupy bodies but potentially decimates them. Notions of pure and impure bodies, hygiene and contamination, have long been bound up in ideas about civilization and its opposites. As Mary Douglas has argued, the deployment of the notion of impurity is an extremely effective means of spreading fear and terror (1966: 13). A viral invader that threatens the pure subject, individual or collective, must be defeated, and infected bodies must be wrapped up, isolated, closed off and hidden away. And bodies that have maintained (or, in some cases, regained) their purity must be immunized.

But the virus resists; it transmutes itself in ways that evade all attempts to contain and eliminate it. Bodies and societies do not have closed borders; rather, the membranes that separate them from the outside are porous, susceptible to crossings that go both ways. That said, although immunological gestures may be doomed to fail, they respond to what seems to be a deeply rooted need on the part of institutions to maintain strict boundaries between selves and others. Infected and dead bodies become targets in these viral wars.

These institutions and the thanatological processes they employ depend intimately on history, geography, social organization, political and economic structures, cultural practices, and beliefs. In Western modernity, as David Sherman points out, cadavers are surrounded by anxiety, revealed as recalcitrant sites of ideological disorientation. What should be done with them? Regulate them, secularize them, modernize them? In new contexts in which the dead are seen as problems that must be dealt with, new laws and procedures are devised, new obligations and values forged, and new authorities come to monopolize the management of the dead. Often, these procedures and their associated institutions and authorities turn out to be hostile to cadaver-subjects, designed to standardize the dead and their resting places, maintain their physical and discursive separation, rather than respect their individual agency and participation in particular social relations (Sherman, 2014: 19). Cadavers, according to Sherman, became illegible and strange, 'more like things to be managed than people to be attended' (2014: 27). This change signified the transformation of a subject–subject relation between the living and the dead into a subject–object relation in which the sick and the dead became the property of medical institutions. In this way, the state amplified its margins of biopower, control over the life and death of its citizens.

According to Sherman, modern cadavers are abject others, catalysts for fear and rejection due to their capacity for infecting life. They have the potential to collapse the division between subject and object, threatening the moral and social order (Sherman, 2014; see also Kristeva, 1982; Bataille, 1991). As a means of managing the anxieties produced by the abject body, modern institutions developed forensic science, among other epistemic practices. And one of the ways in which states demonstrate their power over the lives and deaths of their citizens is the reformation of public health systems, the imposition of public hygiene policies, the implementation of regimens destined to register, control and reduce mortality rates, the creation and relocating of appropriate spaces for the dead, and the bureaucratization of administrative processes (Borneman, 2004).

During the COVID-19 pandemic, sick and dead bodies became vehicles for the deployment of state sovereignty, as governments imposed new rules on health centres, mortuaries and cemeteries. Two constants within the COVID-19 pandemic have been, first, a generalized fear of contagion and, second, the corresponding immunological exercise of state control.

> 'Luckily my grandma didn't die of COVID, because if she had, the *trámites*[3] would have been worse. In the ambulance they kept asking if we were sure that it wasn't COVID, because people didn't want to pick up the bodies.' (Isabel)

> 'During that part of the pandemic, they just wrapped up the coffins in plastic, like when you move, and they pack up your things. He was wrapped in plastic, with packing tape, as if the dead person was going to escape. Then, without uncovering him, we said goodbye, and later they gave us the box with his ashes.' (Antonio)

> 'The only person who could go in and say goodbye to my grandpa was my uncle. No one else, because they didn't let anyone else in. Not even my grandma.' (Marcelo)

Isolating and marginalizing the sick who are in the process of dying is one of the most evident ways in which biopower is exercised. For many of our interviewees, the separation from their loved ones was exacerbated by institutions' control of information and a lack of communication with the health professionals charged with caring for them. In some cases, family members only received information about the sick person's status when it became critical. According to their relatives, many of these patients did not have the opportunity to express their final wishes, as they died soon after being intubated. These difficult conversations led us to reflect on the power of hospitals, of the media and the state itself to control its citizens by means of immunological regulations, orders and decrees. Even the dead must submit to the rules.

The body speaks, tells, remembers. Sick and dead bodies are not simply passive objects; they are, in fact, generative. They exercise agency in the world and have power over the actions of the living, especially over those who must take care of someone who is gravely sick, or deal with the bodies of the dead.

> 'I thought that my dad wasn't so sick. It's hard to imagine that someone who was fine could die so quickly. The last time I talked with my dad was on WhatsApp.' (Álvaro)

'They told me on WhatsApp that my mom was really sick. Since I was in the hospital, they didn't let me check my cell. When I called to see what had happened, they told me my mom had died.' (Rocio)

'My Dad didn't want to take the test because he was afraid of being sick. And he was worried about who would take care of us if he got sick. He thought that if he was sick, he would immediately become useless.' (Diana)

As we mentioned at the beginning of this chapter, one of the things that struck us as we conducted interviews was the way in which people talked about contagion. Again, in Ecuador, the government enforced a stay-at-home rule and a curfew, an extended quarantine with no end in sight which made sickness and contagion legible in a particular way: the sick were seen as *apestados*, or pestilent, and the dead were considered to still be a locus of contagion.

'We were not allowed in to see my mom. The guard at the door even told us not to take her anything, that she already had all she needed. And we told him that my mom was freezing to death, that she had asked for a jacket. And they advised us to take the oldest clothing she had, because the clothing of the sick and the dead were being incinerated. That's how I knew my mom was really sick.' (Diana)

'We knew that they wouldn't let us in, so we didn't even try. My Dad's wife even got sick herself just so she could be in the hospital near my dad, at least during the weakest stage of the disease. When my dad had to go into intensive care, she couldn't be with him, and we sensed that it was the last time we would see him. My Dad died alone.' (Jacobo)

'Everything in the hospital was arranged to keep people out. There were always people outside trying to find out what was happening to their relatives, but no one could get by because of the risk of contagion. Everyone wanted to go in, but they didn't let anyone. It was really sad. My grandfather died alone.' (Marcelo)

The contagious body was relegated, excluded and marginalized, situated in a kind of limbo that made its isolation even more evident. In most Latin American countries, certain hospitals were designated solely for COVID-19 patients, and were organized in such a way as to segregate and isolate people with the disease from the rest of society. In many of these places, patients were not even allowed to have cell phones, and those who were able to maintain telephone contact with their relatives were hospitalized in expensive private clinics.

One of our interviewees was told of her mother's death in the COVID-19 area of the hospital: "Luckily, the doctor, at least on that occasion, behaved decently. He hugged me and told me not to cry anymore, because being sad was going to make it worse. It was the only time he seemed like a human being" (Rocío). Other complaints revolved around the lack of information patients and their families received form doctors, and the frustration people felt because they rarely received daily reports about how their relatives were doing, or because the reports themselves were confusing.

One doctor interviewed by Rosa Inés in Ecuador explained that it wasn't doctors' intention to hide information, but that the problem was one of translating complicated medical terms to members of the general public:

> 'Patients' relatives remember the first and the last words. If you say "He's stable" they interpret it as if he were getting better. If you first say that you're going to give more medicine because there hasn't been a response, people interpret it as if tomorrow he were going to die, and they start asking for other opinions and getting desperate. You also can't use technical terms because they won't understand, and of course when you use simpler language all kinds of details are omitted. So that's what people say that we lied when a patient died because "But you said he was stable", and of course, their anger is directed at the doctor. (Oswaldo)

This doctor emphasized the complexities of practicing medicine during a pandemic. If, during 'normal' life, medical professionals' rule is to avoid involving emotions in their practice, for many the pandemic has depersonalized medical space even more, especially given the overwhelming number of COVID-19 patients during the worst months of the pandemic and the ways in which COVID-19 protocols isolated the sick from the healthy.

However, it is important to note that many of our interlocutors did report instances of empathy and solidarity. This was especially true for patients and family members who were able to commiserate with others who had shared experiences. But, although few, there were also instances of empathy between doctors and victims. Eduardo, for example, after an agonizing series of encounters with medical professionals that were marked by institutional violence, tells of his encounter with a particularly sympathetic doctor when he had to move his brother to another city where he didn't know anyone:

> "'I don't want you to worry. Where are you going to sleep tonight?" the doctor asked. "Well, where else, here, on the damn sidewalk." "Right now, I'm going to tell my son to come and get you. You'll go to my house." [There was a long pause, as Eduardo became visibly

emotional.] "But, Doctor, we don't know each other, how can you offer me your house?" "Forget about whether we know each other or not." His son came about half an hour later, and the doctor said, "Let's go. You don't have to stay here. Your brother is being taken care of, he's in bed, he's hooked up to the machine, don't worry. Tomorrow, come back about this time. I'll take care of it." He told his son, "Give him my room, let him sleep there".' (Eduardo)

Strategies and networks

Just as viruses mutate to evade extinction, our interlocutors strategize and negotiate creatively in response to the protocols and restrictions put in place by the state. When they get sick, as we have seen, they turn to unofficial remedies, trusting in experience and their own conceptions of expertise. When they are forced to deal with institutions, they may take advantage of personal relationships or networks, or, if necessary, they negotiate with authorities by means of bribes. And when treatment fails, they face prohibitions on large gatherings by postponing rituals or organizing alternative forms of grieving.

'Thankfully, we had certain possibilities, and I was able to be hospitalized in the *Hospital Metropolitano*, which had a dedicated COVID wing; I can't imagine [what it was like for] the poor people who had to wait in line for their turn.' (Diana)

'It was because of a friend from the United States, who I had asked for help, that they opened up a bed in Morelia. I got a call from Mexico City, and they told me that they would open up a bed, and that it was a new hospital, recently inaugurated, and that it had a COVID area, and I could take my brother there. Who knows who my friend talked to, or who his contact was?' (Eduardo)

As our interviews show, social networks are key resources in the management of loss and the possibility to negotiate with institutions. Given the widespread corruption to which we have alluded, the payment of bribes, or *mordidas*, is another common strategy when faced with bureaucratic intransigence:

'We had to pay one of the nurses 50 dollars so she would get messages to my dad, or so she would give him the cell for a little while.' (Álvaro)

'The doctor at the private hospital sent me to buy medicines from outside, from a friend of his. The only thing they were attentive to was timely payment of the bill.' (Eduardo)

All our interviewees had negative experiences during the pandemic. Only one of them was willing to use public health services again; most of the rest have decided to pay more for private healthcare even though, as they say, the costs of private healthcare are also a form of violence. But public health services are rife, they say, with institutional violence and corruption. Almost no one was willing to repeat their experiences with the public sector.

> 'They charged us for everything, from the hospital gown to the bedsheets I was lying on.' (Rocío)

> 'They were charging me 20,000 pesos daily to keep my brother there in the hospital. Then they sent me to buy various medicines that, later in the other hospital, they told me they had never given my brother.' (Eduardo)

The tension between 'legal' administrative processes and 'illegal' negotiations is one of these areas, and corruption was mentioned by almost all our interviewees as a phenomenon that envelops their interactions with both state and private health services. Corruption has a language, syntactic codes that citizens become familiar with through experience. It proceeds from disorder, and flourishes in the margin. However, paradoxically, it has an order of its own and may be considered central to the state as an actor in its citizens' daily lives, not through the imposition of rules, but through its multiple and constant exceptions (Das and Poole, 2004: 20).

As we have argued, the procedures administered by the state are often illegible to its citizens. Which procedures are necessary, how and where to fill out forms, whom to ask for guidance: all of these concerns make the experience of managing the sickness or death of a family member even more stressful. And this stress compounds the grief felt by mourners, often converting their feelings of loss into anger and frustration. The lack of control when faced with what may be perceived as an uncaring bureaucracy, as well as what often amounts to considerable expenditures seems to affect men, whose response to illness tends towards the pragmatic, in a particular way when their actions are thwarted. Many of our male interlocutors expressed anger along with their grief. Eduardo, for example, lost his brother, due, at least in part, to medical corruption and inefficiency: "They took away my brother, in the worst way. Those sons of bitches." He told Anne that he came close to taking vengeance but resisted. "Everyone has a family, and maybe those people do, too." Instead, he donated all the equipment he had bought for his brother, trying to find peace through generosity.

Final reflections

We agree with Das and Poole when they argue that 'the margins' constitute a useful position from which to understand the state (2004: 3). They are also a useful position from which to examine what has been described as a pandemic that affects all of humanity, as margins show us how this experience is both collective and individual. We have seen how Latin America (represented partially in this chapter by Mexico and Ecuador) is constituted as part of the global margins, while at the same time it contains and constructs its own internal margins.

Institutions rehearse immunological gestures when faced with spreading contagion, whether the flow of biological viruses, information that circulated on social media, or the transmission of affects such as fear, uncertainty and anxiety. States attempt to impose order by insisting on sanitary protocols, *trámites*, social distancing, stay-at-home orders, and the rational use of statistical data that plot pandemic curves. But states and their institutions, at least in the contexts we discuss, also contain the seeds of their own disorder. Unintelligible administrative processes, contradictory practices and recommendations, seemingly all-pervasive corruption: all of these contribute to the failure of those immunological gestures meant to contain contagion. Of course, individuals and their families also resist containment through the spread of rumour and information from sources that may not be evaluated by institutionally recognized experts, as well as through the contagion of emotions, and the creativity of rituals that circumvent protocols and restrictions.

The people we interviewed seemed to appreciate the opportunity to *desquitarse*, to get things off their chest by talking about their processes, their goodbyes. Collective memory finds a home in the tarot card deck that one young woman inherited from her grandmother, in the 'mafioso car' that one man's children did not want to inherit, in the long conversations that one wife still holds with the ashes of her husband that have pride of place at the head of her bed. One woman, who became a grandmother during the pandemic, is having a hard time getting rid of the things that belonged to her *mamita*. The COVID-19 dead have stayed with their families, sometimes in strange ways, as serendipitous presences capable of generating affects of every kind: tenderness, joy, rage, pain and rancour. Every death, every memory, every pain is unique.

Many of these everyday gestures that people perform not only suspend the absence of their deceased loved ones, but also demonstrate their own agency and that of the dead themselves. And when a farewell is complicated or postponed, mourners develop tools and strategies meant to maintain their relationships, at least temporarily. We have come to see how the virus is itself performative, influencing relations, actions and emotions, in both positive and negative ways. Fear and anxiety surrounding contagion lead to distance and mistrust, but viral crises may also bring about unexpected moments of empathy and new ways of relating. As Emily Martin suggests, following Donna Haraway (1989), perhaps it is time to abandon the notion of the human body as 'the defended self who destroys the foreign intruder lest it be destroyed' and, rather, think of interactions as 'potentially creative situations' that allow us to rethink human and nonhuman relations (Martin, 1990: 422). In this new world in which virus variants appear almost every day, despite vaccinations and other immunological gestures, we have come to see that human experience cannot be contained in a hermetic plastic bag. Viruses, rumours, affects and rituals are always excessive, always spilling over or spilling out.

Notes

[1] Most of the people we interviewed were middle- and working-class Catholics, victims in some way of COVID-19, that we contacted during each of our research projects – Rosa Inés' work on the mortuary industry, and Anne's on precarity and grief.
[2] For a discussion on the human body as a 'police state' that distinguishes between citizens and illegal aliens, see Martin (1990: 412).
[3] *Trámites* is an untranslatable term that refers to the baroque administrative procedures that surround citizens' interactions with the state in many contexts.

References

Bataille, G. (1991) *The accursed share*, vols II and III. New York: Zone Books.

Borneman, J. (2004) Theorizing regime ends. In J. Borneman (ed) *Death of the father and the regeneration: An anthropology of the end in political authority*. Oxford: Berghahn Books, pp 1–32.

Das, V. and Poole, D. (2004) State and its margins: Comparative ethnographies. In V. Das and D. Poole (eds) *Anthropology in the margins of the state*. Santa Fe: School of American Research Press, pp 3–33.

Douglas, M. (1966) *Purity and danger: An analysis of concepts of pollution and taboo*. London: Routledge and Kegan Paul.

Haraway, D. (1989) *Primate visions: Gender, race, and nature in the world of modern science*. New York and London: Routledge.

Kristeva, J. (1982) *Powers of horror: An essay of abjection*. New York: Columbia University Press.

Martin, E. (1990) Toward an anthropology of immunity: The body as nation state. *Medical Anthropology Quarterly*, 4(4): 410–426.

Sherman, D. (2014) *In a strange room: Modernism's corpses and mortal obligation*. Oxford and New York: Oxford University Press.

6

Advertising the Ancestors: Ghanaian Funeral Banners as Image Objects

Isabel Bredenbröker

Introduction

The junction at which one must turn right to enter the town of Peki, an Ewe community in the Ghanaian southeast, branches off an asphalted overland road that leads to the Togolese border. Many *tro tro* minibuses pass by, making the junction a place of high visibility. Here, a couple of recently deceased community members preside as a welcoming committee, conspicuously attempting to catch the eye of travellers (see Figure 6.1). This presence of the dead in the world of the living reflects the elevated importance which the dead and death-related practices hold in Ghana. Of course, these dead at the roadside are not present in the flesh. They are represented by large 'funeral banners': colour-printed posters made out of PVC (polyvinyl chloride), a synthetic polymer-based plastic applied to a fabric-like threaded grid structure.

One will find hundreds more of these funeral banners across town: on the walls of houses, tied to trees or posted to surfaces. They show images of deceased community members, incorporated in digital designs with stock photography, attention-seeking fonts and carefully selected colour schemes. The photographs feature alongside information about the dead, such as their name, age and a headline that indicates whether they died what is locally considered a good or a bad death. Planted onto sticks, these representations of the dead can 'stand', despite their physical bodies no longer allowing them to do so. The PVC, a water-repellent material that is surprisingly heavy, flat and flexible, yet strong, gives the banners support and durability. Other, more difficult qualities of this material are its inability to decompose

Figure 6.1: Obituary banners as welcome committee at the entrance to the town of Peki, Ghana, in November 2016

Source: Photo by Isabel Bredenbröker

organically and its tendency to tear when folded. Throughout the social lives of funeral banners, their material and visual qualities influence the way commemorative practices are conducted and the kind of death that can be socially produced.

This chapter takes a closer look at Ghanaian funeral banners as a popular obituary format in the Ghanaian south. While obituary print products are not completely new, it is difficult to say exactly when they emerged. Obituary pamphlets seem to date back to the late 1970s in Ghana (Budniok and Noll, 2017). Visual and textual announcements with obituary content of the deaths of important people can be dated back to the 1930s (see McCaskie, 2006). Obituary posters preceded banners and are still in use, providing more details on the names of relatives and mourners (Adotey, 2018). Funeral banners have only started appearing over the past decade. Based on ethnographic observation, the chapter will investigate what functions the banners perform for the living. These functions are contextualized with regards to changes in governance, beliefs and mortuary practices that took place over the course of the colonial encounter up until today. Focusing on the materiality and use of these 'image-objects', I will unpack the intertwined relationship between the banners as sculptural but flexible representations of the dead and the image-like but inflexible qualities of dead bodies.

I conducted fieldwork in Peki over eight months between 2016 and 2018. My research investigated the role of materiality in relation to the dead in this community, finding that funerary practices channel complex negotiations over power relations. How then did the dead, and with them the funeral banners, come to acquire such a central position – literally in places of high visibility and structurally as a driving factor in the local political economy?

Death and power

The dead have always been of crucial importance to the living on the African continent and within the African diaspora (Jindra and Noret, 2013; Parker, 2021). Funerals are often big and public social events. Ghanaian funerals have been recognized as remarkable due to their social importance, as initially framed in the work of Jack Goody (1962). Even though it is particularly the Akan in Ghana who are known for their conspicuous funeral celebrations (see McCaskie, 1989; van der Geest, 2000, 2006; Witte, 2002, 2003; Gott, 2007; Parker, 2021), contemporary Ghanaian Ewe communities also place high importance on funerary events. In comparison to the Akan, Ewe practices have received little scholarly attention. Yet, funerary practices across Ghana have all been shaped by a mixing of indigenous social structures with missionary-colonial attempts at executing power by means of regulating death-related activities. In his comprehensive 'History of death and the dead in West Africa', which focuses on Ghana, John Parker dates this emergent 'hybridity of mortuary culture' back to the mid-1900s (Parker, 2021: 322). Parker tells the story of how colonial rule worked towards subjugating its colonial subjects in Ghana, among other things by imposing drastic changes to mortuary practices, such as disallowing home burials and introducing cemeteries. This meant expelling the dead from the places of the living and attempting to replace the worship of ancestors and local deities with Christian religious practice. Forced changes have left a mark on contemporary mortuary practices and demonstrate how, then as much as now, the realm of the dead is related to organizing power structures among the living, as I have written elsewhere (Bredenbröker, 2020).

Funerals in Peki are big and public, drawing large crowds of guests, family and community members. The social importance of death-related practices is visible in the long funeral celebrations and the omnipresence of funeral banners. Peki traditional chiefs, who serve as religious and political authorities at once, have published a funeral calendar, bundling many funerals into dedicated funeral weekends. Channelling the work for the dead by controlling its temporal unfolding here serves as a means of stabilizing local political and religious authorities' institutional claims to power. The elevated importance of death-related events beyond mere economic significance ultimately means that all things to do with the dead affect how community members organize their political structures (see Bredenbröker, 2020). Hence, the Peki community operates a 'political economy of death' (Feeley-Harnik, 1984, 1991). It is the combination of public aspects with numerous, less conspicuous rules, transactions and interactions, which makes the field of death fit to be described as a *total social fact*, following Marcel Mauss (2016). Death serves as a factor which, visibly and invisibly, permeates the social, the economic, the religious and the political sphere (see Figure 6.2). Obituary banners find their place in this omnipotent sphere, often being situated next to market stalls, political campaign posters, advertisements and religious content.

Figure 6.2: Obituary banner placed next to a stall selling cocoyam, which is decorated with an obituary poster, a poster advertising a Christian crusade by a local Pentecostal church and a poster with candidates for the 2016 parliamentary election

Source: Photo by Isabel Bredenbröker

Funeral banners as new ancestral representations

The entangled history of European Christianity and contemporary Ghanaian Christian beliefs, as practised in Peki, marks a specific historical connection between Europe and Ghana. The Peki community and southern Ghana boast an extremely active Christian religious life. These areas were formerly part of the German colonial protectorate and later included in the British Gold Coast. German and Swiss missionaries were active in the entire area. Christianity, however, became locally acculturated and hence adapted to pre-existing indigenous beliefs (Meyer, 1999; Alsheimer, 2007, 2012). Birgit Meyer, who conducted fieldwork in Peki in the late 1980s, describes this intertwined history as a process of negotiation and translation between missionaries and the Ewe population. This process lives on in contemporary funerary practices. While there is a difference between so-called 'traditional' funerals – a term used in Ghanaian English for funerals informed by indigenous codes of conduct – and Christian funerals, both religious practices are blended in funeral settings to prepare the community for all possible eventualities. The reasoning behind choosing a hybrid form of burial is simple. Whenever Christian practice is not considered sufficient for making sure that the deceased will find their place in the beyond and that they will not interfere in any harmful way with the affairs of the living, additional measures, based on indigenous beliefs, can be performed alongside Christian proceedings.

In the banners, traditional and Christian ideas of the afterlife are reflected by indicating indigenous moral categories of death as good or bad, while employing Christian expressions like 'Call to Glory' or 'Rest in Peace'. Visually, white doves, angels, crosses and ladders to heaven meet traditional attire and Western fashion. Mixing visual and textual cues towards both indigenous and Christian beliefs, the banners also blend these different ways of responding to death. The digitally mouldable designs and the durable PVC take this combination of beliefs and practices into a materially and visually modern realm which lends itself to synthesizing different elements with ease. Along the lines of acculturated spiritual practice, the indigenous belief in the dead as ancestors is sustained, while perceived differently by individual members of the Peki community today. Ancestors, from the perspective of most contemporary community members, are often quiet and most notably acknowledged with the ritual pouring of schnapps libation. Formerly, bodies buried in the home served as a material link to the ancestors by way of incorporation. Today, funeral banners can be seen as a new way of manifesting ancestors. They provide a location for the dead right in the middle of the community as opposed to the cemetery. Combined, Christian and indigenous religious elements, as represented in the banners, add to the social importance of funerary practices (see Figure 6.3). The analogy to the

Figure 6.3: Mixing of Christian and traditional imagery in obituary banners

Source: Photo by Isabel Bredenbröker

format of the advertisement or political campaign poster is essentially secular. But while also fulfilling the mundane purpose of advertising the funerals to possible guests and representing the socio-political standing of local families, the banners also frame the deceased as morally good traditional and Christian community members. Synthesizing indigenous and Christian categories of moral personhood and good versus bad death, the banners now make the status of ancestor attainable to those who died a bad death which meant they previously did not qualify for this ideal state.

Transforming bad death through funeral banners

Local indigenous beliefs dating back to pre-colonial times see certain kinds of death as either good (*ku*) or bad (*ametsiava*). These categories still apply today and are easily communicated through the headlines of funeral banners. 'Celebration of Life' or 'Call to Glory' mark a good death, 'Obituary' or 'Call' are more neutral while yet indicating good death, and 'What a Shock' or 'Gone Too Soon' mark a bad death (see Figure 6.4). According to the works of Jakob Spieth (Spieth, 1911), a missionary who lived in Ewe communities, a good death was a death from natural cause such as illness, allowing some time to prepare for death. Good death was followed by visits from sympathizers, the washing and dressing of the corpse and its subsequent burial. Bad death was a sudden death, such as through snakebite, accident, suicide or in labour. Whereas good death could be treated according to a

Figure 6.4: Examples of good and bad death represented on obituary banners

Source: Photo by Isabel Bredenbröker

protocol and resulted in the arrival of the deceased in the land of the souls, a bad death posed problems for the community. Elements of a deceased person's spirit who had died suddenly could split up, linger and potentially be harmful to the living (Parker, 2021: 35). Bad death therefore required a funeral outside of town, the destruction of the deceased's house, the town's purification and revenge in the form of killing what had caused the death (Parker, 2021: 239–240). To counteract haunting, the property of a deceased person could be deposited along the roadside in the bush (Parker, 2021: 249).

Today, the funerary cycle in Peki follows a prescribed 'good death' sequence and multiple alternative 'bad death' sequences which apply if extra measures are required to achieve good death. Good death is death at 'old age', usually above 60, and of natural cause. Qualified community members are those who are seen as contributors to the communal good and do not owe anything to the community. Bad death is untimely and sudden, as for example in a car accident. A death can also be assessed as bad if the deceased is perceived as morally unsound, lazy or otherwise indebted to the community. Obviously, these moral evaluations that are unrelated to the direct cause of death and the age of a deceased may differ in the eyes of the living. Differences in view trigger fierce negotiations over the deceased's moral standing, depending on the relation a living community member has to the deceased and the possible demands made on them to balance that person's remaining debt. The good death sequence aims at establishing the dead as successfully transformed and cleared of all earthly debt or allegations. It involves an ideally lengthy storage at the local morgue. On the weekend of the funeral, the body is washed at the morgue on Friday morning, followed by a ceremonial transport before sunset, an open-casket lying-in-state at a family house, a service with burial on Saturday and a family meeting on Sunday. There are additional events that precede and follow this densely packed week. They often take place over the period of a year up to the first anniversary of a death. Bad death may be treated by an additional soul collection at the site of accident and ritual burial of that soul in the grave. Similar to the deposition of property that Spieth mentions, there are *agbadɔme* places in Peki, bushlands where luggage for the roaming spiritual elements of those who died a bad death are placed. In cases where community members had refused to perform additional rituals, for example because they identified as Christian and reject 'traditional' practice, accidents and bad events that occurred after the bad death of a relative were linked to failure to perform these rituals. Hence, the social pressure to take bad death seriously and act according to protocol is high.

As historical sources (Spieth, 1911), contemporary scholarship (Parker, 2021) and my interlocutors confirm, good death was and is regarded as a trajectory to becoming an ancestor, while bad death is not. Hence, attributions of good and bad death affected the moral afterlife of the deceased. These moral differentiations still apply today, as can be seen in Peki. Yet, they have evolved from what Spieth recorded. Historically, the body would be denied entry to the town in cases of bad death. Today, these bodies can return for a lying-in-state and are buried in a regular cemetery. People who have died badly may also receive funeral banners and thus maintain a prolonged visual-material presence in the community instead of being excluded. Banners are usually left hanging over extended periods of time. Those dead who are represented on them come closer to qualifying as ancestors, no matter their cause of death, since their memory is promoted among the community, as it would be for those on track to ancestor status. That way, funeral banners may help to eventually turn a bad death into a good death, even if the banner initially states that a death is 'bad'. While additional practices and the deposition of gifts at *agbadɔme* help to appease lost spiritual elements, following 'traditional' practice, obituary banners achieve this on a level that is neither decidedly Christian nor traditional. Hence, the banner marks the beginning of the transformative process from bad to good. In cases where the cause of death does not qualify as bad, but allegations regarding the deceased make it difficult to kick off the good death sequence, banners depicting these dead may also help to strengthen the relatives' case for turning their death into a 'good' kind of death.

In combining social negotiations and religious practices, funeral banners help to make ancestor status and morally good death as an ideal kind of death more attainable. For the living, this means that the banners are important tools which help them to gain control over the dead and make them work for their aims. Family names get promoted in association with good death, funerals achieve a higher number of visitors, and all spiritual elements of the deceased are safely contained in their place of destiny. However, this is only possible by closely linking the banners to the dead body and sequences that it undergoes. Bundling human intentions, moral associations and personhood status in bodies and funeral banners, the dead are turned into ideal subjects or 'human indices' of relations (Carroll, 2018: 8), following Alfred Gell's art nexus model (Gell, 1998). The new ideal personas of the dead, which emerge in this process, become locations where the intentions of the living towards a good death are invested and which they help to produce, for example when community members see, read or interact with funeral banners. The banners form part of this nexus of relations that help to manifest the dead's new existence.

The social lives of funeral banners

In the banners, the idealized image of the deceased is represented by a large format photograph, usually featuring one big and one small image, that remind the viewer of the earthly person and the ancestral person. Similarly, the body also takes on iconic shape during the lying-in-state, meticulously dressed and presented in a decorated room. It is not uncommon that a body is changed into different outfits over the course of an evening, propped up into a sitting or standing position. Bright Akosua Brempong, the daughter of the late paramount Chief of Peki, died prematurely following a sudden health incident. But while her banner acknowledged this as a bad death (see Figure 6.5), its aesthetics and presence in public worked towards turning this death into a good kind of death, as did the elaborate presentation of the body at the family house, adorned with heavy gold jewellery and dressed in traditional attire. At lying-in-states, the dead can be interacted with through touch, speech as well as the taking of photos and selfies. Yet, the nature of this presentation is primarily visual. The dressed and propped-up bodies become image-like or sculptural while funeral banners, by being at the same time visual and material, fill in for the deceased persons and give them a temporary new body.

During the funeral of George Yaw Bobi, who died in a car accident at the age of 40, a lively crowd attended the transport of his body from the morgue. As mourners enacted various kinds of work and hobbies related to George, an obituary banner was passed around. Those who got hold of the banner wore it like a cape and received heightened attention while doing so (see Figure 6.7). George's banner could be included in the lively parade, touched, and taken on a bicycle ride, while George's body was loaded on a hearse, rolled up in a body bag and a mat. Due to its flat, light and flexible material, onto which the image of George was printed, the banner replaced his living body as an adaptable effigy. By offering itself to be worn, like

Figure 6.5: Funeral poster and banner for Bright Akosua Brempong

Source: Photo by Isabel Bredenbröker

an item of clothing, the banner was more than simply an effigy figurine, which is usually not flexible. But through the durable and flexible qualities of the PVC, combined with the digitally manipulated image printed on it, the banner acquired the fluidity that spirits possess. Its visual and material qualities rendered it an image-object: not strictly a mask nor sculpture, but a visual representation of a person that contains the possibility of adapting to other forms and contexts materially. Compared to its safely attached state as display object, it was now unchained and became capable of movement and sight, two qualities which David Freedberg identifies as life-like powers transferred onto images (Freedberg, 1957: 33). Later on, while the body was being prepared for viewing, people danced with George's banner, reviving the deceased as a guest of his own funeral. While this was happening, the dancers frenetically wiped the image with a piece of cloth, in a performative effort of cleaning it (see Figure 6.6). This kind of treatment would certainly not have been fitting for George during his lifetime. Rather, it reflects the cleaning of his body that took place earlier that day and invests the image with an idol-like quality, making it the subject of adoration and preservation. In other instances, banners proved to be similarly versatile, for example when standing in as temporary headstones before the finishing of a grave (see Figure 6.8).

Figure 6.6: Cleaning of George's funeral banner during dancing at the evening of the lying-in-state

Source: Still from funeral video. Photo: Terry Multimedia

The afterlives of funeral banners

After the funerals, banners are either removed by kin, especially when they trigger painful memories, or they are left to their own devices.

Figure 6.7: Banner of Bobi worn by participant during the picking up of his body from the Peki morgue in 2017

Source: Photo by Isabel Bredenbröker

Many of my interlocutors voiced that banners were no longer important after some time on display. But since the PVC as a synthetic material does not rot, banners do not disappear but linger as trash. They have fulfilled their purpose and lost their function as ideal representations of the dead. Interestingly, the popularity of synthetic materials in the town's funerary practices helps to maintain the memory of the dead, but denies them disappearance (Bredenbröker, forthcoming 2024). Often, synthetic materials that resist transformation and organic decay are used with the intention of transferring qualities of permanence and control onto the dead. In some cases, though, this also backfires and elements of the dead linger out of context. One example are gifts made of synthetic materials at *agbadɔme* sites, which do not decay, thus producing a permanent material presence of the wandering spirits that are supposed to live here. (Bredenbröker, forthcoming 2024).

Like these gifts to the spirits, banners can also develop an afterlife of their own, one that resides between the controlled space that the living have materially carved out for the dead, and their transformation into immaterial presence. As trash that does not disappear, elements of the dead remain in an uncertain state of afterlife, durable yet no longer useful (see Figure 6.9). The practice of purposefully leaving effigy statues and portraits of the dead to

Figure 6.8: Banner used as temporary headstone in the Peki-Avetile cemetery in 2016

Source: Photo by Isabel Bredenbröker

decay has been noted in other ethnographic studies, such as of the *malanggan* of Papua New Guinea (Küchler, 1998; 2002). Letting these artfully carved wooden sculptures of the ancestors rot amounts to a sacrifice, a partaking in the 'gifts to gods' economy (Küchler, 2002; also Gregory, 1980). Küchler describes *malanggan* as skins, in line with local beliefs and terminology. They contain life energy and assist in its transfer and transformation (Küchler, 2002). The idea of an effigy as a skin relates to the use of funeral banners as wearable effigies. But whereas the making of a *malanggan* entails an intimate form of sharing knowledge along kin lines and the making of Akan terracotta heads used for similar purposes was performed by distinguished female potters (Parker, 2021: 92–106), often in a secretive process, contemporary obituary banners can simply be ordered from designers. Anyone who has a computer and the necessary software can offer their services to bereaved families, which includes taking care of the printing process and delivery of the finished product (Reverend Media, 2020). In Peki, designing obituary banners and posters has become a popular job, fuelling the political economy of death and serving to feed the living.

Figure 6.9: Banner left on the roadside as trash

Source: Photo by Isabel Bredenbröker

Conclusion: between advertisement and ancestors

This chapter has described how the dead in Peki are made into ideal subjects, which serve as indices of various intentions invested into them by the living (Gell, 1998). Funeral banners make good death and ancestor status attainable by means of their ubiquitous presence in town and their mediating position between indigenous 'traditional' beliefs, Christianity, economic function, political context and tangible goals of the living. They reveal the powerful position that the dead have in the local political economy in which they are embedded through historical context as well as the visual similarities and proximity to other advertisement formats in public space. The banners advertise funerals for which relatives seek to attract many guests. It is also not uncommon to see an obituary banner right next to an advertisement for beer or a huge poster featuring the candidates for the presidential election (see Figure 6.10). Another aspect that imbues them with power is their relation to the bodies of the dead as these undergo transformation during funerary activities. By reading material processes of transformation alongside processes of transforming significations and social transformation, I suggest that funeral

Figure 6.10: Funeral banner placed in the company of presidential election campaign advertisement

Source: Photo by Isabel Bredenbröker

banners are in fact more than images, namely image-objects, due to their material properties and their incorporation into practices of commemoration and mourning. They provide new flexible bodies for the dead, replace them in the world of the living and transfer durable and morally good properties onto the dead as ancestors. Through the use of digital technologies and synthetic materials, the banners offer multiple possibilities at generating new ideal representations of the dead that are easy to interact with and display. Bodies, on the other hand, are often kept in the deep freeze of a morgue for extended periods of time until their presentation during lying-in-states. Hence, their material and moral qualities impose limitations on the kinds of interactions that can take place between the living and the dead. Banners and bodies stand in a mutually generative relationship that serves the remaking of the dead into safely contained and morally good persons, a practice that marks a contemporary way of relating to ancestors.

Acknowledgements

Research on which this chapter is based was funded by the DFG (Deutsche Forschungsgemeinschaft) graduate training group 'Value and Equivalence' at Goethe University Frankfurt (Germany). I dedicate this text to the memory of my late grandmother, Ingrid Wilde, who died while I was writing it.

References

Adotey, E. (2018) Where is my name? Contemporary funeral posters as an arena of contestation and (re)negotiation of chiefly relations among the Ewe of Ghana and Togo. *History in Africa*, 45: 59–69.

Alsheimer, R. (2007) *Zwischen Sklaverei und christlicher Ethnogenese: Die vorkoloniale Missionierung der Ewe in Westafrika (1847 – ca. 1890)*. Münster: Waxmann.

Alsheimer, R. (2012) Missionarsethnologie und Tribalismus: Ewe in Westafrika. In U. van der Heyden and A. Feldtkeller (eds) *Missionsgeschichte Als Geschichte Der Globalisierung Von Wissen: Transkulturelle Wissensaneignung Und -Vermittlung Durch Christliche Missionare in Afrika Und Asien Im 17., 18. Und 19. Jahrhundert*. Stuttgart: Steiner, pp 21–32.

Bredenbröker, I. (2020) The last bath: Cleaning practices and the production of good death in an Ewe town. In I. Bredenbröker, C. Hanzen and F. Kotzur (eds) *Cleaning and value: Interdisciplinary investigations*. Leiden: Sidestone Press, pp 69–88.

Bredenbröker, I. (forthcoming 2024) *Rest in plastic: Death, time and synthetic materials in a Ghanaian Ewe community*. Oxford: Berghahn.

Budniok, J. and Noll, A. (2017) Tod Und Druckerschwärze: Begräbnisbroschüren Als Erinnerungsorte Der Ghanaischen Mittelklasse. *Ethnoscripts*, 19(1): 37–58.

Carroll, T. (2018) *Orthodox Christian material culture: Of people and things in the making of heaven*. Abingdon: Routledge.

Feeley-Harnik, G. (1984) The political economy of death: Communication and change in Malagasy colonial history. *American Ethnologist*, 11(1): 1–19.

Feeley-Harnik, G. (1991) *A green estate: Restoring independence in Madagascar*. Washington, DC and London: Smithsonian Institution Press.

Gell, A. (1998) *Art and agency: An anthropological theory*. Oxford: Clarendon Press.

Goody, J. (1962) *Death, property and the ancestors: A study of the mortuary customs of the LoDagaa of West Africa*. London: Tavistock Publications.

Gott, S. (2007) 'Onetouch' quality and 'marriage silver cup': Performative display, cosmopolitanism, and marital *poatwa* in Kumasi funerals. *Africa Today*, 54(2): 79–106.

Gregory, C. (1980) Gifts to men and gifts to God: Exchange and capital accumulation in contemporary Papua. *Man*, 15: 626–652.

Jindra, M. and Noret, J. (eds) (2013) *Funerals in Africa: Explorations of a social phenomenon*. New York and Oxford: Berghahn.

Küchler, S. (1988) Malangan: Objects, sacrifice and the production of memory. *American Ethnologist*, 15(4): 625–637.

Küchler, S. (2002) *Malanggan: Art, memory, and sacrifice*. Oxford: Berg.

Mauss, M. (2016) *The gift: Expanded edition*. Chicago: Hau.

McCaskie, T. (1989) Death and the Asantehene: A historical meditation. *The Journal of African History*, 30(3): 417–444.

McCaskie, T. (2006) Writing, reading, and printing death: Obituaries and commemoration in Asante. In K. Barber (ed) *Africa's hidden histories: Everyday literacy and making the self*. Bloomington: Indiana University Press, pp 341–384.

Meyer, B. (1999) *Translating the devil: Religion and modernity among the Ewe in Ghana*. Trenton: Africa World Press.

Parker, J. (2021) *In my time of dying: A history of death and the dead in West Africa*. Princeton and Oxford: Princeton University Press.

Reverend Media (2020) How to design Ghana funeral banner tutorials II Photoshop CC. *YouTube*. https://www.youtube.com/watch?v=Bgu46mjQLYs (accessed 11 February 2022).

Spieth, J. (1911) *Die Religion Der Eweer in Süd-Togo*. Leipzig: J. Brehmer.

van der Geest, S. (2000) Funerals for the living: Conversations with elderly people in Kwahu, Ghana. *African Studies Review*, 43(3): 103.

van der Geest, S. (2006) Between death and funeral: Mortuaries and the exploitation of liminality in Kwahu, Ghana. *Africa: Journal of the International African Institute*, 76(4): 485–501.

Witte, M. (2002) *Long live the dead! Changing funeral celebrations in Asante, Ghana*. Amsterdam: Aksant.

Witte, M. (2003) Money and death: Funeral business in Asante, Ghana. *Africa: Journal of the International African Institute*, 73(4): 531–559.

7

Dying Apart, Buried Together: COVID-19, Cemeteries and Fears of Collective Burial

Samuel Holleran

Introduction

In April of 2020, as New York City's COVID-19 death toll soared, a photographer used a drone to capture images of dozens of pine coffins being lowered into trenches. The picture underscored the grim reality of a virus which had started to kill hundreds per day. The pictures – soon followed by others of mass graves in Iran and Brazil – drove home the reality of accelerating fatalities. They also spoke to a deeper fear of the loss of individuality in death.

The images of mass graves were taken from a drone hovering over New York's Hart Island, a 40-hectare speck of land off the Bronx that has been used as a sanatorium and potter's field for over 150 years. It has been the final resting place for most of the city's unclaimed dead, including the very poor and the incarcerated. Hart Island is one of the oldest continually operated 'potter's fields' in the United States, yet it is completely unknown to most New Yorkers. It is not served by a ferry and its access is restricted. George Steinmetz, the photographer who took the photos of coffins being loaded into the trench on 15 April 2020, had his drone confiscated and was briefly detained by police for trespassing (Robbins, 2020). Before Steinmetz's drone photos were published, the island was non-existent for all but a handful of New Yorkers, those tasked with burying the bodies. Those people were, almost without exception, prisoners from nearby Riker's Island.[1] Hart Island is not merely 'abstracted from public view' (Denyer Willis, 2018), it is secreted away as a matter of policy. While its outline appears on some city maps it is rarely labelled. In recent years, some openness has arrived in the form of compassionate visits for families of the dead interred there; although this required a significant amount of paperwork and visitors were made to surrender their mobile phones so very few photos of the site exist (Walshe, 2015). Trench burial on Hart Island is nothing new. At the height of the AIDS crisis, there were more than 1,200 annual interments there with only a number given to identify the individual dead in trenches holding 150 plain coffins. In recent years, the city council has recognized the island as one of the largest cemeteries in the world for victims of AIDS and put forward a plan to turn it into a park with a special ferry and a new memorial (Spivack, 2019).

Starting in 2008, the artist-activist Melinda Hunt began The Hart Island Project to digitize 58,000 burial records acquired through a Freedom of Information request. The project's website presents a textual record for those buried after 1980[2] and, since 2018, has added georeferencing information. In December 2019, New York's mayor officially signed over control of the island to the city's Parks Department, a possible first step towards the creation of a publicly accessible memorial space. The mayor and city council also agreed to a hearing that would examine all public burials with some advocating the closure of Hart Island and a shift to cremation only. Just months after the hearing was scheduled COVID-19 emerged in New York City, halting plans to rethink public burial, and significantly increasing Hart Island's intake of bodies.

This chapter has its origins in research conducted in late 2020 and early 2021 that focused on the impact of the COVID-19 pandemic on workers in the Australian 'deathcare' industry, including: palliative care staff, funeral directors, cemetery and crematoria workers, celebrants, and memorial makers (Gould and Holleran, 2021). While the focus of interviews was on the resilience of the deathcare sector under duress, conversations (which took place mostly over the phone because of physical distancing restrictions) often came back to images of mass death from outside Australia. Communal burial represented an uncontained system-wide shock, and a major concern we heard from deathcare workers was that they would not be able to 'uphold' the integrity of their sector if things took a turn for the worse as they had abroad. A full 30 per cent of Australians were born overseas (Australian Bureau of Statistics, 2021), and Melbourne is home to significant immigrant groups from China, Italy, Iran and the United States – countries where mass casualty events occurred in 2020. Images of burial *en masse* in these places appeared in the news and arose in our interviews. In the first year of the pandemic, mass graves became a stand-in for loss of dignity and individuality in death. This chapter builds on interviews with deathcare professionals and engages with literature in Death and Media Studies to understand how news coverage of mass burial works as a shorthand for social fissures. This chapter does not seek to catalogue all imagery of mass burial and sets aside catastrophic events like war and famine to focus on peacetime 'breaks' that illustrate precarity in deathcare infrastructures.

This chapter provides historical background and context to contemporary fears of mass burial and introduces more singular projects that bring co-burial into the deathcare discourse as a communal, or green, alternative to existing methods of bodily disposition. It has a particular focus on media representations of makeshift morgues, cooling trucks and trench burial. Images of mass burial from countries hit hard by COVID-19 loomed in the consciousness of interviewees. To understand the shock of contemporary collective burial this chapter starts with a short history of cemeteries and the removal of the dead from more localized burial sites. It moves on to discuss images of mass burial, including photographs from the pandemic; it ends by examining new services that reframe communal burial.

The public option

Historically, Hart Island, and other paupers' grave sites across the world, were the solution for the interment of people so marginal they could not pay for – or were not recognized as deserving of – a proper burial. While some paupers' grave sites contain individual burials and grave markers, trenches exist in most sites because of the ease by which they can be filled. While administrators of burial grounds for the indigent emphasize their 'solemn responsibility' (Purcell, 2014) to the dead they typically opt for arrangements that are not just cost-sensitive but, sometimes, deliberately austere, differentiating the 'public option' from market-based burials.

Groups around the world have advocated for city-sponsored burials that give more dignity to the dead, including religious organizations and charitable groups like the Collectif les Morts de la Rue who have, since 1999, mobilized volunteers to provide burials for Parisians without means (Guffanti, 2015). In some countries, basic burial fees are included in local tax assessments. In Sweden, a *Begravningsavgift* (funeral fee) is levelled by municipalities with a tax equal to 2.5 per cent of a person's income; it ensures a basic funeral rite and cemetery plot (with a 25-year renewable tenure) for all citizens (Nordh et al, 2021). The management and care of unclaimed bodies reveals fissures in the safety net of the state and in public conceptions of those 'deserving' of care, even if that care comes after one's life is over.

The potter's field is often seen as the final resting place for those who have already died a 'social death' above ground; their lack of kinship ties and resources has made caring for their body a matter of 'disposal', and not 'disposition'. They lack what Judith Butler calls 'grievability' (2010: 50); meaning that lives not recognized as worthy of protection are also seen as unworthy of memorialization. Those suffering from a new disease have often been buried collectively and in haste. In the early years of the AIDS epidemic, when the postmortem contagion risk of the virus was unknown, many funeral directors demanded sealed coffins or refused to handle bodies outright (Troyer, 2020). The stigma around the disease often meant that patients, many of them gay men ostracized by their families, died, and were buried, without ritual or mourners.

The COVID-19 pandemic has, like the European plagues of early modernity and the Spanish Flu of 1918–1920, necessitated collective burial and has strained deathcare practices. Western fears of mass burial go back to the plague pits of Europe. The multiple waves of bubonic plague that swept over European cities underscored the shaky state of medical knowledge and tenuousness of social bonds. Daniel Defoe described London's 1665 plague as a great equalizer; carts dumped men, women and children – naked but for their nightshirts – into hastily dug holes. Here, rich and poor went in together 'to be huddled together into the common Grave of Mankind' (Defoe, 2005). However, our more recent experiences of mass death show that it is precisely the poor (as well as religious and ethnic minorities) who are likely to die, while the well-to-do tend to both evade death and, when they do succumb, they are celebrated with a far greater level of memorialization.

Cemeteries and the city

Before the advent of the parklike, 'hygienic' cemetery at the city's edge, the dead were buried in overfull churchyards often with wooden, and brittle stone, markers that quickly disintegrated. In this way the 'common' people became part of a whole when they were both literally and figuratively 'inscribed' into landscapes. As the historian Thomas Laqueur notes, the 'majority of the parish (that is, the poor) were thus visible as a collective; their bodies changed the shape of the land; they were constitutive of the "mould'ring heaps" that are the churchyard's surface' (Laqueur, 2015: 138). The Old Jewish Cemetery in Prague is an archetypal example of a churchyard cemetery (although not actually connected to a 'church') in which the materiality of many monuments comes together in one churning whole. By the early 19th century, churchyards were seen as unhygienic, unsightly and the source of miasmic fumes. Modern municipal cemeteries were built at the edge of cities, churchyards were closed, and new regulations were passed to standardize interment practices (Laqueur, 2015). Burial moved from a religious practice at the centre of cities to a municipally managed process at the urban periphery.

Individual graves situated in the consecrated ground of the cemetery hold in their size and permanence a good indication of who was viewed as 'fully human'. For a long time, this excluded the destitute and people from historically marginalized groups who were relegated to trench burial at the cemetery's periphery, or burial on unconsecrated ground.[3] Within the taxonomy of interment spaces, the unmarked burial ground sits at the very bottom – these are sites where the dead are 'thought' to be but (unless remains are exhumed) there may be no surface markers; a step up are pauper's fields where a fence, plaque or column attest to the presence of bodies and suggest a potential roster. Burial grounds, largely forgotten, can lay dormant for years before re-emerging, as did New York's African Burial Ground and London's St. James's Burial Ground.[4] Bodies that had done without 'proper' memorialization for hundreds of years became problematic in the public consciousness; teams of archaeologists were deployed for exhumation, documentation and, in the case of New York, reinterment.

The notion that cities are 'built on bones' – literally in the sense of Paris with its famous catacombs or figuratively in the case of other densely settled cities where unmarked burial grounds could one day 'pop up' – is unsettling to many. The discovery of remains at sites slated for development is often accompanied by public processes to determine how to memorialize and reinter remains. Decision-making can take years, time that is not afforded when collective burial happens during moments of societal crisis.

Cemeteries as sites of mass burial

Early in the 2020 outbreak of COVID-19, Australian health departments asked cemetery managers and other deathcare workers to confirm the mortuary capacity of their facilities. News reports state that officials were also drawing up plans to transform key landmarks – like the Melbourne Convention and Exhibition Centre (Towell et al, 2020) – into temporary hospitals and morgues. While large-scale morgues were, thankfully, not needed, the inventorying process highlighted concerns about the capacity to manage the deceased.

Executives from the deathcare sector noted that, while stock-taking constitutes a part of their job,[5] their sector has not always been part of disaster planning processes. At the beginning of the COVID-19 pandemic this changed. State leaders contacted cemetery directors asking them to map their sites and note the amount of available acreage – not for convention burial, but for pit graves. One cemetery chief executive officer (CEO) described gathering "a very small group of people" who determined "how many transport vans they had, where mass burials would occur, and how many could occur in one day". The key, the CEO stated, "wasn't to be alarmist but ... to do what needed to be done". Extending trench burial, known as 'pauper burial' in some legal frameworks, to all victims both highlights the unprecedented nature of the pandemic and the inequities already present in infrastructures of deathcare.

The early focus on cemetery space turned out not to be necessary. Melbourne's extended lockdowns meant that death rates actually went down and while funeral attendance was severely curtailed (at times to ten people) the infrastructures of deathcare held up under the strain of COVID-19. However, the news that public spaces in the city were considered for temporary morgues alarmed the public and helped to pull back the curtain, exposing the fragility of a system that promises individualization and abundant options, but is also vulnerable to sudden shocks.

Images of body storage and mass burial

Because they shock and upset, images of mass death are thought to break into the brains of the public in a way that images of single deaths cannot. They can also threaten governments and upset the structure of civil society (Rabinowitz, 1994). This is one of the reasons why the images of the coffins, and bodies, of fallen soldiers have a history of being excised from news reporting (Trachtenberg, 2008). The American Civil War was one of the first conflicts to show images of the dead, both on the battlefield and in transport. It broke with the pageantry of regimental paintings and Romantic battlefield tableaus and introduced the cold and sober eye of wet-plate photography. The images coming out of Antietam were 'so nearly like visiting the battle-field' as to bring out 'all the emotions excited by the actual sight of the stained and sordid scene' (Holmes, 1872). The intervening years have sought greater and greater realism in the depiction of war, with the virtual reality-anticipating panoramas used to commemorate the Franco-Prussian Wars and the filmic depictions of fighting in the First World War. Even as images from battlefields have been increasingly circulated, images of the dead have often been banned by army censors, perhaps because they tally the final sum extracted by wars.

War and violence may be increasingly on display, particularly on television, but once the dead have fallen, conventions of photojournalism generally dictate that images of bodies should be taken from a distance, unrecognizable from their facial features, and, increasingly, paired with a content warning when published. Only a small proportion of war-related images will show dead or injured people up close, and those are usually limited to seconds-long television clips, not print-based publications that are publicly displaced and have more implied permanence in their tactile form (Silcock et al, 2008). The wide circulation of an image of a dead Kurdish boy on a Turkish beach was met mostly with unease (Papailias, 2019). While some have supported the distribution of such images because of their ability to 'break through' to otherwise numbed publics, scholars have also argued that perhaps it is the world's surfeit of 'endangered, dehumanised life' that 'sustains documentary' photographic practice (Rangan, 2017). During the COVID-19 crisis, some advocated (Rosenthal, 2020) for more images of intubated patients and overflowing morgues to shock scofflaw citizens into compliance with mask mandates, social distancing measures and vaccination drives.

The first images of mass graves to emerge from the pandemic were not from a photojournalist's camera but from the data-gathering activities of satellites. Aerial photos of pre-dug trenches taken on 1 March 2020 over Qom, Iran confirmed 'the worst fears about the extent of the epidemic and the government's subsequent cover-up' (Borger, 2020). The images were obtained by the *New York Times* from the geospatial imaging company Maxar Technologies. Unlike the Hart Island footage, the images exist at a resolution that makes individual bodies imperceptible. The grainy photos were only intelligible when paired with the headline 'mass graves'. This moved them into the humanitarian space of death and memorialization, giving context to rows of bodies that were improperly 'farewelled' and suggesting the far greater number of families grieving their loss.

Helicopters, and increasingly drones, give news outlets access to sites they would normally be barred from; allowing for a role reversal in which journalists can 'survey' the state institutions typically associated with surveillance. In some cases, this has confirmed the existence of disturbing practices; for example, when aerial images taken by the station KFOX14 in El Paso, Texas showed bodies being stacked in temporary morgue trailers in November of 2020. Underneath the translucent white gowns of the body transport workers one can clearly see black and white prison stripes, and it was later confirmed that inmates were brought in for the job at a rate of US$2 per hour (Rocha, 2020). The appearance of refrigerated trailers in a particular community could, in and of itself, become a news story, indicating an uptick in cases and deaths (Hay, 2020). In the United States, dozens of news stories reported on the approval of trailer purchases and the arrival of trailers in hospital-adjacent parking lots; these are assumed to be 'temporary morgues' and their image is now a reliable shorthand for mass death in the COVID-19 era.

Seeing images of the dead doesn't necessarily make people interrogate the real cause of deaths during a natural disaster. As the sociologist Eric Klinenberg (2002: 218) noted in his study of the 1995 Chicago heatwave that killed hundreds, '[t]here is little evidence that the photographs helped audiences to understand the sources of the trauma that was happening around them or to establish connections between the social and political conditions in the city and the emerging public health crisis'. The availability of these images may also serve the opposite intention, becoming a gateway into 'virtual disaster tourism' (Kaussen, 2015) where the line between 'getting involved' and rubbernecking is considerably blurred. In many cases, newspaper images have been accused of helping to create a sense of panic but doing little to illuminate the social failures that lead to scores of excess deaths. Nonetheless, local governments have also worked to tighten their control of media, 'governing by public relations' (Klinenberg, 2002), and tried to block the release of sensitive imagery. The Reuters 'photo of the week' from 20 November 2020 shows the blurred hand of a sheriff in the foreground as he tries to block photographs from being taken at the El Paso temporary morgue. As previously mentioned, photographers have had their drones and cameras seized (Robbins, 2020) and others have had their attempts to document burial sites blocked.

The introduction of COVID-19 vaccinations in early 2021 shifted the context for images of mass casualties. Photos of cooling trucks and temporary morgues could be used by leaders not just to encourage citizens to 'stay home and flatten the curve' but to make the case for a very specific ask: to get vaccinated. In late 2021, the mayor of the Aboriginal Shire of Palm Island, off the Australian state of Queensland, posted a photo to the local government area's Facebook page of a nondescript grey shipping container. The image is captioned by a text informing community members, 90 per cent of whom are of Australian Aboriginal or of Torres Strait Islander descent, that it is, in fact, a 'temporary morgue sent to Palm Island ... [where] [w]e have very ill people in our community and low vaccination rates'. He goes on to say that 'I know this is confronting but it's time for tough advice to be listened to. ... Let's make sure we never need to use it please'. It is difficult to measure the efficacy of these appeals and to thanatological angst, but the use of cooling containers, in particular, speaks to an emergent vocabulary of disaster.

Co-burial reimagined

COVID-19 exposed fears of dying alone and being buried together. However, communal burial is not always neglectful or dehumanizing. Many cultures, particularly in Central and Southern Europe, have a process by which ashes or bones of the deceased are collectively interred in a vault or ossuary after a defined period of burial (Laqueur, 2015). The rise of cremation and the relative lack of established rites around cremated remains (cremains) in Western countries has led some to experiment with mixing cremains together or with other substrates to create new types of memorials (Kohn et al, 2019). While this mixing of cremains is materially different from co-burial, it has helped to redefine the define the spectrum of acceptability, opening the door to co-burial and more radical forms of bodily disposition for those interested in alternatives to individual burial.

Ashes as a form of materiality are 'highly ambiguous' (Prendergast et al, 2006: 884); they can be divided up, scattered, combined or compressed into discrete objects like jewellery and figurines. Compared to bodies, there are few rules governing cremains, allowing them to be posted in the mail or mixed with the remains of other family members or a favourite pet (an option that is increasing in popularity). The comparative 'lightness' of ash allows for a 'necrosociality' (Kim, 2016) that would be difficult to achieve with bodies. In some East Asian cultures where grave visitation is important, it is common for ashes to be interred together, often under a family headstone, to make sure that no family member is inadvertently abandoned.

In Japan, communal burial societies are increasingly common (Rowe, 2011). Some have their roots in live-in houses for people with disabilities and socially marginalized groups, such as the Kotobuki Welfare Workshop, a place where many homeless and former day labourers have found refuge (Kim, 2016: 844); others are targeted at more middle-class constituents. By joining up, individuals help to offset the costs of grave sites and distribute the ongoing caretaking that would otherwise fall onto their family alone. In a rapidly ageing country, *hakatomo* (a compounding of 'grave' and 'friend') groups are a new form of civil society, with monthly meetings and activities. The cremated ashes of members are interred in mounds, underground vaults or statues of the Buddha – undifferentiated and unlabelled – and this is not viewed as dehumanizing. Burial societies offer a new form of voluntary association 'based on choice rather than obligation' (Rowe, 2011: 226) and they spread the onus of grave-tending and memory-keeping to a group that extends beyond kinship ties. In this context, the individuality in death that is seen as the bare minimum in Anglo burial culture could be seen as a failure of sociability in life.

The co-burial of bodies has been a harder sell in North America, yet there are emergent practices that have moved in that direction. The Seattle-based start-up Recompose has tried to persuade Americans to re-examine their feelings towards individualized death and communal burial. What started as a speculative design project by the company's founder, Katrina Spade, has launched as an ecological alternative to traditional mortuary care. Recompose works to transform bodies into soil through a process similar to composting, thereby reconnecting 'the end of life to the natural world' (Recompose – Ecological Death Care, 2022). In its current model, bodies are placed into individual, temperature-controlled pods between layers of woodchips and alfalfa but in Spade's original iteration, called the Urban Death Project, bodies were placed together at the top of a single large vault, where they slowly travelled down through layers of organic matter, decomposing and, eventually, yielding a mass of soil.

In her original design, Spade was not only critical of the environmental cost of conventional burial practice, but also of American culture's 'obsession with individualism' (Ross, 2016) when it comes to the integrity of remains. However, the idea was met with intense critique. Catholic leaders across the United States vociferously objected, saying that the process denies 'the uniqueness of the human person' (Grondelski, 2019). This is in keeping with the Church's position on cremation, which is tolerated, while ash-scattering is explicitly forbidden. The individual must be maintained *in toto*. Even in the US's Pacific Northwest, where the 'death positive' movement is rooted, initial plans for communal decomposition may have been too much for future clients. In 2017, Recompose shifted the design of its system to seal each person's remains in an individual vault for treatment, ensuring that families receive soil that can be traced back directly to their loved one.

Co-burial rhetorically aligns with movements for co-working and co-housing. A new collectivity that is both forced by the precarious finances of the Millennial generation (many of whom will cohabit with roommates for decades not so much as a lifestyle choice but as necessity to maintain a foothold in increasingly expensive cities [Holleran, 2021]) and imagined as an alternative to the 'Me' generation ethos of Baby Boomer parents. Recompose was forced to navigate this divide by providing both a sense of 'community' with the later addition of individualized vaults to maintain the unity of each decomposing body. Instead of burial *en masse*, the option to 'donate your soil, [so] it becomes part of the collective and is no longer tracked as individual soil' is presented at the end of the process, not the beginning (Recompose – Ecological Death Care, 2022), treating the soil much as ashes from cremation are treated.

Recompose has been innovative in its direct lobbying in Washington State to amend laws to allow its process, and it is currently moving forward with the first 'organic reductions'. Similar bills have passed into law in Colorado, in 2021; in California, in 2022; and in New York, in 2023. The imagery used by the company has shifted considerably since Spade's Urban Death Project, which foregrounded renderings of a space where a helical ramp snaked up a large silo in which bodies would be deposited (Kiley, 2015). This 'human composter' has been replaced by more oblique imagery of forest floor underbrush laid out artfully across pastel-coloured screens. This points to a Millennial generation that, while ready for a different kind of burial, is not keen on being confronted with the process of burial and decomposition.

While Recompose and other 'death disruptors' have been able to shake up an industry widely perceived as outmoded, it is still uncertain if their products will find a sizeable market. Still, their presence within the sector has begun to shift norms related to the way taphonomic processes are talked about in the imagery of deathcare that is displayed in public-facing materials. Objects that are normally 'backstage' now appear in the foreground. A promotional video for Return Home, a Recompose competitor in Washington State, shows the company's CEO in front of an industrial shelving that holds three storeys of 'vessels', each containing a body in the process of turning into soil (Return Home, 2022). The vessels, unadorned grey boxes, are marked only by number. They resemble industrial equipment. They are accessible to families to visit during the decomposition process. "We want them to feel welcome to come visit the facility and pay their respects to their loved one anytime they want", says Brie Smith, the Services Director. The site is not near a cemetery or garden but in a light industrial terrain, directly adjacent to e-waste recycling and self-storage facilities. Here, the lack of memorializing flair also seems radically honest. However, the enthusiasm for human composting is not animated by a desire for collectivity in death, like the Japanese *hakatomo*, but by a desire to be closer to the earth.

Conclusion

Collective burials during the COVID-19 pandemic do indeed tap into our 'worst fears' but they also point to the changing nature of interment. Trench burial, a public option thought by many to be relegated to the distant past, was shown to be very much with us today. Refrigerated trucks and shipping containers, commonplace workhorses in the global supply chains that get us fresh food and new electronics took on *unheimlich* qualities when they appeared parked next to hospitals and city morgues. These images of deathcare infrastructure at the point of breaking caused distress and were later marshalled by some authorities to back up health mandates. Representations of mass death in the media have focused a spotlight on a changing deathcare sector and shifting notions of individuality and permanence in final disposition.

While the COVID-19 pandemic appears to be in recession, the memories of crisis in the hardest-hit regions are still very much with us. Death at a large scale without the accompanying ruins of war or hurricanes can be jarring; but with the initial shock also comes the realization that deathcare infrastructures have always been at work in the background of urban life. The appearance of bodies on nightly news and social media streams may percolate into conversation on what a 'good death' looks like. New modes of disposition like *hakatomo* and human composting offer an alternative to existing practices and chip away at fears of co-interment. While human composting remains both illegal and difficult to envisage in most jurisdictions, it troubles notions of propriety and tradition in deathcare. Images of the new technology in action suggest a lack of individuality in stacks of vessels for 'organic reduction'; suggesting a togetherness that goes against the grain of cemetery-based individuation in death.

Notes

[1] Until 2019, the Hart Island burial site was managed by the city's Department of Corrections. It was transferred to the NYC Parks Department.
[2] All records prior to 1980 were destroyed in a fire.
[3] Also included in this group are the unclaimed dead from public hospitals, mental health centres, prisons and aged care homes
[4] The grounds re-emerged as the result of excavation linked to major construction projects in 1991 and 2018, respectively.
[5] In the state of Victoria cemetery trusts are self-funding institutions operating on a not-for-profit basis. So, the sale of new plots, and the continued availability of plots (primarily in newly developed sites at the urban growth boundary), is their main source of income.

References

Australian Bureau of Statistics (2021) 30% of Australia's population born overseas. Media release. 23 April. https://www.abs.gov.au/media-centre/media-releases/30-australias-population-born-overseas (accessed 1 March 2022).

Borger, J. (2020) Satellite images show Iran has built mass graves amid coronavirus outbreak. *The Guardian*, 12 March. https://www.theguardian.com/world/2020/mar/12/coronavirus-iran-mass-graves-qom (accessed 1 November 2020).

Butler, J. (2010) *Frames of war: When is life grievable?* London: Verso.

Defoe, D. (1995) *A journal of the plague year*. Project Gutenberg EBook. http://www.gutenberg.org/files/376/376-h/376-h.htm (accessed 1 March 2022).

Denyer Willis, G. (2018) The potter's field. *Comparative Studies in Society and History*, 60(3): 539–568.

Gould, H. and Holleran, S. (2021) An essential service: Experiences of Australian deathcare workers during Covid-19. Report. https://deathtech.research.unimelb.edu.au/2021/09/05/an-essential-service/ (accessed 2 July 2023).

Grondelski, J.M. (2019) Calling a spade a spade: 'Recomposing' human remains promotes sacrilege. *National Catholic Register*, 15 March. https://www.ncregister.com/commentaries/calling-a-spade-a-spade-recomposing-human-remains-promotes-sacrilege (accessed 2 July 2023).

Guffanti, L. (2015) Volunteers and the French public pauper burial: Do it yourself? *Mortality*, 20(1): 67–82.

Hay, A. (2020) Pandemic-hit Arizona, Texas counties order coolers, refrigerated trucks for bodies. *Reuters*, 17 July. https://www.reuters.com/article/us-health-coronavirus-usa-casualties-idUKKCN24H3HK (accessed 2 July 2023).

Holleran, M. (2021) Millennial 'YIMBYs' and boomer 'NIMBYs': Generational views on housing affordability in the United States. *The Sociological Review*, 69(4): 846–861.

Holmes, O.W. (1872) *Soundings from the Atlantic*. Boston: J.R. Osgood and Company. https://www.loc.gov/item/15010188/ (accessed 2 July 2023).

Kaussen, V. (2015) Zooming in: Virtual disaster tourism in post-earthquake Haiti. *Social and Economic Studies*, 64(3/4): 33–77.

Kiley, B. (2015) The architect who wants to redesign being dead. *The Stranger*, 3 March. https://www.thestranger.com/features/feature/2015/03/03/21792773/the-architect-who-wants-to-redesign-being-dead (accessed 30 October 2020).

Kim, J. (2016) Necrosociality: Isolated death and unclaimed cremains in Japan. *The Journal of the Royal Anthropological Institute*, 22(4): 843–863.

Klinenberg, E. (2002) *Heat wave: A social autopsy of disaster in Chicago*. Chicago: University of Chicago Press.

Kohn, T., Gibbs, M., Nansen, B. and van Ryn, L. (2019) *Residues of death: Disposal refigured*. London: Routledge.

Laqueur, T. (2015) *The work of the dead: A cultural history of mortal remains*. Princeton: Princeton University Press.

Nordh, H., House, D., Westendorp, M., Maddrell, A., Wingren, C., Kmec, S. et al (2021) Rules, norms and practices: A comparative study exploring disposal practices and facilities in Northern Europe. *OMEGA - Journal of Death and Dying*, 0(0): 1–29. https://doi.org/10.1177/00302228211042138

Papailias, P. (2019) (Un)seeing dead refugee bodies: Mourning memes, spectropolitics, and the haunting of Europe. *Media, Culture & Society*, 41(8): 1048–1068.

Prendergast, D., Hockey, J. and Kellaher, L. (2006) Blowing in the wind? Identity, materiality, and the destinations of human ashes. *The Journal of the Royal Anthropological Institute*, 12(4): 881–898.

Purcell, A. (2014) Hart Island holds a million graves of babies and unidentified and poor people. *The Sydney Morning Herald*, 30 March.

Rabinowitz, P. (1994) *They must be represented: The politics of documentary*. New York: Verso.

Rangan, P. (2017) *Immediations: The humanitarian impulse in documentary*. Durham, NC: Duke University Press.

Recompose – Ecological Death Care (2022) https://recompose.life/who-we- are/ (accessed 13 January 2022).

Return Home (2022) https://returnhome.com/ (accessed 13 January 2022).

Robbins, R. (2020) NYPD seizes drone of photojournalist documenting mass burials on Hart Island. *Gothamist*, 17 April. https://gothamist.com/news/nypd-seizes-drone-photojournalist-documenting-mass-burials-hart-island (accessed 13 October 2020).

Rocha, A. (2020) Incarcerated Texans enlisted to work in county morgue as Covid-19 deaths overwhelm El Paso. *Texas Tribune*, 15 November. https://www.texastribune.org/2020/11/15/coronavirus-texas-el-paso-inmates-morgue-deaths/ (accessed 2 July 2023).

Rosenthal, E. (2020) It's time to scare people about Covid. *The New York Times*, 7 December. https://www.nytimes.com/2020/12/07/opinion/covid-public-health-messaging.html (accessed 2 July 2023).

Ross, R. (2016) Inside the machine that will turn your corpse into compost. *Wired*, 25 October. https://www.wired.com/2016/10/inside-machine-will-turn-corpse-compost/ (accessed 13 October 2020).

Rowe, M.M. (2011) *Temples, burial, and the transformation of contemporary Japanese Buddhism*. Chicago: University of Chicago Press.

Silcock, B.W., Schwalbe, C.B. and Keith, S. (2008) 'Secret' casualties: Images of injury and death in the Iraq war across media platforms. *Journal of Mass Media Ethics*, 23(1): 36–50.

Spivack, C. (2019) Hart Island will become publicly accessible parkland: The City Council passed a package of bills to make the island more accessible. *Curbed*, 14 November. https://ny.curbed.com/2019/11/14/20963508/hart-island-new-york-public-parkland (accessed 1 November 2020).

Towell, N., Harris, R. and Preiss, B. (2020) 'Jeff's shed' earmarked for giant Covid-19 hospital and morgue. *Sydney Morning Herald*, 26 March.

Trachtenberg, A. (2008) Through a glass, darkly: Photography and cultural memory. *Social Research*, 75(1): 111–132.

Troyer, J. (2020) *Technologies of the human corpse*. Boston: The MIT Press.

Walshe, S. (2015) 'Like a prison for the dead': Welcome to Hart Island, home to New York City's pauper graves. *The Guardian*, 4 June. https://www.theguardian.com/us-news/2015/jun/03/hart-island-new-york-city-mass-burial-graves (accessed 1 November 2020).

8

Spirit Mediums at the Margins: Materiality, Death and Dying in Northern Zimbabwe

Olga Sicilia

This chapter is part of an ethnography primarily exploring the relations between materiality, corporeality and death, objects, and the multiple pasts in which spirits and mediums are involved in their communities in Zimbabwe. It focuses regionally on the mid Zambezi Valley in northern Zimbabwe, and historically on current mediums of spirits of clans that claim to have ruled this area in the long past (*mhondoro* ancestors).

My ethnography builds on long-term fieldwork in the Angwa and Kanyemba areas in Zimbabwe (including Mozambican border-villages) within a PhD programme and subsequent short visits to the area. Research methods were based on open-ended interviews with mediums and their kin-group (both consanguineal and ritual), headmen, and other key informants in the community. In addition, my observation and documentation of discussions and consultations at the shrines (mediums possessed) were *post-actum* reconstructed and contextualized in text. They became an invaluable source of qualitative data on local politics, ritual and performative practices. Archival data, photographic and film materials added to this ethnographic record.

Scholarship on mediums and spirits in Zimbabwe is extensive and cannot be summarized in this brief introduction. It informs about rich regional variations from historical and anthropological perspectives covering considerably long timeframes such as the 'precolonial', colonial and post-independence periods. In particular, materiality and human bones in Zimbabwe's colonial and postcolonial violent state contexts have gained relevance in recent scholarship. It links the materiality of human remains to aspects of 'emotion' and 'affect' arguing that human bones' agency is related both to representations of the past, and to 'their "emotive materiality" as substances and their "affective presence" as dead persons; spirit subjects which continue to make demands upon society' (Fontein, 2010: 431) in the present. In line with this, others have focused on 'what bones do to people' in the sense of what they do to constrain or allow in various social and material contexts. Hence it has been suggested to consider bones as ambivalent subject/objects. Bones as subjects 'provide a physical reminder or indicator of how well the wishes of the deceased are being fulfilled'. Bones as objects 'have "agency" as materials and things', that is, they 'do things' (Krmpotich et al, 2010: 372–373).

The present chapter focuses on two aspects of the dying process of mediums: the complexities of disgust as well as mourning as a response bound to the materiality of the corpse (but not only that). The proposed accounts of disgust aim to discuss this experience in relation to decaying bodies and death going beyond cultural representation (Durham, 2011) and the sensorium. As hosts of spirits and ritual practitioners, the death and remains of mediums are differentiated. This affects the mourning process of relatives who often struggle due to the ambiguity between the spirit and the person of the medium. Thus, attention is paid to the subjective experiences of the medium's close kin and those involved in their burial and dying journey to show practices of death in relation to meaning, matter, substances and spirits. Corporeal substances (in particular human blood) and the material traces of death pose a threat to mediums. Blood and corpses as well as any medicalized form of their dying thereby represent strong taboos.

Mourning the absent body: emotion and the materiality of the corpse

Public display of the deceased is a widespread practice at regular funerals in the mid Zambezi Valley. As compared to regular funerals, no 'body viewing' is carried out for a deceased medium. Instead, the corpse is kept secluded for some days awaiting mediums of the clan to gather for funeral, and for its preparation for burial transport. Subsequently it is discussed how both the absence and presence of the remains has an emotional impact upon relatives. Furthermore, no particular objects of the dead medium are viewed and handled as part of a response to mourning and loss, as has been demonstrated for other cases (Miller and Parrott, 2009; Newby and Toulson, 2019).

Beyond being instrumental for the identification of the deceased, 'body viewing' is primarily linked to demonstrating respect during the last farewell, and to provide an occasion for public mourning before the body is buried. Therefore, at regular funerals, 'body viewing' can be read as part of a ritualized farewell, as a setting for gestures of condolence to mourners.

Here the preparation of the corpse for burial is undertaken by funerary aides (*madzisahwira*) of the family. As a polluting object/subject, the corpse has to be cleaned and prepared in a presentable manner. Sprinkling water or rubbing it with a wet cloth during the funeral aims at keeping it cool. Lastly, the funerary aides wrap the whole body in cloths, except for the head. Towards the end of a funeral the corpse is brought outdoors on the coffin or casket for public viewing, and the spokesperson of the family invites to approach those who wish 'to say goodbye to the deceased' or 'to see the body for the last time'. Relatives then may take the chance to tell the deceased that they hope to continue being looked after and protected.

Being confronted face to face with the deceased at 'body viewing' provokes in many relatives a strong emotional reaction. Despite their anticipation of this effect, the need to approach the corpse and pay their last respects is equally strong for most of them. As a witness put it, "[S]ometimes people collapse, they faint when they see the face and others have to assist them. People cry, men also but women more [often]". Mourning is understood as part of the funeral and it is a public act. The community mourns[1] the loss, thereby empathizing with the relatives of the deceased. During the funeral, crying, wailing, joking forms of drama imitating the deceased when alive, as well as singing, dancing and showing sadness, are all expressions of mourning. Mourning is seen primarily as a public community act. In some parts of southern Zimbabwe, for example, 'traditional' community mourning for some chiefs includes a ban on all farming work for a few weeks (Fontein, 2015: 55). Private or personal experiences of grieving within the family after the funeral seem by contrast less salient and expressed in restrained ways. These are personalized activities for which the community no longer can give any direct support.

As a key informant stated:

> '[At the funeral] people come to you [the bereaved] at various times doing things, crying, saying words of empathy [condolences at *kubata maoko*], making jokes about grieving. All this recalls the memory of your relative and makes it difficult to take distance. This is what is grieving since others [the mourning community] can see it. After the funeral, though sometimes elders of the family might assist counselling those grieving in the family, mourning fades slowly and the mourner accepts the death of the relative. He finds his own means to accept the situation and move forward with life.' (Interview with R. Chitsiko, 19 November 2021, Angwa)

The topic has triggered some wider debates in anthropology. Lambek, for instance, in response to an article by V. Despret, points to the need for 'a comparable distinction between kinds of endings, one in which the conclusion of specific acts is distinguished from finality in an ontological sense' (Lambek, 2019: 254). As he continues, the ending of a task is different from the ending of a life: ending may either be experienced as something that is completed, or as something final and irreversible. Mourning has above all to do with death loss, yet for many it has to do with closure, which, as Lambek shows, 'is necessary precisely so that life in all its indeterminacy can continue' (2019: 255). The assumption of closure, and the idea that mourning the loss implies to cut the emotional attachment with the deceased and thus accept death as irreversible, has, as Robben observes, been challenged by a number of scholars from diverse disciplines. They sustain 'that mourners may refashion their affective relationships with the deceased into meaningful continuing bonds' in various ways (Robben, 2018: xvi). Connerton (2011) also refers to aspects of bonds' continuity when discussing mourning and memory in the context of historical traumas and suffering.

In addition, it has been shown elsewhere that grief and mourning can be experienced as an open-ended process based on shared mutualities between the dying, the dead and the living rather than as closure (Danely, 2018). Drawing on Connerton's work about embodied or habit-memory (performative forms of memory), Hallam and Hockey (2001: 43–44) noted that previous bodily proximity and engagement with the deceased may at different postmortem situations awake both 'a painful sense of loss' as well as some comfort, depending on the memories the survivor re-enacts which would speak for continuity after death rather than as something final. 'Embodied memories of the dead', they maintain, 'which are produced in the actions of the living, can emerge as habitual repetitions of bodily interactions developed through prior interactions with the deceased—thus loved ones might continue their presence through the bodies of those who survive them' (2001: 43). Within these larger frameworks that are distinguished from assumptions of closure, Fontein (2018) also draws attention to the potentially unfinished and incomplete nature of death, such as in cases of violent deaths in colonial and postcolonial Zimbabwe. He demonstrates how human remains (as material substances) and the dead are imbricated in ongoing contested processes of (re)constitution of the past in what he calls Zimbabwe's 'politics of the dead'.

It has been noted in discussions about 'the unburied dead' how difficult it is to mourn relatives and thus to reconcile with their death when their corpses are absent and lost as a consequence of terror, wars and accidents (Weiss-Krejci, 2013). In these contexts the corpse 'in its materiality' matters as it enables families to properly grieve (Newby and Toulson, 2019: 1). Relatives of mediums report similar challenges due to the absence of the corpse at these specific funerals in northern Zimbabwe. Indeed, immediately after a medium's death and in contrast to regular deaths, his or her closest relatives are denied transitional passing or staying at the medium's homestead. A special shelter is made for them to participate in the funeral from a distance. Yet they are strictly disallowed to take part in the burial itself. As I have shown elsewhere, a ritual protocol is put in place immediately after death that markedly differentiates the corpse of a medium from that of an ordinary person (Sicilia, 2015). Two critical aspects affect relatives' mourning at these funerals. One is the fact that the corpse of their relative is taken away and concealed until being transported for burial. From the moment of death, the next of kin therefore will not be able to communicate with and experience their deceased relative's presence. An additional critical aspect is the emotional restraint of sorrow that dominates at mediums' funerals (and burials), which are performed as a celebration. Here, public display of grief (explicit wailing or crying) is strictly disapproved of.

The corpse of a spirit medium indicates a double absence at funerals. Not only is it out of sight. In addition, relatives cannot claim and appropriate it, because the corpse belongs to the spirit (*mhondoro*) for whom the medium has been the host during their lifetime. Hence the lack of visibility of the remains also signifies the absence of any right of claim by the family and others. The spirit rules the medium's body both in life and death. Therefore, the medium's funeral and burial is arranged not by members of his or her family but by the spirits of the clan (to which the spirit that the medium hosted belongs) through their respective mediums. In fact, it is not the recently deceased medium that is buried. The ceremony is performed as if burying the human being that was in the long past the spirit hosted by the deceased medium. In this sense, the funeral and burial of a medium seems to be performed not as a unilateral event of loss, closure and irreversible end, but as an event predominantly pervaded by happiness and celebration. The community gives verbal condolences to relatives for their loss (*kubata maoko*), while at the same time community members 'celebrate' the spirit in each medium they bury. This may trap close kin into uneasy contradictions and ambiguities when mourning their relative, as the son of the last medium of the spirit Chimaku explained:

> 'When my father died we had nothing to say about the corpse [*mutumbi*]. I was personally very pained that I was not allowed to see my dead father. At one point [at the funeral] I had the impulse to go and see his body, and give him my last respect [to cry my father for the last time].[2] I was refused by my senior relative. ... As family members we were not allowed to join the other group of mourners [funeral attendees]. We were given our own place, and my senior relative was the only person I could lean and talk to release my emotions. ... At a relative's funeral I could show my grief unlike at my father's. We were forced to show some kind of happiness when in actual fact deep in

our hearts we had pain. We were forced to appear in the same way as those who were at the funeral celebrating.' (Interview with Bhito Dzumbunu and T. Gomwe, 21 October 2021, Kafamauro village)[3]

A son of the last medium of Nyamupahuni who died abruptly in January 2019 in his 90s also reported similar struggles at his father's funeral both with conflicting emotions and with the obligation of emotional restrain of sorrow, which reveals the complexities of coping with mediums as individuals with dual identity and ambiguous meanings:

> 'Since it was a touching moment [the funeral] when you [himself and those close relatives in the same situation] felt that your emotions would come out and be seen, you would go out of the place we were given and come back when you were settled because this was not allowed at the funeral. … Once a person [medium] gets possessed [becomes a medium] you [he as a son] will discover that even the relationship [that of father–son in his case] changes. The relationship becomes that of *mhondoro* one [the spirit]. You would call someone [another medium] "father" when you are even not related to that person. Even when two mediums [*homwe*] gather they call themselves according to their *mhondoro* relationship.[4] For example son's son, father, brother. So, there is exploitation[5] [by the spirit] and you [as family member] get used to it. Your own relationship [consanguine one with the medium] might not be recognized at all. No wonder why you have nothing to say to your relative [no farewell at the funeral].' (Interview with Someone Bhachi, 20 November 2021, Muyengwa village)

Death disgust and changes in the postmortem body: putrefaction and dry bones

Funerals and burials in the Zambezi Valley are set to be concluded within 24 hours as temperatures are high most of the year, and any chances to effectively keep the corpse cool are extremely low. In many cases, however, burials are delayed while waiting for relatives and other relevant attendees to arrive, which considerably affects the corpse. Primarily for reasons of logistics, burials of mediums are more often than not such delayed events, since mediums live quite dispersed in the area. They (those organizing it and those invited to attend) have to be informed and then travel to the funeral site. On average 3–4 days are spent waiting for all mediums to gather.

Most residents are familiar with the sight and stench of death in daily funerals. Nevertheless, the experience of disgust, which is not openly admitted, is no less familiar for them in this context. To be used to the proximity of human decay is not identical with control over its physical rejection; a rejection that often conflicts with feelings of dehumanizing and degrading effects about the deceased who is always a neighbour or close kin.

As a visceral rejection, disgust in relation to the decaying body and to dying was often experienced not as 'pure' disgust in absolute terms but came to be associated with other equally strong emotions such as affection, anger or fright. The following commentators may illustrate this. Their experiences point to the ambivalence inherent to encountering the corpse (as an ambivalent subject/object), capable to provoke simultaneous attraction and repulsion, and how they struggled with this ambivalence. In the context of postmortem transformations, an almost unbearable aversion to the stench of decomposing bodies at funerals and 'body viewing' situations was admitted, however, as a sensitive issue. As a headman noted:

> '[T]he smell of that body is terrible. You know ... here [in the Zambezi Valley] it is hot and we might have to wait until relatives come. Many people cannot stay close to where the body is; they cannot stand that smell. Some cover their nose, but the *madzisahwira*[6] cannot, they have to stay there. Often you see at crowded funerals that only some people are closer to where the body is and a bigger group gathers at a distance [from it] because of that smell. They even go without food.'[7] (Interview with headman D. Mugonapanja, 17 November 2021, Angwa)

With regard to the extent of social acceptance of this rejection, he added, "[S]ome people are patient and do understand it, others don't. Some people [relatives of the deceased] spray perfume on the body and in the room [the hut where corpse lies]". And he continued:

> 'Sometimes the body of the dead one [*mutumbi*] changes so much that it all swells, head, face, arms, legs, trunk ... the whole body. You might even not recognize the person. The relatives doing the funeral might be then shy and don't want to do "body viewing". They wrap then the whole body covering the face also because people might think there's a witchcraft issue involving the deceased or that he had an unresolved problem with someone.' (Interview with headman D. Mugonapanja, 17 November 2021, Angwa)

As another commentator stressed the display of disgust triggered off by the sensory properties of the corpse was taken as morally improper:

> '[W]hen showing others your dislike[8] people might take it as you are showing pride, liking too much yourself. You would be showing everyone that you don't like the smell as if you are the only one who

is smelling that. ... No one disputes that the smell of decaying body is awful but don't show it in public [at funeral], it is disrespectful[9] to the attendees and the deceased himself [herself].' (Discussion with R. Chitsiko, 14 November 2021, Angwa)

Thus at funerals attendees are generally expected to display restrained expressions related to disgust, and to govern their emotions in this regard. Covering the nose, facial expressions or even involuntary retching tend to be disapproved of. The commentator continued:

'If uncontrollable, people should better remove themselves from funeral place. It would be inhuman to show rejection of that smell ... it [the stench] is because of unavoidable reasons like waiting for a relative, or the person might have died in the bush and remained there for some time, or have died alone unattended.' (Discussion with R. Chitsiko, 14 November 2021, Angwa)

This resonates with what some authors have discussed as the need to regain and maintain dignity (humanity) when dealing with a corpse, 'to think about death practices as about restoring and reclaiming our humanity as distinct from animals' (Posel and Gupta, 2009: 303).

From a comparative legal perspective the corpse is both a person and a thing. For legal scholars the corpse is an unstable object as they conceive its transient thingness (Stroud, 2018). Experiencing death disgust nevertheless tackles the subject–object divide in a conflicting way, namely, to experience the corpse as both affective subject and repulsive object. It is through the process of objectification, Miller suggests, that objects and subjects are made. They do not exist *a priori* as differentiated from each other (2005: 9). As a repudiated thing, the corpse seems to be alienated from the animated person's subjectivity. For many confronted with a corpse, it provokes a phenomenal tension that challenges attempts to overcome the subject–object dualism: being no longer a subject, the corpse can neither be fully taken as an object (as merely passive and rotting flesh). In his analysis of disgust and human remains, philosopher McGinn (2011) makes an interesting, almost implicit wet/dry distinction: The object of disgust, he argues, is the fleshy-leaky-putrid corpse, as being neither in the previous stage (the recently dead) nor in the last stage in the transformation of human remains (dry bones) awaken disgust.[10]

In his 2001 version of 'Thing theory', philosopher Bill Brown asked about the possibility to imagine 'this matter of things', 'as the amorphousness out of which objects are materialized by the (ap)perceiving subject, the effect of the mutual constitution of subject and object, a retroprojection'. 'Temporalized as the before and after of the object, thingness', he claims, amounts to a latency (the not yet formed or the not yet formable) and to an excess (what remains physically or metaphysically irreducible to objects). But this temporality obscures the all-at-onceness, the simultaneity, of the object/thing dialectic and the fact that, all at once *the thing seems to name the object just as it is even as it names some thing else*. (Brown, 2001: 5, original emphasis)

Endeavours concerned less with offering 'an alternative *theory* of things' but with 'methodologies that "think through things"' (Henare et al, 2007: 5, original emphasis), propose that meaning and thing could be treated as an identity. These authors argue that '[r]ather than accepting that meanings are fundamentally separated from their material manifestations ... *things might be treated as* sui generis *meanings*' (Henare et al, 2007: 4, original emphasis). My 'death disgust' ethnography may be interpreted as a southern African case exploring the approaches suggested by Henare, Hollbraad and Wastell that recognize thingness in heuristic rather than in analytic terms. Recent scholarship, in addition, points rightly to the complexities of human remains and substances that challenge and simultaneously need strategies 'of subjectification and objectification and remain ambiguously at once both subject and object yet neither wholly one nor the other' (Fontein and Harries, 2013: 120).

The cases of the mediums of Chizombi and Nyamupahuni also illustrate other aspects related to disgust and death. Towards the end of her life, the last female medium of Chizombi had to be nursed as she became seriously ill; no relative did this but a neighbour in the role of a caregiver. The lady in charge of her had to cope at stages with some form of revulsion derived from handling a body terminally ill and thus in the process of dying. As a matter of fact, the medium's demise in December 2005 was a fairly predictable death.[11] The nursing lady reported having experienced disgust about bodily wastes of the incontinent medium, as well as anger and indignation because of a perceived lack of recognition for her dedication to the medium. As a neighbour and out of friendship, she had accepted doing house chores for the medium on her request, already some time before she became fatally ill. As she recalled during our interview in an upset tone:

'She [the medium] then got ill. The illness lasted for almost a year and throughout this time I was assisting her. She became seriously ill and I continued assisting. Divers [current medium of the spirit Chimau] later came to me and said, "Please could you go on with what you are doing?" but he never gave me anything [a reward]. She got [ill] to an extent that she was unable to go to the toilet alone and would pee herself. ... I was the only one who washed her cloths when she peed on them day and night, but I didn't receive anything from anyone.

On the day she died, I had left her in her hut in the evening and came to my homestead to give some instructions to prepare dinner. When I returned [to the medium's hut] it was already dark. I entered her hut and was surprised to step on her legs that were blocking the way to the door. I then said to her, "What kind of sleeping is this, let me help you". I then moved her legs and placed them back to her mat. Came then out of the hut and took some grass and lit the fire to give light in the house. This is when I realized that she had just died. I then went to Jackson [relative of the medium of Chimau] and told him that Chizombi [the spirit] had done *kuparura* [killed the medium].' (Interview with mai Sithole, 11 November 2021, Muzeya village)

During the medium's funeral at the ritual sessions held at the shrine, the nursing lady was not chosen to act as burial aide as she expected, which would have most probably occurred after having cared for a terminally ill person throughout. However, this is so if that person is not a medium, in which case the spirits choose at the funeral the burial aides from the descendants of the clan; yet the nursing lady was not related to the Nyamapfeka clan to which Chizombi belongs. As a matter of fact, she was asking for recognition of her effort and dedication to the ill medium until death. Her assistance as an end-of-life carer looked as if it was perceived by others as meaningless. It is arguable whether community recognition would have shaped her experience and memories of disgust, transforming them into an experience beyond rejection. The spirits, in her view, could at least have given her a token of appreciation. This, materially, translates into ritual money or a piece of (usually black) cotton cloth, which are common objects as payments or transactions at the shrine. As she continued:

'At the funeral they [the spirits] only said, I should guide them [the burial aides] into the hut where the corpse was. After the burial my colleagues [the two female funeral aides] were paid 20 [Zimbabwe] dollars and they shared 10 each. I was given nothing. Kamota [*mutape*[12] for the spirit Chimau] had already warned me earlier on that Chimau does not appreciate the work done for him. I only realized this during that time.' (Interview with mai Sithole, 11 November 2021, Muzeya village)

After this experience, she abandoned her loyalties to the spirits and joined a local branch of the Johanne Masowe (Apostolic) church where she still remains.

Following the death of the last medium of Nyamupahuni (senior spirit), his corpse was no longer in good condition. It had been lying for four days in his hut, waiting for nine mediums distributed between Zimbabwe and the border in Mozambique whose presence at the funeral was required, and who had to be notified and then strove to reach the homestead of the deceased.[13] "By then", as the officiant leading the funeral and a member of the *dungwe*[14] of the Nyamapfeka clan stressed, "the body had already turned bad. … At the funeral we [himself and the two male funeral aides] had courage enough, you know … to handle the situation, but the body had turned bad".[15] The old but healthy medium had suddenly died, collapsing at his homestead in the morning of 4 January 2019 after being probably bitten on his legs by a scorpion or a snake during the night. He was in his area one of the few remaining mediums from the senior generation, belonging to those who went through the last period of the colonial era and the war for independence. As this commentator continued, the presence of the corpse of the medium and the handling of a decomposing body involved not only disgust but also frightening moments. It provoked a mix of reverence and rejection. In contrast to everyday deaths, "fear", he said, "is always there the first time you witness the *homwe* [medium] dead since this [the body] is the medium of a *mhondoro* [spirit], and you would always think of the actual *mhondoro* [ancestral lion]. But as time goes on [during the funeral] you get used [to it]". Indeed, after possessing a medium, it is said that the spirit returns to the bush where it wanders, inhabiting a lion. Often residents report the roaring of lions in the vicinity when a medium dies. In this commentator's imagery it was likely that a *mhondoro*, an actual lion (ancestral lion), could come out of the hut where the corpse of the medium for the spirit Nyamupahuni lay: a fright-provoking presence for him.

The treatment of a medium's corpse aiming to delay putrefaction is simple and does not include sophisticated forms of manipulation beyond that of 'keeping it cool' with ritual water (water with herbs and snuff handed out at the shrine) throughout the funeral, away from the gaze of attendees. This is the task of the funeral aides or *madzisahwira* for the clan to which the spirit of that medium belongs. They do not form part of an experienced group with specialized ritual knowledge. If chosen, they might have the chance to perform this task once or probably twice in life, preparing the medium's corpse for transport and burial after following strict instructions of the spirits of the clan that are communicated to them at the shrine during the funeral. In their hands, the medium's body is stretched, cleaned, 'kept cool', and lastly clothed, that is, wrapped for burial from head to feet with cotton cloths of the spirit.

Regular burials are burials of bodies in the flesh. Here the corpse is placed in a simple wooden coffin (or a more solid casket) to then go through a process of underground 'wet' decomposition in village cemeteries. In contrast, the medium's corpse is transported to a site in the forest for temporary deposition on a wooden platform (temporary burial) where it undergoes an air-dry putrefaction process. Through passive excarnation (natural defleshing) by 'dry' putrefaction and the agency of predators, the medium's corpse transforms into dry bones that are ready for final burial in the forest. For this purpose, after some months following the temporary burial (which includes a rainy season) the dry bones from the skeleton are recovered and collected at the burial site. Most of them lie dispersed on the ground while others are on the temporary platform. The most important piece is the skull that cannot be missing. Unlike smaller bones, the burial of the medium's bones cannot take place without this part. "If you don't find the head [*musoro*] it means you didn't find the person", argued a headman[16] and member of Nyamupahuni's ritual group of support, who had buried the last medium of this spirit. The collected dry bones are subsequently placed on the soil underneath the temporary platform, and covered with leaves (final burial). This is the *rusonzo*, the ancestral burial place. In line with Lan's structural analysis (1985: 93–94), the distinction wet/dry indeed matters. Dryness is a quality of the ancestors. In addition, 'dry' burials (that is, those of merely bones as compared to those of body in the flesh) seem to have been reserved for 'precolonial' rulers and members of royal descent in the mid Zambezi Valley. As a matter of fact, though it is materially the medium who is buried, the burial is meant to be for the *mhondoro* (the ancestor). The corpse, and subsequently the dry bones of the medium, are imagined and treated as if those of the human being (of royal descent) who the spirit was in the long past (Sicilia, 2015).

Conclusion

Many authors have observed how death practices have changed considerably across sub-Saharan Africa over the last century or more (see Fontein, 2018). *Mhondoro* mediums' death and funerary practices as well as those of regular deaths in the mid Zambezi might not be an exception to this, including the affective responses to death loss. Mourning as an emotional response is not always related to closure but to continuity of bonds and open-ended processes as mediums' death suggest. No regular community mourning is performed for mediums whose remains are concealed from the public in a funeral that disallows public displays of grief, and celebrates the spirit while burying its host. If mourning can be linked to boundness, disgust represents almost the opposite as one of the strongest forms of rejection, which in relation to dying and the deceased manifests in complex ways as human remains and substances are ambiguously both subjects and objects shifting in radically unstable ways between both. The particular case of spirit mediums in northern Zimbabwe may illustrate this complexity.

Acknowledgements

I am indebted to the Angwa and Kanyemba communities for their helpful support throughout my research. For their generous comments and stimulating remarks I am grateful to Joost Fontein, Andre Gingrich, Estela Weiss-Krejci, and to the editors of this volume for their invitation to contribute.

Notes

1. *Kuchema mufi* (to cry the dead one). It is understood as 'showing others your grief'. The sole presence of attendees at a funeral, regardless of their emotional state, is taken as grieving. Interviewees did not make a distinction between mourning and grieving.
2. *Kuchema baba vangu kekupedzisira*.
3. Mediums are part of the 'traditional' leadership in rural communities. Therefore, not only relatives and residents take part at the funeral but also most community leaders are expected to attend (that is, village heads, chief, councillors and others) and follow the procedures of the ritual sessions taking place at the shrine of the spirit the deceased medium was the host for. Here is where the mediums attending the funeral get possessed and their spirits talk.
4. Ritual kinship (that of the spirits of the clan that possess the mediums) is at play not only in ritual settings (shrines) but dominates off-shrine over the medium's consanguine kinship and relationships in everyday situations. Therefore, the medium is mostly ranked and addressed by the kinship within the clan of the spirit (*mhondoro*) s/he is the host of.
5. *Kupamba* translates as 'to take without consent or by force'. Since mediumship is understood not as a choice of the medium but of the spirit that possesses, relatives of mediums live out possessions and the ritual medium-spirit relation as a burden that constrains their family relationships. Possessions coexist with relatives' rejection of the medium-spirit bond. They often report that the spirit abuses or oppresses the medium and his family, forcing them to comply with rules. As the commentator stressed, "to do things we would not do … not allowing us to cry when we actually need to release our emotions [at funerals]" (interview, S. Bhachi, 20 November 2021). The son of the last medium of Chimaku reported a similar view when complaining that he was not allowed to see the corpse of his father, noting, "you know these spirits do *kupamba*. When they possess, that *mhondoro* immediately exploits us, we will now be following its instructions and we'll have nothing to say" (interview, Bhito Dzumbunu, 10 November 2021, Kafamauro village).
6. Funeral aides (sing. *sahwira*) or 'friends'.
7. A funeral meal is offered to attendees. This is carried out at the homestead of the decedent at a short distance to the hut lodging the corpse.
8. *Kusema* translates as 'to dislike'. To do *kusema* means to make evident to others your dislike.
9. Doing *kutsvinya* (to show contempt or disrespect by words or actions).
10. This well-written and informed book did unfortunately not make any use of anthropological theory that could have enhanced it beyond cultural representation. Particularly the discussion on dirt could have benefited from classical anthropological work, but also more recent studies on death, materiality and corporeality could have contributed to some arguments in the book. My claim is that the author leaves out the subject/object problem when discussing disgust in relation to 'a conscious self', 'the corpse' and 'the body' at large. To a great extent my critic reinforces what some anthropology scholars have already noted, that 'disgust' should rather 'serve as a heuristic, something to prompt us to ask questions, not an object in and of itself' (Durham, 2011: 135).
11. The neighbourhood attributed her death to the consequences of HIV/AIDS. For details on this case, and on the ritual burial of this medium, see Sicilia (2015).
12. Ritual assistant of the medium.

[13] Interview with C. Nhamoyemari and R. Kapamara, 4 May 2019, Chikondoma village. Interview with Someone Bhachi, 8 April 2019, Muyengwa village.
[14] Group of ritual support and obligations to the spirit (*mhondoro*). For a detailed discussion about some dynamics of the *dungwe* within the Nyamapfeka clan in the Angwa area, see Sicilia (2017).
[15] He expressed disgust in a subtle and respectful way. Interview with R. Kapamara, 19 November 2021, Chikondoma village.
[16] Interview with *sabhuku* Chimufombo, 12 November 2021, Chimufombo village.

References

Brown, B. (2001) Thing theory. *Critical Inquiry*, 28:1–22.

Connerton, P. (2011) *The spirit of mourning: History, memory and the body*. Cambridge: Cambridge University Press.

Danely, J. (2018) Mourning as mutuality. In A.C.G.M. Robben (ed) *A companion to the anthropology of death*. Oxford: Wiley Blackwell, pp 131–143.

Durham, D. (2011) Disgust and the anthropological imagination. *Ethnos*, 76(2): 131–156.

Fontein, J. (2010) Between tortured bodies and resurfacing bones: The politics of the dead in Zimbabwe. *Material Culture*, 15(4): 423–448.

Fontein, J. (2015) *Remaking Mutirikwi: Landscape, water and belonging in Southern Zimbabwe*. Suffolk: James Currey.

Fontein, J. (2018) Death, corporeality, and uncertainty in Zimbabwe. In A.C.G.M. Robben (ed) *A companion to the anthropology of death*. Oxford: Wiley Blackwell, pp 337–355.

Fontein, J. and Harries, J. (2013) The vitality and efficacy of human substances. *Critical African Studies*, 5(3): 115–126.

Hallam, E. and Hockey, J. (2001) *Death, memory and material culture*. Oxford and New York: Berg.

Henare, A., Holbraad, M. and Wastell, S. (2007) Thinking through things. In A. Henare, M. Holbraad and S. Wastell (eds) *Thinking through things: Theorising artifacts ethnographically*. London and New York: Routledge, pp 1–31.

Krmpotich, C., Fontein, J. and Harries, J. (2010) The substances of bones: The emotive materiality and affective presence of human remains. *Material Culture*, 15(4): 371–384.

Lambek, M. (2019) The ends of the dead. *HAU: Journal of Ethnographic Theory*, 9(2): 253–256.

Lan, D. (1985) *Guns and rain: Guerrillas and spirit mediums in Zimbabwe*. London: James Currey.

McGinn, C. (2011) *The meaning of disgust*. Oxford: Oxford University Press.

Miller, D. (2005) Materiality: An introduction. In D. Miller (ed) *Materiality*. Durham, NC: Duke University Press, pp 1–50.

Miller, D. and Parrott, F. (2009) Loss and material culture in South London. *Journal of the Royal Anthropological Institute*, 15: 502–519.

Newby, Z. and Toulson, R. (2019) Introduction: Emotions and materiality in theory and method. In Z. Newby and R. Toulson (eds) *The materiality of mourning: Cross-disciplinary perspectives*. London and New York: Routledge, pp 1–20.

Posel, D. and Gupta, P. (2009) The life of the corpse: Framing reflections and questions. *African Studies*, 68(3): 299–309.

Robben, A.C.G.M. (2018) An anthropology of death for the twenty-first century. In A.C.G.M. Robben (ed) *A companion to the anthropology of death*. Oxford: Wiley Blackwell, pp xv–xi.

Sicilia, O. (2015) Neither tombs nor weeping: The death of Mhondoro lineage ancestral mediums in the mid-Zambezi Valley. In G. Delaplace and F. Valentin (eds) *Le Funéraire: Mémoire, protocoles, monuments*. Paris: Éditions de Boccard, pp 209–222.

Sicilia, O. (2017) Ritual, history, and logics of ancestrality: An ethnography of mhondoro ancestors in northern Dande, mid-Zambezi Valley (Zimbabwe). Unpublished PhD thesis. University of Vienna.

Stroud, E. (2018) Law and the dead body: Is a corpse a person or a thing? *Annual Review of Law and Social Science*, 14: 115–125.

Weiss-Krejci, E. (2013) The unburied dead. In S. Tarlow and L. Nilsson Stutz (eds) *The Oxford handbook of archaeology of death and burial*. Oxford: Oxford University Press, pp 281–301.

PART III

Troubling Agencies

9

Rehabilitate or Euthanize? Biopolitics and Care in Seal Conservation

Doortje Hoerst

Each autumn, seals with lungworm infection are common 'patients' at Sealcentre Pieterburen, a seal rehabilitation centre in the Netherlands. They are among one of three groups that the seal rehabilitation centre takes in. The other two groups are pups that have lost their mothers – often due to human disturbance – and seals harmed by pollution in the sea. The centre aims not only to rehabilitate seals, but also to educate their visiting public on the Wadden Sea ecology, including relations with humans (Hörst, 2021). Caretakers and veterinarians work to remove the internal lungworm parasite from seals and release the seals back into the Wadden Sea. Paradoxically, the common seal population in the Netherlands is at 'carrying capacity', meaning it has stopped growing because of limited food availability (Van der Zande et al, 2018: 4–5). As such, despite the effort of caretakers and veterinarians, many seals – which are the top predators – may die because of pressure on food resources (Van der Zande et al, 2018: 4–5). While animal welfare advocates argue for continued rehabilitation of individual seals to prevent the animal's suffering, ecologists call for a strategy that considers the health of the whole population (Felix, 2018; Van der Zande et al, 2018). Those at the seal rehabilitation centre try to navigate both positions. They have undertaken a science project which I will call 'Project B', asking *which* of those sick seals should be rehabilitated.[1]

Inspired by multispecies approaches (Haraway, 2008; Van Dooren, 2014; Tsing, 2015; Lowe and Münster, 2016), I ask how lungworms, seals and humans navigate life and death with science Project B at the seal centre, as they become participants in practices of care and biopolitics. To help focus on how different beings are involved, and how they influence each other's actions, I draw on material semiotics. In this framework, the actor-enacted (human or nonhuman) *acts* and influences others intentionally or unintentionally and is simultaneously *enacted* by others in a network. The 'actor-enacteds' are not in control but *become* in relation to others (Law and Mol, 2008: 58). Using this framework to analyse the research conducted by seal rehabilitation centre scientists reveals a different approach to biopolitics, wherein biopolitics can be extended to more-than-human lives. I question the dominant position of humans in relation to nonhumans (Haraway, 2008: 271), including the role of nonhumans in biopolitics to draw out the complexity of power relations that play out between more-than-humans. While multispecies studies of nature conservation include more-than-humans in frameworks of agency, they tend to position humans as the ones with biopolitical power (Blue and Rock, 2010; Lorimer and Driessen, 2013; Srinivasan, 2014). I argue that lungworms challenge that power, resulting in attempts at multispecies collaboration between seals, humans and lungworms in navigating death and care.

Beginning with a more detailed theoretical discussion on care and biopolitics, I consider these concepts in the context of a seal rehabilitation centre in the Netherlands. Drawing on fieldwork and interviews carried out from September to December 2018, I show how lungworms, humans and seals are closely entangled in the Dutch Wadden Sea area. By focusing on the lungworms' lifeways and the moments different lifeways meet through practices of care, humans become decentralized, creating a network in which seals and lungworms along with humans become actor-enacteds. Going into the specifics of Project B, I include the role of science and technology as a way of communicating across difference, making possible a biopolitics as shared multispecies practice. Finally, a discussion follows on how this research project raises ethical considerations of deciding between life and death through practices of care. In a situation of carrying capacity, when life may lead to death and death to life in different temporalities, science takes a precarious ethical position.

Biopolitics and care

The seal rehabilitation centre practices science as a means for both biopolitics and multispecies interaction. By extending the concept of biopolitics with the concept of 'multispecies collaboration', I reconsider biopolitics as a dynamic process that can be shared with nonhuman species, such as lungworms.

As initiatives that intervene in life for the protection of the species, nature conservation organizations are inherently involved in biopolitics. Foucault (1978: 139) describes biopolitics as a technique of biopower, power over life. Biopolitics is a technique aimed at controlling bodies on the level of species and populations. Among other things, it focuses on elongating life through changes in mortality and birth rates (Foucault, 1978: 139). Biopower, and especially biopolitics, are at the core of nature conservation, which often aims to prevent species from becoming extinct. Some authors have shown how nature conservation can make an intervention into the lives of one species, which might necessitate death for another species (Bocci, 2017; Crowley et al, 2017; Hodgetts, 2017). To protect turtles on the Galapagos Islands, several organizations assigned hunters with the task to kill hundreds of goats (Bocci, 2017). In the United Kingdom, grey squirrels have been killed in favour of the survival of red squirrels (Crowley et al, 2017; Hodgetts, 2017). Care is never innocent (Puig de la Bellacasa, 2011; Murphy, 2015). When attending to care, it is important to keep in mind who is excluded from care, or, as in several cases of nature conservation, at whose expense care is practised (Murphy, 2015: 726). Killing or compromising lives can become a justified sacrifice if it is necessary to make prioritized nonhumans live (Van Dooren, 2014: 117).

The seal rehabilitation centre practises science to decide which seals will be prioritized over other seals. Science is a core practice of biopower. Medical knowledge has given humans a sense of control or power over life (Foucault, 1978: 142). Possibilities to extend sick or elderly lives through medical care have extended medical interventions into birth and mortality rates of human populations. Veterinary care, likewise, intervenes in mortality rates of nonhumans (Law, 2010). Moreover, nature conservation organizations use science as an authority for policy, while science does not necessarily lead to a definitive decision or 'good' policy. Different studies can be used to argue for divergent positions in complex issues, with multiple parties using the authority of science as a political tactic for persuasion (Ozawa, 1996; Dickson and Adams, 2009). With such a dominant position of science in nature conservation, this chapter draws attention to the practices of scientific research that are foundational for caretaking policies. The seal rehabilitation centre, as will be illustrated in this chapter, attributes a central importance to science that, according to them, has the potential to provide good care because it is based on *facts*.

One of the challenges for the concept of biopower to include possibilities of shared power with nonhumans is a reconsideration of agency. Biopower is mostly attributed to humans, as nonhuman animals seem to undergo disciplining techniques of humans (Blue and Rock, 2010; Lorimer and Driessen, 2013; Srinivasan, 2014). In practice, nonhuman agency is difficult to account for in more-than-human relationships, especially when agency is thought to include intentionality. To step away from intentionality, Anna Tsing (2015) develops a concept that allows for open-ended, surprising multispecies relations, such as those between seals, humans and lungworms. Building on multispecies collaboration as 'working across difference' and relying on one another (Tsing, 2015: 28; Haraway, 2016: 87), Tsing explains it as 'unintentional engineering': '[T]he overlapping world-making activities of many agents, human and non-human. ... But none of these agents have planned this effect' (Tsing, 2015: 152). That is, in entangled lifeways, beings change one another and their environment, without necessarily consciously doing so.

In this chapter, I let go of the full unintentionality Tsing presupposes and let unintentional and intentional doings merge as paths cross. This can be exemplified by the work of Timothy Hodgetts (2017). He analyses how pine martens enact biopolitics by living in a certain place, making the place less attractive to grey squirrels and more attractive to red squirrels (Hodgetts, 2017: 23). This dynamic is utilized by humans, who try to attract pine martens to 'collaborate' in environmental management (Hodgetts, 2017: 20). In other words, he focuses on practices of martens, squirrels and humans to analyze the enactment of biopolitics, by affirming who (or what) makes a difference in a particular situation. Importantly, this approach opens theoretical space to include nonhumans, such as pine martens, as actors with biopolitical power.

Practising nature conservation in the Netherlands

Project B is undertaken in relation to recent changes and public discussions around seal rehabilitation in the Netherlands. At the start of 2018, a report on seal rehabilitation policy was published by the Scientific Advisory Committee (Van der Zande et al, 2018). This report states that the common seal population may be at carrying capacity, therefore rehabilitation should be limited (Van der Zande et al, 2018: 4–5). It continues that seals who are compromised by human activity should be rehabilitated – humans are responsible and can be held accountable – while seals dying because of 'natural causes' should be left to die to ensure a natural selection process. A lungworm parasite infection falls under 'natural causes'.

The report sparked a public debate that is part of a wider commitment to nature conservation by people in the Netherlands. For example, at the Oostvaardersplassen, a rewilding experiment introduced bovines and horses (Lorimer and Driessen, 2013). However, when harsh winters in 2005 and 2009 caused starvation, animal welfare organizations filed court cases and public protest ensued (Lorimer and Driessen, 2013: 176–177). The state agency largely responsible for the area responded with a tactic to regain public support (Lorimer and Driessen, 2013: 177), but the discussion about the Oostvaardersplassen flared up again following the harsh winter of 2018. Public protests demanded to feed the bovines and horses – activists even illegally fed the animals themselves (Barkham, 2018). Simultaneously the outcome of the Scientific Advisory Committee fuelled public discussion on limiting seal rehabilitation at the Wadden Sea and an animal welfare association successfully petitioned the national parliament to discuss seal conservation (Tweede Kamer der Staten-Generaal, 2018).

As an institution funded by public support *and* holding science in high regard, the seal rehabilitation centre finds itself in a double bind. Accommodating both ideals, rehabilitating all seals, and not rehabilitating any seals who have lungworm, are ruled out as options by the centre, at least in the short term. As an answer to this double bind, they trouble the opposition between animal welfare and population management through Project B.

Parasitical collaboration

Project B is a research project that hopes to give more insight into lungworm infection of seals. The first aim of the project, as the researchers explained in interviews, is to assess the degree of lung damage to quickly establish a prognosis and potential for rehabilitation through care and medication. If seals are projected to die, euthanasia is considered because it is supposed to relieve suffering. The aim is to reduce the suffering of seals by euthanizing those who are so heavily infected that they have no chance of survival even with medical care.

The second, more speculative aim is to assess if seals are so heavily infected that they have no chance of survival *without* the help of rehabilitation. If that could be assessed, the medical practices would have no dramatic effect on the 'natural selection' process. Those who would have died 'in the wild' would be euthanized and those who would have lived would be rehabilitated. Suffering could be eased for all, either through medication or euthanasia.

Both aims involve intensive multispecies collaboration. Lungworms are biopolitical actors, as they influence population dynamics of seals. As such, to reach either of the aims, the seal rehabilitation centre needs to understand lungworms better. Moreover, to reach the second aim, collaboration is necessary, as the seal rehabilitation centre aims to assist the lungworms, rather than act on their own – itself a biopolitical act. Delving into the speculative lifeways of nematodes and parasites (Von Uexküll, 1934; Tsing, 2015: 156), in this case lungworms, decentralizes humans to analyse Project B as a collaborative multispecies project. Though not much is known about their lifeways, there have been several studies on lungworms that reside in the lungs of young common seals (Dailey, 2006; Lehnert et al, 2010; Ulrich et al, 2015; Rhyan et al, 2018). Using these studies, we can get to a closer understanding of the multispecies interrelationships of lungworms, seals and humans.

Lungworms are nematodes that reside in the respiratory system of a host, in this case a common seal. Adult lungworms reproduce in seal lungs and give birth to larvae (Rhyan et al, 2018: 91). These larvae forage in the lungs, grow until they have matured and may then reproduce further. Some of the larvae are coughed up by the seals and then potentially swallowed and excreted through the faeces, after which – if they live long enough without the host – they float around until fish, such as turbot, eat them. Turbot, in turn, is regularly on the menu of young seals who have just learned to hunt (Lehnert et al, 2010: 847). The lives of these lungworms are hidden. They play out in the darkness of seal lungs, deeply entangled in the tissue. Their presence can be revealed through some laborious techniques, for example during a necropsy (Dailey, 2006: 589), using a serum and translation into numbers (Ulrich et al, 2015), or extracting them from faeces (Mesquita et al, 2018). Sometimes, seals reveal adult lungworms by coughing them up.

Another way in which lungworms make themselves known is through the bodily response of a seal. If the immune system of a seal is not capable of countering the migration of larvae to the lungs and their subsequent growth and reproduction, the lungs get filled with worms. With less lung capacity, seals have trouble diving for food, which often leads to underfed, skinny seals. Also, seals are hydrated by the fish they eat. As their food intake decreases, these seals begin to dehydrate, leading to thin and curly whiskers, dry eyes, and crusty, bloody noses. Sometimes, damage caused by lungworms leads to subcutaneous emphysema. Besides being incredibly painful, subcutaneous emphysema can be fatal for a seal. Blood, dry eyes, skinny and curly whiskers can all be visually observed, and subcutaneous emphysema can be felt through the skin by experienced veterinarians. Sound also matters; seals' breathing sounds differently when their lungs are filled with lungworms or when the lungs are damaged. With the right technology, such as a stethoscope, these sounds can be recognized and may point to the presence of lungworms in the seal. Furthermore, faeces of lungworm-infected seals have a sour, pungent smell.[2] Through all of those sensory ways, presence of lungworms in a seal can be suspected.

The lifeways of seals, lungworms and caretakers thus intersect at the seal rehabilitation centre. Lungworms make themselves known through movement or damage they cause in the tissue of seals. At the same time, lungworms are enacted, as both seals and technologies make the lungworms' presence known and detectable. Lungworms become biopolitical actors as they have an influence on seals at a population level. Moreover, lungworms find themselves in a powerful position, as caretakers at the seal rehabilitation centre must reckon with them in their own biopolitical practices. Understanding this intersection of lifeways as a form of collaboration, seals and lungworms open up unexpected opportunities for humans in further biopolitical action and medical care as humans involve themselves with the rehabilitation of 'lungworm patients'.

Science, technology and worms

Opportunities for unintentional collaborations between seals, lungworms and humans expand through science and technology during Project B.

> **FIELD DIARY**
> *October 2018*
> Project B started when the new technological equipment came. During an intake, the researcher shows the new stethoscope. It has digital recording and Bluetooth. With this, they can record the lungs' sounds, which is necessary for research on the respiration system. With Bluetooth they can transfer the sounds to the computers, where assistants annotate the recordings. They can listen to and notate the small, specific differences and eventually, when more is known, vets can do a better diagnosis of the degree of lung damage. During the intake, they take the new stethoscope and listen to each lung by putting the stethoscope on either side of the thorax and record them for thirty seconds each.

In the next intake, more technology is involved.

> **FIELD DIARY**
> *November 2018*
> When the research assistants listened to the previous recordings, they could not determine if the sounds were made because of movement of the seal, by the researcher, or by what was happening inside the lungs. This intake a research assistant squats in front of the seal and records the stethoscope procedure with a video camera. In this way, they can record when the seal inhales or exhales and when the seal struggles or the researcher moves, thereby moving the stethoscope and making additional sounds. The seal struggled frequently during the recording, so the researcher had to put the stethoscope recurrently back in the right place.

In this process of recording, the use of technology is adjusted to the behaviour of seals in the intake. Seals do not freely collaborate. The researchers must come up with an extra device, the camera, because the stethoscope recorder is sensitive to other sounds as well. Although a veterinarian would be able to make sense of the sounds during the intake, it would be difficult to use the recording for research purposes when it was later replayed to add annotations.

With the recordings, the sounds of the lungs are translated into digital data. The researchers attempt to create an algorithm, so the computer can analyse future recordings and make a prognosis of a seal's health based on them. The differences are so tiny that a strictly systematic comparative analysis must be done, based on an enormous amount of data. The researchers hope they will be able to support a clinical diagnosis with algorithms and the systematic processing of data for a prognosis.

For potential collaboration, researchers try to attune to lungworms (Despret, 2004), making them noticeable through sounds, video, graphs and numbers. Understanding how lungworms play a role as biopolitical actors makes possible a careful consideration of aligning the biopolitical goals and actions of the seal rehabilitation centre. Using technology and systematic analysis, the researchers aim to understand lungworm infection better. Initially, an increased understanding might help reach the first aim of the project: to reduce suffering for seals who are in such an advanced stage of lungworm infection that they will die even with medical care.

For the second aim of the project, there is need for further 'collaboration' between humans and lungworms, one that might lead to a different biopolitical strategy for the seal rehabilitation centre. Through Project B and the activities of close, technologically mediated listening that accompany it, biopolitics may become shared, transgressing species boundaries, a trans-biopolitics (Blue and Rock, 2010). Ideally, the lungworms would show the seal rehabilitation centre which seals should live and which should die to allow seal rehabilitation according to 'natural selection processes'. If so, lungworms would become leading biopolitical actors. Caretakers and researchers will then gain a mediating function to 'listen' to the lungworms and speed up the process of living a healthy life or dying what would otherwise be a slow death.

Giving lungworms a leading position could dramatically alter the position humans take in relation to nonhuman biopolitics. Rather than dominating or 'mastering' the 'natural world' that is 'other' (Plumwood, 1993), this technique might provide for an opportunity to listen to what is already happening. Moreover, it means taking up the role of assistance, and as such not keeping fully 'out' of the ecological circle but influencing it in a way that relieves suffering of those who live through it (Plumwood, 2012). It could result in a practice of care that does not prioritize either the population or animal welfare but sits in the middle. It could be an approach that 'stays with the trouble' (Haraway, 2016).

Science and ethics

Using science and technology, a different care policy might be possible that foregrounds animal welfare together with ecological population management. Science is valued centrally by the seal rehabilitation centre to (re)evaluate policy. As one of the researchers said: "We need to do it [change] slowly and with proper science. So that is what I would like to develop, some scientific based criteria to really help the animals properly. ... I think it is important to have facts and the way to have a fact is with science." They point to the relevance of science specifically to changing commitments with lungworm patients. To know how, it is important that science creates facts and brings knowledge.

Using science for policy has an extra advantage in heated public discussions such as those in 2018. To convince a donating public of the 'right' care policies of the seal rehabilitation centre, they draw more generally on scientific 'evidence'. 'Science' can be negatively defined as *not* an opinion (Stengers, 2000: 28). With this definition of science, opinions become directly discredited to critique science on an equal basis. "Scientific facts", as the researcher calls them, would be able to surpass popular opinions about which seals should be rehabilitated, which should not and how to do so, without lingering indecisively in 'unempirical' ethical public debates. However, the answer to what is good to do ethically can get hidden by scientific facts. Taking a position in ethical debates, science itself becomes an ethical practice of care, with an authority that can only be challenged by science.

Recognizing how ethics are still implicated despite the heavy emphasis on science, a researcher details the dilemma:

> 'I think if the population is in carrying capacity and they are not endangered and if you would let it happen, these animals will die. I think there is a reason for it. So, we should not save them all. ... But it is not that simple. And it is also not easy to euthanize an animal that you know you can probably save. But yeah, should you save it? That is the question, but it is not easy to answer.'

Veterinarians still make decisions about life or death of seals. To which extent they want to share biopolitical power with lungworms is an ethical decision, one they had not yet made during my research. In the situation of carrying capacity, every seal life is a potential 'sacrificial life' (Van Dooren, 2014: 114). Due to pressure on resources, a seal life saved at the seal rehabilitation centre might cost the life of another because there might not be enough food in the sea to feed them both. Although these deaths happen at different temporalities, they are interacted with in the same decision. Care is not innocent. Providing medical care and withholding it both result in death, albeit not for the same seal.

Project B does not ask the ethical question, but it is implicated in its practices. In a time when the population is at carrying capacity, death of one may well be a 'gift of life' (Rose, 2012) to another. However, who receives that gift of life remains contentious. The project assumes that 'natural selection' is the best approach to seal rehabilitation and tries to ensure that lungworms will perform their balancing act of nature. This informs a biopolitics in which immuno-compromised seals will become the sacrificial lives for the wellbeing of the population. The researcher from the seal rehabilitation centre emphasizes their doubts about the ethics implicated in Project B. Is the final, speculative aim 'right'? Is it 'good' to consciously reject helping seals who might be cured with the help of medication? These are real and difficult questions that scientific research takes an authoritative position on, but is not able to solve. However, by doing Project B, the first steps are taken in a certain ethical direction. It explores if sharing biopolitical power with lungworms is possible, meanwhile alleviating suffering for individual seals. Thereby, it prioritizes the lives of seals who can counter lungworms over others.

Conclusion

With science Project B, lungworms, seals and humans navigate life and death in collaboration. In contrast to most cases in nature conservation (Blue and Rock, 2010; Lorimer and Driessen, 2013; Bocci, 2017), Project B allows biopolitical power to shift to nonhuman beings. Lungworms set the parameters for a seal population at carrying capacity. While lungworms are already actor-enacteds in the existing network with seals and humans, their biopolitical role might be enhanced through 'trans-biopolitics'. Science and technology become critical mediators in this multispecies interaction. With these dynamics, the seal rehabilitation centre reconsiders its own biopolitical role. They explore a different stance to 'nature', one that does not place humans outside of the ecological circle, but as having an assisting function within it. By implication, this different attitude accepts death as part of life. It considers decisions about deaths of known seals in the rehabilitation centre and unknown ones in the population as related in one ecology.

With a new biopolitical approach, the seal rehabilitation centre might find a way to deal with their double bind, by combining care for the population and animal welfare. Dying becomes a process that the seal rehabilitation centre can medically ease, but not avoid. Decisions to contribute to certain deaths and not others still remain. Science will not prevent the entanglement in threads of ethics and politics, but rather tends to contribute to it. Firmly grounded in non-innocent care, ethical questions of how to go about seal rehabilitation remain contested and open-ended.

Notes

[1] This research project is anonymized because it was in its early stages and speculative when I was there.
[2] While this is not confirmed by scientific research, it was mentioned by both caretakers and volunteers.

References

Barkham, P. (2018) Dutch rewilding experiment sparks backlash as thousands of animals starve. *The Guardian*, 27 April. https://www.theguardian.com/environment/2018/apr/27/dutch-rewilding-experiment-backfires-as-thousands-of-animals-starve (accessed 3 February 2022).

Blue, G. and Rock, M. (2010) Trans-biopolitics: Complexity in interspecies relations. *Health*, 15(4): 353–368.

Bocci, P. (2017) Tangles of care: Killing goats to save tortoises on the Galápagos Islands. *Cultural Anthropology*, 32(3): 424–449.

Crowley, S.L., Hinchliffe, S. and McDonald, R.A. (2017) Killing squirrels: Exploring motivations and practices of lethal wildlife management. *Environment and Planning E: Nature and Space*, 1(1–2): 1–24.

Dailey, M.D. (2006) Restoration of parafilaroides (Dougherty, 1946) (Nematoda: Metastrongyloidea) with description of two new species from pinnipeds of Eastern Central Pacific. *The Journal of Parasitology*, 92(3): 589–594.

Despret, V. (2004) The body we care for: Figures of anthropo-zoo-genesis. *Body and Society*, 10(2–3): 111–134.

Dickson, P. and Adams, W. (2009) Science and uncertainty in South Africa's elephant culling debate. *Environment and Planning C: Government and Policy*, 27(1): 110–123.

Felix, N. (2018) Knuffelen we onze wilde dieren dood? *Nederlandse Omroep Stichting*, 15 March. https://nos.nl/op3/artikel/2222550-knuffelen-we-onze-wilde-dieren-dood (accessed 3 July 2023).

Foucault, M. (1978) *The history of sexuality volume 1: An introduction.* New York: Pantheon Books.

Haraway, D.J. (2008) *When species meet.* Minneapolis: University of Minnesota Press.

Haraway, D.J. (2016) *Staying with the trouble: Making kin in the Chthulucene.* Durham, NC: Duke University Press.

Hodgetts, T. (2017) Wildlife conservation, multiple biopolitics and animal subjectification: Three mammals' tales. *Geoforum*, 79: 17–25.

Hörst, D. (2021) Caring for seals and the Wadden Sea: Multispecies entanglements in seal rehabilitation. *Maritime Studies*, 20: 305–316.

Law, J. (2010) Care and killing: Tensions in veterinary practice. In A. Mol, J. Pols and I. Moser (eds) *Care in practice: On tinkering in clinics, homes and farms.* Bielefeld: Transcript Publishers, pp 57–72.

Law, J. and Mol, A. (2008) The actor-enacted: Cumbrian sheep in 2001. In C. Knappen and L. Malafouris (eds) *Material agency.* Berlin: Springer Science and Business Media, pp 55–77.

Lehnert, K., Samson-Himmelstjerna, G., Schaudien, D., Bleidorn, C., Wohlsein, P. and Siebert, U. (2010) Transmission of lungworms of harbour porpoises and harbour seals: Molecular tools determine potential vertebrate intermediate hosts. *International Journal for Parasitology*, 40(7): 845–853.

Lorimer, J. and Driessen, C. (2013) Bovine biopolitics and the promise of monsters in the rewilding of Heck cattle. *Geoforum*, 48: 249–259.

Lowe, C. and Münster, U. (2016) The viral creep: Elephants and herpes in times of extinction. *Environmental Humanities*, 8(1): 118–142.

Mesquita, J.R., Mega, C., Coelho, C., Cruz, R., Vala, H., Esteves, F. et al (2018) ABC series on diagnostic parasitology part 3: The Baermann technique. *The Veterinary Nurse*, 8(10): 558–562.

Murphy, M. (2015) Unsettling care: Troubling transnational itineraries of care in feminist health practices. *Social Studies of Science*, 45(5): 717–737.

Ozawa, C.P. (1996) Science in environmental conflicts. *Sociological Perspectives*, 39(2): 219–230.

Plumwood, V. (1993) *Feminism and the mastery of nature*. London: Routledge.

Plumwood, V. (2012) *The eye of the crocodile*. Edited by L. Shannon. Canberra: Australian National University Press.

Puig de la Bellacasa, M. (2011) Matters of care in technoscience: Assembling neglected things. *Social Studies of Science*, 41(1): 85–106.

Rhyan J., Garner, M., Spraker, T., Labourn, D. and Cheville, N. (2018) *Brucella pinnipedialis* in lungworms *Parafilaroides* sp. and Pacific harbor seals *Phoca vitulina richardsi*, proposed pathogenesis. *Diseases of Aquatic Organisms*, 131: 87–94.

Rose, D.B. (2012) Multispecies knots of ethical time. *Environmental Philosophy*, 9(1): 127–140.

Srinivasan, K. (2014) Caring for the collective: Biopower and agential subjectification in wildlife conservation. *Environment and Planning D: Society and Space*, 32(3): 501–517.

Stengers, I. (2000) *The invention of modern science*. Minneapolis: University of Minnesota Press.

Tsing, A.L. (2015) *The mushroom at the end of the world: On the possibility of life in capitalist ruins*. Princeton: Princeton University Press.

Tweede Kamer der Staten-Generaal (2018) Stichting DierenLot biedt petitie 'Samen voor zeehonden' aan. 12 June. https://www.tweedekamer.nl/debat_en_vergadering/commissievergaderingen/details?id=2018A02038 (accessed 12 October 2022).

Ulrich, S.A., Lehnert, K., Siebert, U. and Strube, C. (2015) A recombinant antigen-based enzyme-linked immunosorbent assay (ELISA) for lungworm detection in seals. *Parasites and Vectors*, 8: Article 443.

Van der Zande, E., Van Alphen, A.N., Goodman, J.J.M., Meijboom, S.J., Stegeman, F.L.B., Thompson, A.J. et al (2018) *Advice of the Scientific Advisory Committee on Seal Rehabilitation in the Netherlands*. Wageningen: Wageningen Environmental Research.

Van Dooren, T. (2014) *Flight ways: Life and loss at the edge of extinction*. New York: Columbia University Press.

Von Uexküll, J. (1934) *A foray into the worlds of animals and humans*. Minneapolis: University of Minnesota Press.

10

Troubling Entanglements: Death, Loss and the Dead in and on Television

Bethan Michael-Fox

This chapter utilizes a form of diffractive analysis (Barad, 2007) to outline several conceptual relationships between television as a medium and death, and to examine how one televisual text – the French supernatural drama *Les Revenants* (2012–2015) – functions to explore a range of sociocultural ideas about death, loss and the dead. According to Huddleston and Rocha (2018: 27) popular cultural texts or 'objects' are ideal candidates for diffractive analysis. Diffraction, they argue, is 'a way to glimpse into the entangled nature of our world', and popular cultural texts can facilitate an understanding of some of the 'complicated entanglements' that exist both within texts and in their connections to the social worlds they inhabit (Huddleston and Rocha, 2018: 27). As this chapter will show, the thematic engagement with death in the television series *Les Revenants* is directly and allusively entangled with a range of sociocultural ideas about death, loss and the dead. These are in turn entangled with complex relationships to death, both metaphorical and literal, enmeshed within the medium of television itself. By unpicking some of these entanglements, it is possible to explore different perspectives informing the series and its potential receptions, and to consider material-discursive meanings about mortality that popular cultural texts can expound. The relationships outlined between television and death and the ideas enmeshed within the series *Les Revenants* can both be understood to trouble conventional, established and often reinstated assumptions and perceptions about death, loss and the dead.

Barad's conception of a diffractive methodology is focused on placing 'understandings that are generated from different (inter)disciplinary practices in conversation with one another' (Barad, 2007: 92–93). This involves 'thinking insights from different disciplines (and interdisciplinary approaches) through one another' in a way that is attentive to their discrete and nuanced differences. This means reading them not against each other, but together in a way that acknowledges the 'material-discursive boundary-making practices' that produce both those disciplinary definitions, texts and more broadly 'objects' and 'subjects' (Barad, 2007: 93). Though Barad (2007) has critiqued Butler's work from a new materialist perspective, Butler (2006a: x) has also championed the practice of drawing on the ideas and approaches of authors and methods from different disciplines, referring to this as a form of 'intellectual promiscuity' involving reading 'together, in a syncretic vein' the work of intellectuals who have few alliances with one another, might not read each other and might not particularly care to be read together. Here, I suggest death studies represents a field of inquiry that demands a diffractive methodology more than others, given death is a subject that refuses to be consigned to one discrete discipline or area of study. Like other academic fields and disciplines, it is one that is constructed and has highly contested and shifting boundaries. A diffractive analysis allows for insights to be drawn from a range of different perspectives that inform death studies as they are read together, while their tensions are also acknowledged. Television is also an ideal medium for diffractive analysis because television is emblematic of the ways in which popular culture can become what Butler calls a 'new venue for theory' (Butler, 2006a: ix–x). This is a venue that is 'necessarily impure', but where theory 'emerges in and as the very event of cultural translation' (Butler, 2006a: ix–x). *Les Revenants* is an example of this through its engagement with ideas about death, loss and the dead. Drawing diffractively on literature informing the field of death studies, including examples from psychoanalysis, psychology, poststructuralism and hauntology, this chapter considers social and cultural entanglements between television and death, and explores how one televisual text functions as a 'new avenue for theory' (Butler, 2006a: ix–x) to extend and engage with a range of shifting sociocultural understandings about death, loss and the dead. The first section sets out numerous relationships that exist between death and television as a medium, before going on to consider how *Les Revenants* can offer a venue through which complex, competing and troubling ideas can circulate and function in material-discursive ways to destabilize normative perceptions about death, loss and the dead.

Death and television

Elsewhere, I have argued that television is a medium especially hospitable to the presence of the dead (Michael-Fox, 2020a, 2023). Television is well recognized as having brought death into the home (Durkin, 2003;

Wheatley, 2006). This phantasmagoric entry into the home via television has been concurrent in England and many other countries with the shift of material, physical death (and the dead body) out of the home and into various institutions and privatized locations. But as Hay (2001) has argued, television is a complex site. The term television is to some extent arbitrary in that it refers, like the broader term media, 'to the assemblage and interdependence of various technologies and practices' (Hay, 2001: 205). Television has also escaped the home, having become part of an ecology of 'new media', meaning that the images and voices of the dead (both real and imagined) can emerge in several other contexts, such as on portable tablets and smartphones. In this way, television and the dead it represents become entangled in many different local and personal material contexts. The practices involved in producing television have an impact on the environment at a global scale, and in this television becomes embroiled in discourses about the role of human agency in climate crisis and its attendant death – literal and metaphorical, as well as human and nonhuman. Steps are being made to address this by, for example, the organization albert, which offers training and certification aiming to inspire the film and television industries to produce sustainable content and eliminate waste and carbon emissions in production (albert, 2022). In the context of television series like *Les Revenants* which, as this chapter will show, raises questions about the impact of humanity upon the environment, tensions emerge between television's capacity to provoke ideas about concepts such as climate crisis and the very practice of television watching, which ultimately contributes to environmental harm.

There are also several direct entanglements between television and human death. The devices on which television is watched have been explicitly connected to highly exploitative working practices and to suicides in the factories that produce them, in particular Apple products (see Mielach, 2012). Globally there are many whose living depends on risky roles that exist within the production and disposal of products and devices associated with television. These are often products characterized by planned obsolescence, built not to last but to fail in only a few years – a different kind of death. One study shared widely in the media reported that audiences themselves may die as a consequence of watching television, with the sedentary hours required to 'binge' a series increasing the risk of a blood clot in the lung (Griffin, 2016). Focusing such a study on television watching rather than the sedentary hours spent staring at a screen while working in a role deemed economically productive is political, underpinned by the positioning of television watching as an unproductive leisure activity. Yet it also signals Baudrillard's (1993 [1976]: 127) argument in *Symbolic exchange and death* that 'a culture of death' has emerged in the context of a capitalism where 'the factory no longer exists because labour is everywhere'. This argument has taken on a new relevance in the context of engrained capitalism and under the weight of neoliberalism, where the divisions between work and leisure are increasingly complex (see Pfannebecker and Smith, 2020) and television can seem to 'magically' appear on devices at the tap of a screen or click of a button. Perhaps only the occasional message to audiences alerting them to 'buffering' will draw attention to the highly complex and ephemeral processes taking place, or to the many human and nonhuman actors required to fulfil them. Parikka (2012: 97) offers the term 'medianatures' to help make sense of the 'continuum between mediatic apparatuses and their material contexts in the exploitation of nature', emphasising the complex and often destructive relationships at the foundation of medianatures. Yet the representational contents of television (what is being watched, what is being streamed) are equally as imbricated in the politics of death as the material (and seemingly immaterial and ephemeral) technologies that facilitate that representation.

Deterministic discourses have consistently positioned television as contributing factors in violence and murder, with perpetrators' pasts often investigated as to whether they consumed content that might have emboldened them or informed their behaviour. Giroux (2009: 4) has argued that television has been central in leading the living to resemble 'armies of zombies', who 'tune in to gossip-laden entertainment, game, and reality TV shows, transfixed by the empty lure of celebrity culture'. Here, Giroux's (2009) argument is concerned with the content of television as much as the medium and signals the positioning of television as of less value, significance and 'seriousness' than, for example, film. As Wheatley (2006: 202) has made clear, there have long since been societal and cultural concerns about 'the propriety of television viewing'. These entanglements between television and death are all brought out, though perhaps rarely at a conscious level, by the material practices of consuming television as a commodity. Yet as Penfold-Mounce (2018) has argued, cultural texts can function to produce provocative morbid spaces that encourages, prompts and facilitates very conscious engagement with mortality that might be uncomfortable or troubling. In the next section, *Les Revenants* is positioned as an example of a television series that can function to produce a provocative morbid space and explicit reflection on death and loss, while ultimately remaining deeply entangled within the ideas about death and television discussed here, and in the continuum of connections between media and their exploitation of nature that Parikka (2012) signals with the term 'medianatures'.

Les Revenants

Les Revenants (2012–2015) is a French supernatural television drama created by Fabrice Gobert. It aired in France for the first time in 2012. The series focuses on a close-knit community in a mountainous alpine town where the dead begin to return to their homes – not as the conventionally reinscribed zombies that audiences might expect, but as their former selves. The series was adapted from an earlier film of the same name directed by Robert Campillo. The television series, of which there are two seasons, was broadcast with subtitles in the United Kingdom as *The Returned*. It was remade (with much of the series' nuance removed) for audiences in the United States, also titled *The Returned* (2015). *Les Revenants* received critical acclaim (Mangan, 2014; Luckhurst, 2016) and won an International Emmy for its first season. Next, I will examine how agency and power come to the fore in the series through two different dichotomies that *Les Revenants* troubles and disrupts: alive/dead and now/then.

Alive/dead

While *Les Revenants* centres on the potential consequences of a material return of the dead as organic matter and as agentic individuals, the power and agency of the dead are not what might be expected from a series where those who have died come back, because the dead are not the stereotypical or conventional zombies of horror genres. Penfold-Mounce (2018: 68) has argued that it is through resistance to clear categorization that the (un)dead demonstrate agency, their 'continual renewal and change' stopping them from being 'typecast as a particular type of reanimated corpse'. The dead in *Les Revenants* defy categorization. Establishing whether a character is dead or alive is difficult both for characters and, at times, audiences, troubling conventional boundaries of alive/dead. *Les Revenants* is one of several texts engaged in this destabilizing of alive/dead categories, exploring what might happen if the dead returned as people largely like their former selves. It is similar in premise to the British television series *In the Flesh* (2013–2014) and *The Fades* (2011), US series *Resurrection* (2014–2015) and Australian series *Glitch* (2015–2019). Each of these series is concerned with the practical consequences of the return of the dead as well as philosophical questions their return would raise, and all can be seen to disrupt normative ideas about death and the dead. Notably, none of them is associated with the horror genre or with the kinds of representations discussed previously that tend to be implicated in arguments about media violence and its potential harms. Each of the series, instead, offers a more meditative exploration of mortality.

Narratives like and including *Les Revenants*, focused on the dead returning as 'themselves', perhaps suggest a broad sociocultural concern about the enduring agency and power of the dead in life and about what it means to be alive/dead, tied to shifts in the technologization, medicalization and enduring politicization of living and dying. This is in contrast to the concerns associated with cultural texts about insensate zombies, which are often understood as symbols of other kinds of social anxieties typically around race, migration, capitalism and globalization (see, for example, Comaroff and Comaroff, 2012), or theorized as allegories for a predatory neoliberal capitalism, playing on concerns about population growth and globalization (Birch-Bayley, 2012; Michael, 2016). Such concerns seem not to be being signalled overtly in a series as intimate in tone as *Les Revenants*, where the focus is very much on notions of selfhood, loss and grief, and on the ways that people constitute themselves through and in their relationship to significant others. The series is engaged in exploring what Butler explains as the way in which loss and its accompanying experiences of grief challenge 'the very notion of ourselves as autonomous and in control' (Butler, 2006b: 44). It is personal, existential ideas such as these about death, loss and what it means to be alive/dead that permeate the series, as characters tussle with the emotional consequences of loss and the return of the dead, their own sense of agency and power challenged by this inexplicable return. What the alive/dead characters of *Les Revenants* highlight is both the enduring hold of the dead upon the living, and the sometimes-problematic power that the living hold over the dead in terms of how they are remembered.

Throughout *Les Revenants*, questions about what it means to be alive/dead are just beneath the surface, and life and death are both counterposed and combined. For example, in the opening credits a young heterosexual couple are featured kissing in a fertile field before the camera pans to two graves marked with wooden crosses and flowers, suggesting the passage of time and connoting life, reproduction and death. Yet it is notable that the camera pans left, not right, disrupting established and expected (though entirely socioculturally constructed and culturally specific) timelines by positioning death before life, not after. Several other disruptions of established and normative divisions between life and death also emerge within the series. The character Adele has experienced hallucinations after her fiancé's suicide. When he does return, she assumes her visions of him are hallucinations. In some ways he was very much alive for her when he was dead, so his physical return adds another layer of complexity to the haunting she was already experiencing. Julie, a character who barely survived a brutal knife attack years previously, suspects she too is one of the dead. Having experienced a kind of living death because of profound trauma, Julie finds it difficult to accept she is alive. These examples demonstrate how the series complicates conventional wisdom about life and death and constructed divisions between then/now and alive/dead, offering different ways of thinking about the power of the past and the agency of the dead. They also function to demonstrate how the series is entangled with broader sociocultural ideas theorized within but not confined to academic disciplines including psychology and sociology. For example, diagnostic definitions of post-traumatic stress disorder and complicated grief, and notions of continuing bonds with the dead (discussed in the next section). In this way, the series functions to demonstrate the cultural power and agency of a range of ideas about the self and about the dead that circulate within popular culture.

Now/then

The enduring power of the past on the present is a key thematic feature of *Les Revenants*, often centred around the town's human-made dam. The dam used for the television series is the visually striking Tignes dam in southeastern France, which was created despite protest from locals whose village was submerged by its creation in 1947 (Tignes, 2022). The development of the dam meant the death of the village and represented a significant loss for those whose lives and histories had been tightly connected to it, and whether this was a factor in selecting the dam for use in the series or not, it adds another entanglement of meaning to the series in terms of its connections to death. *Les Revenants* makes clear its concern with the natural world – itself a construction that positions the human *outside of* nature (Kirkby, 2017) – when taxidermized cats and pinned butterflies come back to life and escape their mountings, evading human control and troubling notions of permanency. Similarly, water and flooding play a primary symbolic role in the series representing both life and death. New materialist approaches often challenge 'longstanding assumptions about humans and the non- or other-than human material world' and 'routinely emphasize how matter is "alive", "lively", "vibrant", "dynamic", "agentive"' (Gamble et al, 2019: 111). In *Les Revenants*, water in particular takes on power and agency, and the waterbody of the human-made dam around which the series centres functions consistently within the series to trouble normative divisions between then/now.

A merging of now/then is evident in the series in at least three different ways in the series. First, the dead return, just as they were. Some of them have died a few short years before, others have been dead for decades. In this sense, the past quite literally comes back and melds with the present. When the dead return, it is often from the dam or its edges, and the waterbody functions in this sense to offer rebirth, symbolic of the potential fertility of the 'natural world' as well as of its capacity to endure far longer than the people who inhabit it. Second, historical moments of disaster reoccur. When the dam's water level drops but no cracks can be found in the structure, audiences discover that the dam flooded the town 35 years before the time when the series is set, and at the culmination of season one another flood occurs. These disasters, ultimately products of human intervention but also inexplicable, complicate the boundaries of the human-made and the natural disaster, as is increasingly the case in terms of real natural disasters within the context of climate emergency (Oxfam, 2021). Third, through the Gothic trope of the uncanny return or 'temporal loop', which is often used to signal 'personal and socio-cultural trauma re-enactments' (Juranovszky, 2014: 4).

For example, characters who try to leave the town drive for hours but find themselves in a disconcerting loop, always back on the same road and never able to cross the body of water that would put them outside of the town. This body of water is a product of human intervention, created through human power and agency. Yet the water here takes on agency and power of its own, blocking the town's residents from leaving. This is suggestive of the cultural idea of nature seeking revenge for the losses incurred by human intervention and for the environmental damage humans have wrought on the planet. More broadly, the repetition of the flooded dam and the return of the dead all function as temporal disjunctures in which then/now divisions collapse and trauma – personal, social, environmental – reoccurs.

Les Revenants and its numerous ways of bringing the past to bear on the present make it susceptible to being read hauntologically. Fisher (2014: 9), whose work has been central in bringing the notion of hauntology to bear on popular culture, presses the relevance of hauntological readings to a cultural moment where temporality is askew and in numerous ways 'time has folded back on itself'. Shaw (2018: 3) describes hauntology as a 'critical practice' that 'turns to the past in order to make sense of the present'. The term hauntology emerges in Derrida's *Specters of Marx* (1994). Its difference and similarity to the term ontology functions to undermine any then/now binary. The effect works better in the original French, where the term *l'hantologie* is a closer homonym for ontology than hauntology is. As hauntology has evolved, it has become 'shorthand for the ways in which the past returns to haunt the present' (Coverley, 2020: 7). The series' engagement with hauntological themes is illustrative of their increasing prevalence in contemporary popular culture, a site that has both been instrumental in generating and responding to the development of hauntology as a concept. In *Les Revenants*, the power of the past on the present is closely tied to the natural environment in terms of the repeated flooding of the town by the human-made waterbody of the dam, which as discussed previously has an agency of its own. Yet the capacity of the past to inform, complicate and change the present is also evident in the series in the relationships between the returned alive/dead characters and the living. It is also in these relationships that the series can be seen to challenge normative assumptions about grief as, initially, the dead who come back are those for whom someone remains 'stuck in the past'.

For example, the first episode of *Les Revenants* introduces a support group for the parents of children who died in a bus crash four years earlier. One of the couples announce that they are expecting a baby. They express thanks to the group, which they feel helped them to 'not exactly get over our loss but to carry on … move forward', echoing the conventional language of 'moving on' still dominant in many cultural messages about grief (though certainly, this is not the case in all cultures). In contrast Claire, the mother of another girl who died in the crash, does not attend the group at all. Claire keeps her daughter's room as it was. When Camille is the first to return, it seems to be being suggested that Claire's inability to 'move on' has been powerfully generative, leading to her daughter's return. Those parents who have 'moved on' have not experienced the return of their children, in what seems to be being positioned as a kind of punishment (though later in the series, almost all of the dead do return, complicating this notion). Eng and Kazanjian (2003: 3–4) explain that in classic conceptions of mourning 'the past is declared resolved, finished, and dead', whereas 'in melancholia the past remains steadfastly alive in the present'. Melancholia, then, is positioned as a type of grief that undermines the notion of then and now as linear – instead, time folds on itself as a consequence of loss. In this series, melancholia is initially posited as generative, as capable of bringing the dead back through its complication of then/now. This is an idea that is entangled in a wide range of academic literature from various different disciplines informing death studies.

In particular, it was Freud's early theorizations about what constitutes a 'healthy' approach to loss that have filtered into dominant understandings in the sociocultural imaginary about the importance of 'moving on', and 'the post-Freud paradigm for understanding grief' has perpetuated 'the idea that the primary goal of grieving is to cut the bond with the deceased so that new attachments can be formed' (Silverman and Klass, 1996: 7). However, the notion of 'moving on' from grief has been widely challenged from a range of cultural perspectives both theoretical and practical. For example, Derrida (1989: 38) has argued for the 'sublimity of a mourning without sublimation'. He offers what Kirkby (2006: 461) has positioned as a model that 'depathologises mourning and sees it as the opportunity for a continuing engagement with the legacy of the dead who remain within us and yet beyond us'. Klass et al's (1996) theory of 'continuing bonds' suggests the bereaved might 'hold the deceased in loving memory for long periods, often forever', and argues that 'maintaining an inner representation of the deceased is normal rather than abnormal' (Silverman and Nickman, 1996: 349). These perspectives all challenge conventional understandings of grief derived from Freud's early conception of mourning and melancholia (though it is important to note that Freud himself also came to understand the melancholy identification he initially deemed pathological to be a 'normal' part of mourning – see Freud, 2001 [1923]; Clewell, 2004). The fact that little attention has been paid to the similarities between Derrida (1989) and Klass et al's (1996) conceptualizations of grief demonstrate how tensions and antagonisms can be 'disciplinary rather than intellectual' (Michael-Fox, 2020b: 187), and emphasizes the usefulness of a diffractive analysis (Barad, 2007) for exploring entangled cultural ideas that can come to the fore within popular cultural texts. Reading these different theorizations together and alongside a television series makes it possible to see how notions of grief and mourning are shifting across a range of different cultural coordinates in both material and discursive ways. While *Les Revenants* is illustrative of what hauntology as a critical practice has often emphasized – that the past and the dead hold significant power over the present – it is also illustrative of how ideas about loss, and about conventional notions of then/now and how they should function, are being destabilized and troubled in different venues. Within the context of popular culture, theoretical ideas become entangled with conventional wisdom and find a new avenue through which to enter the sociocultural imaginary. In *Les Revenants*, tensions between alive/dead and then/now offer a breadth of troubling ways of thinking about death, loss, and the power and agency of the dead that challenge normative assumptions.

Conclusion

In cultural texts, meanings are configured in various ways and are then reconfigured by audiences (always plural and always complex) whose own life experiences, hopes and material circumstances inform their engagement. As Barad (2003: 818–819) argues, 'meaning is not ideational but rather specific material (re)configurings of the world'. Television series such as *Les Revenants*, which raise significant questions about the power of the past and the agency of the dead, offer a popular cultural venue through which audiences can encounter challenging ideas about death, loss and the dead that are entangled with a range of academic, practical and theoretical ideas that challenge normative assumptions. Reading cultural texts alongside and through – and with an awareness of how they may have been *informed by* – both discourses about and material experiences of death and loss can illuminate the ways in which they function as provocative morbid spaces (Penfold-Mounce, 2018) within the context of a broader sociocultural imaginary. At the same time, a material-discursive analysis of television considers the myriad ways in which the medium, its content and consumption all form part of medianatures (Parikka, 2012) and are imbricated in environmental change. While the television series *Les Revenants* raises questions about death, loss, and the power and agency of the dead in its thematic engagement, its concern with humanity's impact on the environment, evident in the metaphor of the agentic human-made waterbody of the dam, also raises ethical questions about the entangled role of media like television in environmental change that may trouble audiences.

References

albert (2022) we are albert. https://wearealbert.org/ (accessed 7 February 2022).

Barad, K. (2003) Posthumanist performativity: Toward an understanding of how matter comes to matter. *Signs*, 28(3): 801–831. DOI: https://www.jstor.org/stable/10.1086/345321

Barad, K. (2007) *Meeting the universe half way*. Durham, NC and London: Duke University Press.

Baudrillard, J. (1993 [1976]) *Symbolic exchange and death*. London: SAGE.

Birch-Bayley, N. (2012) Terror in horror genres: The global media and the millennial zombie. *Journal of Popular Culture*, 45(6): 1137–1151.

Butler, J. (2006a) *Gender trouble*. 2nd edition. New York and London: Routledge.

Butler, J. (2006b) *Precarious life: The powers of mourning and violence*. London: Verso.

Clewell, T. (2004) Mourning beyond melancholia: Freud's psychoanalysis of loss. *Journal of the American Psychoanalytic Association*, 53(1): 43–67. doi: 10.1080/13576270801954351

Comaroff, J. and Comaroff, J. (2002) Alien-nation: Zombies, immigrants, and millennial capitalism. *The South Atlantic Quarterly*, 101(4): 779–805.

Coverley, M. (2020) *Hauntology: Ghosts of futures past*. Harpenden: Oldcastle Books.

Derrida, J. (1989) *Memoires for Paul de Man*. Translated by C. Lindsay, J. Culler, E. Cadava and P. Kamuf. New York: Columbia University Press.

Derrida, J. (1994) *Specters of Marx*. Translated by P. Kamuf. New York and London: Routledge.

Durkin, K.F. (2003) Death, dying, and the dead in popular culture. In C. Bryant (ed) *Handbook of death and dying*. London: SAGE, pp 43–49.

Eng, D.L. and Kazanjian, D. (2003) Introduction: Mourning remains. In D.L. Eng and D. Kazanjian (eds) *Loss: The Politics of Mourning*. Berkeley and Los Angeles: University of California Press, pp 1–28.

Fisher, M. (2014) *Ghosts of my life*. Winchester: Zero Books.

Freud, S. (2001 [1923]) The ego and the id. In *The standard edition of the complete psychological works of Sigmund Freud*. Translated by James Strachey. London: Vintage, pp 19–27.

Gamble, C.N., Hanan, J.S. and Nail, T. (2019) What is new materialism? *Angelaki*, 24(6): 111–134. DOI: 10.1080/0969725X.2019.1684704

Giroux, H. (2009) *Zombie politics and culture in the age of casino capitalism*. New York: Peter Lang.

Griffin, A. (2016) Binge watching TV can actually kill you, study finds. *The Independent*, 25 July. https://www.independent.co.uk/news/science/binge-watching-tv-can-actually-kill-you-study-finds-a7155351.html (accessed 23 June 2020).

Hay, J. (2001) Locating the televisual. *Television and New Media*, 2(3): 205–234.

Huddleston, G. and Rocha, S.D. (2018) Don Draper, teacher-as-artist: A diffractive reading of *Mad Men*. *Taboo, The Journal of Culture and Education*, 17(3). https://doi.org/10.31390/taboo.17.3.05

Juranovszky, A. (2014) Trauma reenactment in the gothic loop: A study on structures of circularity in gothic fiction. *Inquiries Journal/Student Pulse*, 6. http://www.inquiriesjournal.com/a?id=898 (accessed 30 June 2023).

Kirkby, J. (2006) 'Remembrance of the future': Derrida on mourning. *Social Semiotics*, 16(3): 461–472. doi: 10.1080/10350330600824383

Kirkby, V. (ed) (2017) *What if culture was nature all along?* Edinburgh: Edinburgh University Press.

Klass, D., Silverman, P.R. and Nickman, S.L. (1996) *Continuing bonds: New understandings of grief*. Abingdon and New York: Routledge.

Luckhurst, R. (2016) *Zombies: A cultural history*. London: Reaktion Books.

Mangan, L. (2014) *The Returned* – box set review. *The Guardian*, 20 February. https://www.theguardian.com/tv-and-radio/2014/feb/20/the-returned-box-set-review-french-drama (accessed 23 June 2020).

Michael, B. (2016) The return of the dead: Fears and anxieties surrounding death and resurrection in late postmodern culture. In I. Dixon, S.E.M. Doran and B. Michael (eds) *Fears and anxieties in the 21st century*. Leiden: Brill, pp 31–43

Michael-Fox, B. (2020a) Dead chatty: The rise of the articulate undead in popular culture. In M. Coward-Gibbs (ed) *Death, culture and leisure: Playing dead*. Bingley: Emerald, pp 111–124.

Michael-Fox, B. (2020b) Present and accounted for: Making sense of death and the dead in late postmodern culture. Doctoral thesis, University of Winchester. https://winchester.elsevierpure.com/en/studentTheses/present-and-accounted-for (accessed 30 June 2023).

Michael-Fox, B. (forthcoming 2023) (Un)dead together: Hospitality, hauntology and the 'happily ever after'. In M. O'Thomas and R. Hand (eds) *American horror story and cult television: Narratives, histories and discourses*. London: Anthem Press.

Mielach, D. (2012) Is it ethical to own an iPhone? *Scientific American*, 3 February. https://www.scientificamerican.com/article/is-it-ethical-to-own-an-iphone/ (accessed 7 February 2022).

Oxfam (2021) 5 natural disasters that beg for climate action. *Oxfam International*. https://www.oxfam.org/en/5-natural-disasters-beg-climate-action (accessed 7 February 2022).

Parikka, J. (2012) New materialism as media theory: Medianatures and dirty matter. *Communication and Critical/Cultural Studies*, 9(1): 95–100. DOI: 10.1080/14791420.2011.626252

Penfold-Mounce, R. (2018) *Death, the dead and popular culture*. Emerald: Bingley.

Pfannebecker, M. and Smith, J.A. (2020) *Work want work: Labour and desire at the end of capitalism*. London: Zed.

Shaw, K. (2018) *Hauntology: The presence of the past in twenty-first century English literature*. Basingstoke: Palgrave Macmillan.

Silverman, P.R. and Klass, D. (1996) Introduction: What's the problem? In D. Klass, P.R. Silverman and S.L. Nickman (eds) *Continuing bonds: New understandings of grief*. Abingdon and New York: Routledge, pp 3–27.

Silverman, P.R. and Nickman, S.L. (1996) Concluding thoughts. In D. Klass, P.R. Silverman and S.L. Nickman (eds) *Continuing bonds: New understandings of grief*. Abingdon and New York: Routledge, pp 349–355.

Tignes (2022) Le Barrage de Tignes. https://en.tignes.net/discover/glacier-lake-dam/le-barrage-de-tignes (accessed 7 February 2022).

Wheatley, H. (2006) *Gothic television*. Manchester: Manchester University Press.

Television

Glitch (2015–2019) Created by Tony Ayres and Louise Fox. ABC. Television series.

The Fades (2011) Created by Jack Thorne. BBC Three. Television series.

In the Flesh (2013–2014) Created by Dominic Mitchell. BBC Three. Television series.

Resurrection (2014–2015) Developed by Aaron Zelman. ABC. Television series.

The Returned (2015) Developed from the French series *Les Revenants* by Carlton Cuse. New York: A&E Studios. Viewed on Netflix.

Les Revenants (2012) Created by Fabrice Gobert. Paris. Haut et Court. Viewed on DVD.

11

Material Entanglements of the Corpse

Marc Trabsky and Jacinthe Flore

Introduction

The International Consortium of Investigative Journalists (ICIJ) published an incendiary report in 2012 on a thriving global market for cadaveric human tissue. The transnational conglomerate of journalists tracked across 11 countries how 'donated' corpses are obtained in Ukraine, processed into biomedical products in Germany and then distributed in the United States for a consumer market spread across the world. In mapping the journey of the corpse and its parts from Eastern Europe to North America, the ICIJ revealed how a variety of commonly used medical treatments involve the recycling of cadaveric tissue. From cruciate ligament reconstructions to penis enlargements, heart valve replacements to orthopaedic surgery, and skin transplants, bone grafts and bladder slings, the dead body materializes as a lucrative vessel for the harvesting of skin, flesh and bone.

This 'shadowy market' in the supply and demand of cadaveric tissue resembles the practice in the 18th and 19th centuries of trafficking indigenous peoples' remains in the United Kingdom, and African American cadavers in the United States (Richardson, 2001; Sappol, 2004). The most notorious 'body brokers' in the colonial market for human cadavers were the 'resurrectionists', who until the enactment of the *Anatomy Act 1832* (UK), resorted to any means available, including grave robbing and even murder, to procure specimens for medical schools. The Anatomy Act legalized the trade of cadaveric tissue only in the situation where a person had lawful possession of a corpse. In other words, where a corpse remained unclaimed by the next-of-kin, a person could lawfully supply it to medical schools in exchange for a fee, which was ostensibly exploited by workhouses, prisons, hospitals, morgues and funeral houses to sell the cadavers of mostly paupers, prisoners and indigenous people.

Modern 'body brokers' still operate today around the world to supply 'donated' corpses not only to medical schools, but also profit-making companies, which then sell or lease body parts to research institutes, pharmaceutical corporations, and medical training companies. What has changed however, since at least the 1980s, is that the global market for cadaveric tissue has diversified into different revenue streams (Gow and Shiffman, 2017). Although selling and buying organs and tissue for transplantation remains illegal in most countries around the world, multinational corporations have commodified the 'tissue-processing' industry for the purposes of transplantation, and created a secondary market for the recycling of human organs, tissue, skin and bone for medical research (Willson et al, 2012). The allegations made by the ICIJ against RTI Surgical (formerly known as RTI Biologics), for its role in procuring so-called 'donated' tissue and supplying it to for-profit companies for manufacturing a range of biomedical products, suggests that body brokering is still a profitable enterprise in the 21st century, and cadaveric human tissue has become a valuable commodity for sustaining human life.

This chapter examines how the recycling of cadaveric tissue in the 21st century problematizes legal epistemologies of the corpse. Its point of departure is how legal doctrine on proprietary interests in the corpse has increasingly become disrupted by technologies that repurpose cadaveric tissue for a global market of medical devices, implants, treatments, and pharmaceuticals. We argue that the technologies involved in recycling necro-waste in the creation of biomedical products invite an alternative perspective of knowing the corpse. The chapter does not discuss the problem of regulating a global market of cadaveric tissue, and it moves beyond the question of whether necro-waste can be lawfully owned by legal persons. Rather, we call for a rethinking of how the corpse is conceptualized in law, not in terms of whether it is a person or a thing, but to borrow from feminist theoretical physicist Karen Barad (2007), with regards to its intra-activity with matter, discourse and institutions. We explore how the vitality of necro-waste that emerges through intra-action challenges legal understandings of how the corpse becomes materially entangled with legal discourses.

The chapter begins by examining the development of legal doctrine on proprietary interests in the corpse since the 17th century. Jurists have questioned in common law countries, such as Australia, the United Kingdom and the United States whether the 'no property' rule in human body parts persists in the 21st century. They have asked if law is to define the corpse as a thing, what obligations, if any, could pertain to owning, trading, gifting and exchanging cadavers. While, if law is to conceptualize the corpse as a person, they have queried whether it is possible to endow the dead body with legal personhood, and if so, whether any rights or duties survive posthumously. The chapter first considers the current status of the 'no property' rule, and then suggests that it imagines a dead body that is *a priori* unique, whole and bounded. We subsequently explain how the recycling of cadaveric tissue undermines legal doctrine by transforming the human body and its parts into lucrative waste. Recycling necro-waste in the manufacturing of biomedical products invites an alternative perspective of knowing the corpse by revealing the human cadaver to be fragmented, relational and entangled. The chapter concludes by calling for a rethinking of how the corpse is conceptualized in law through its intra-activity with matter, discourse and institutions.

Legal epistemologies of the corpse

The question of the legal status of the corpse has long been unsettled in the common law. The *Haynes Case* was the first to define the corpse as neither a person nor a thing (*res nullius*), 'but a lump of earth hath no capacity' (1614: 1389). William Haynes was caught disinterring graves, stealing the winding sheets found within and reburying the dead bodies he exhumed. The crucial issue in this case was whether the deceased person possessed the winding sheets. If they were owned by the executor of the estate, Haynes could be found guilty of theft, however, if they merely belonged to the dead body then Haynes was innocent. The court held that a corpse was not capable of owning anything, and thus Haynes was guilty of theft because the winding sheets formed the property of the executors of the estate. Even though the corpse was defined as 'a lump of earth', it was unequivocal, as William Blackstone noted, that it was 'not to be subject to the laws of property in the same manner as real earth' (Davies and Naffine, 2001: 107). In other words, the corpse could not own things, but neither could it be considered property in itself.

Jurists have debated the amorphous contours of the doctrine dividing the corpse into a person and a thing in several significant cases since the 17th century. In *Gilbert v Buzzard* (1820), also called the *Iron Coffin Case*, the ecclesiastical court rejected Mr Gilbert's claim to bury his wife in an iron rather than a wooden coffin, because it defined the cemetery as merely a 'holding medium'. If any right to possess a corpse was said to exist under the common law, it was not a proprietary right in perpetuity, but rather a limited right of possession constrained by irreversible processes of putrefaction. The court held that an iron coffin was not an appropriate vessel for burial, because it would impede the 'natural' decomposition of the corpse. In *R v Stewart*, which concerned a dispute about who was responsible for paying for the burial of the deceased, the court declared that '[e]very person dying in this country ... has *a right to Christian burial*; and that implies the right to be carried from the place where his body lies to the parish cemetery'

(1840: 1009, original emphasis). While it was evident from both *Gilbert* and *Stewart* that the right to possess a corpse was not proprietary, it was unclear throughout the 18th and 19th centuries how the duty fitted into existing categories of law.[1]

The High Court of Australia decision of *Doodeward v Spence* (1908), however, articulated an exception to the 'no property' rule, whereby the work or skill of the living can transform the corpse into a thing that can be owned. The court reasoned that the possession of an unburied human corpse was not necessarily unlawful, in fact it could be 'permanently possessed', because medical schools, museums and moribund sideshows would simply cease to exist if they could not enforce their ownership of their anatomical displays. While a corpse could never constitute a thing in itself, if

> a person has by the lawful exercise of work or skill so dealt with a human body or part of a human body in his lawful possession [such] that it has acquired some attributes differentiating it from a mere corpse awaiting burial, he acquires a right to retain possession of it, at least as against any person not entitled to have it delivered to him for the purpose of burial, but subject, of course, to any positive law which forbids its retention under the particular circumstances. (*Doodeward v Spence*, 1908: 414)

Recent case law in Australia has applied the *Doodeward* decision to justify that a spouse may possess human gametes extracted from their deceased partner either prior to or after their death.[2] And when faced with the theft of 35 human body parts from the Royal College of Surgeons, the English Court of Appeal in *R v Kelly and Lindsay* (1998) relied upon *Doodeward* to find that converting a corpse into a preserved specimen transformed it into a thing that could be owned and subsequently stolen. But the 'work and skill' exception to the *res nullius* doctrine sits unsteadily alongside the long-standing concept that only a contractual right to burial exists in common law, that is, an 'irrevocable licence', as cited in the *Beard* case to remain undisturbed 'at least until the natural process of dissolution' (1986: 278) is complete. It also remains incongruous with the jurisprudence of succession law, which since at least the 12th century has developed rules by which the dead may exert proprietary rights over future generations.

The question of the legal status of the corpse has also been subject to much debate among philosophers, bioethicists and legal scholars since at least the 18th century. In advocating that the corpse is a thing that can be owned, and theoretically traded, exchanged and abandoned, they have asked what obligations, if any, pertain to a proprietary right in a dead body or body parts. Indeed, scholars have argued that although the human corpse is 'a messy, maybe dangerous, perhaps valuable, often useful, and always tangible thing', as Ellen Stroud (2018: 117) writes, it is undoubtedly an object in law. On the other hand, in arguing that the corpse cannot and should not be categorized in law as a thing, others have explored whether it is possible to endow it with legal personhood. Several legal theorists have argued that the modern law of testation demonstrates how the dead could be said to exercise their legal personality over the living, while some have questioned whether the 'death of the body is not [in fact] the end of the biographical person' (McGuiness and Brazier, 2008: 303). The problem with conceiving of the corpse as a thing is that it presumes that death is a distinct event in time rather than an entangled process. Whereas the problem of conceptualizing the corpse as a person is that it relies upon a rationalist imagination of the dead body as *a priori* unique, whole and bounded. The idea of posthumous personhood idealizes the physical cadaver as an undivided 'natural given' and either locates its personality in a disembodied will that transcends matter or assimilates it into the dead body itself.

The lucrative waste of death

Funeral industries produce an abundance of waste. The corpse is disinfected, cleansed, shaved, stitched, bleached and tinted. Arterial embalming involves pumping a formaldehyde solution through the body's arteries, while draining its veins of blood and other fluids. Cavity embalming makes use of a 'trocar', which collects fluids, matter, gases and bacteria from organs and injects chemical preservatives into the body's cavities. Cremation burns the body into bone grit, which is commonly referred to as ashes, but it also leaves behind heat-resistant medical implants, fine bone dust and vaporized mercury. Necro-waste designates the by-products of different applications of work on a corpse in death-related trades (Olson, 2016). It includes an ensemble of materials – fluids, gases, tissue, bone, skin, implants, chemicals and effluence – discarded from postmortem examinations, medical research and training, transplantation procedures, plastination techniques and technologies for the disposal of human remains.

Cremation has emerged as the most popular method for the disposal of dead bodies in the West in the 21st century. While burial practices remain important rituals for many communities in the West, and they consume a significant slice of the billion-dollar revenues generated by the funeral industry, low-cost cremations have become the preferred disposal method for most families. Cremation, though, relies upon the consumption of an abundance of energy and questions have been raised both about mercury emissions from the incineration of dental amalgams, and the recycling of metal pacemakers, splints, implants and joints.[3] Consequently, more environmentally friendly disposal methods have emerged, such as alkaline hydrolysis, which involves dissolving cadavers in a potassium hydroxide-water solution, heating the solution to 93 degrees Celsius for four hours and crushing the bones into a fine calcium phosphate substance. There has also been a grassroots movement for natural burial, partly fueled by a diversification of revenue streams, the increasing costs of burial services and a concomitant desire to hasten the 'natural' process of decomposition. Despite the differences between the various modalities for disposing human remains, funeral service providers have begun to emphasize how the corpse can be 'gifted' to the environment, while ignoring the array of waste products produced by each disposal technology.

Necro-waste describes the refuse of different applications of work on a corpse in death-related trades that do not necessarily result in a gift for nature or society. These waste products, as highlighted by the ICIJ case study at the beginning of this chapter, are not always flushed into sewage drains or integrated into the environment. They are increasingly recycled in a global economy for cadaveric tissue. While discussions of necro-waste should not be confined to the funeral industry – for example, waste is generated by postmortem examinations, transplantation procedures, and through medical research and training – it provides the most obvious example of how waste is produced, its use-value in a global economy for cadaveric tissue and how it transforms legal epistemologies of the corpse. Philip Olson writes in his analysis of embalming practices and technologies in the United States and Canada that the business model of the funeral industry is structured around draining the corpse of 'unwanted, useless, or obstructive matter' in the course of creating 'a product of industrial art, an object to which new matter is added' (Olson, 2016: 331). He provides the following example of the embalming process:

> During arterial injection, the embalmer drains blood from the corpse (typically by way of the incised jugular vein), while pumping diluted, pigmented embalming fluid (arterial fluid) into the body (usually through the carotid artery). The blood, along with some embalming fluid, flows down the embalming table and into a slop sink, which usually drains into either the municipal sewer system or a septic system. (Olson, 2016: 331–332)

The purpose of embalming is to arrest the visceral effects of death, to temporarily suspend the process of decomposition, and through the application of mechanical treatments and chemical substances, present the corpse as if it was living, even if only for a couple of days prior to its disposal. Formaldehyde, methanol, phenol, putty, piping and plastics are inserted into the corpse in a futile attempt to arrest the ravages of decay, which will, once the body is disposed of in the ground, contaminate the area around the gravesite. This means any objects deemed by the embalmer to be unnecessary to 'beautifying' the corpse (or even hasten the decomposition process), such as blood, fat, tissue, organs, bone or eyes, are removed and discarded as necro-waste. Funeral industries are highly regulated in different parts of the world, however, as Olson (2016: 330) points out, that does not mean that all aspects of its practices, such as the disposal of waste from the embalming table, are scrutinized by professional societies or state-based regulators.

The production of necro-waste through funeral embalming fragments the corpse into *lucrative* waste. Waste is something deemed no longer useful for human consumption, yet as Myra J. Hird explains, it is also 'an inherently ambiguous linguistic signifier: anything and everything can become waste, and things can simultaneously be and not be waste' (2012: 454). For John Frow, waste is both negative value and its constitutive structure, 'it is residually a commodity, something from which money may still be made' (2001: 21). We add the adjective 'lucrative' to the concept of necro-waste to signal the profitability of its circulation in global trade (Troyer, 2020), but we are also indicating that necro-waste *exceeds* the meanings ascribed to the corpse in law. As Olson writes, it 'represents a different way of *knowing* the corpse, and no one body concept serves as the true and proper way of knowing the dead human body in all contexts or for all purposes' (2016: 327).

The notion that the corpse could constitute in law either a thing or a person, or even both at the same time, reiterates how legal epistemology is founded upon a search for the cadaver's facticity. The objectivity of the corpse, its matter, the apparent naturalness of its 'inanimate physicality', is complicated by the recycling of cadaveric tissue. Even if its material existence could be located prostrate in a grave, splayed on the dissection table or plastinated in an anatomy museum, its 'apparent unity', as Bruno Latour reminds us, 'is only the superficial impression left by the routine of life' (2002: 127). The remainder of this chapter will show that doctrinal analyses of the legal status of the corpse are unable to account for how repurposing flesh, skin and bone for biomedical products problematizes legal epistemologies of the dead body. The recycling of cadaveric tissue divides the human body into ever more parts that can bought, sold, lent and exchanged. The circulation of these practices around the world punctures the legal status of a corpse as a person or a thing, and they reveal how the human cadaver is immanently fragmented, relational and entangled. If the central question in law has been how to fit the corpse within the existing legal categories of person or thing, this chapter explores instead whether the corpse can be rethought through a critical examination of its material entanglements.

Necro-legal entanglements

Central to feminist new materialist perspectives is an endeavour to redefine the relationalities of human and nonhuman. In this frame, the remainder of this chapter considers the materiality of the corpse and its entanglements in social and legal worlds. However, materiality is not inert matter; instead, it is 'always something more than "mere" matter: an excess, force, vitality, relationality, or difference that renders matter active' (Coole and Frost, 2010: 9). We can, through this perspective, view the corpse as generative of discourse and law. Thus, entanglements with matter, knowledge and more-than-human practices are foregrounded. Such an approach emphasizes how the entanglements of human and more-than-human emerge *within* encounters with matter.

The concept of entanglement has been harnessed in feminist new materialism and science and technology studies to shed light on the inextricability of concepts, objects and practices that have been generally approached as 'separate', for example, humans and nonhumans, the living and the dead, and waste and recycling. 'What often appear as separate entities (and separate sets of concerns) with sharp edges', writes Karen Barad, 'does not actually entail a relation of absolute exteriority at all' (2007: 93). Entanglement ushers in questions of ontology and epistemology and how certain things become 'known', or how certain forms of knowledge attain a privileged status in society. This suggests a mode of thought whereby objects, agency and identity, and their emergence, are radically transformed. In rethinking how knowledge is produced, entanglement refers to more than 'to be intertwined with another' (Barad, 2007: ix). It renders limited ideas of 'connection' or 'relation', rather, entanglement is *intra*-active and not *inter*-active. On this view, matter is agentic, it enacts vitality in its intra-activity with humans and objects. When applying a feminist new materialist perspective to legal epistemologies of the corpse, the dead body and its parts appear as 'emergent propert[y] … in [its] ability to make things happen' (Bennett, 2009: 24). Indeed, the conversion of the corpse into waste and its repurposing in biomedical products circulates in our world in a network of objects, practices, economies, humans and laws, where it affects and is affected by multiple agents.

We suggest applying a feminist new material perspective to understand how legal epistemologies of the corpse are challenged by the recycling of cadaveric tissue in the world. This work requires more than mapping the trajectory of the corpse in social and legal worlds. In fact, such an approach risks merely recasting the corpse as a passive and inert object in a network functioning independently. Rather, we approach the recycling of cadaveric tissue as entangling the corpse into a tethering of matter, discourse and institutions. Thus, much like Jane Bennett's (2009) case studies of trash, electrical networks and food, the corpse enacts an intensity or force that may enable or stymie the will of humans. For writers who engage with feminist new materialism, entanglement emphasizes how 'individuals emerge through and as part of their entangled intra-relating' (Barad, 2007: ix).

Where *inter*action suggests the coming-together of pre-existing objects, intra-action posits that agents – in our example, the corpse, tools used to dissect it, embalming practices and disposal technologies, legal institutions, regulatory bodies, funeral service providers and blood, fat, tissue and organs discarded as waste – do not precede their encounters with one another, they *emerge through* intra-action and remain inextricable (Barad, 2007: 33). The corpse is not limited to a unitary or undivided physicality or personhood, its material agency is distributed. Intra-action presents a critique of the separation between the technology (or apparatus) and the person wielding the technology in the making of scientific knowledge. Thus, matter – and indeed the corpse – can be considered a dynamism of *forces*.

These perspectives challenge attempts made by legal doctrine to fit the corpse within pre-existing categories of 'thing-ness' or personhood. By holding that the corpse is a thing, jurists attempt to disentangle it from a network of discourses and relations, and the agency of the corpse itself. While scholars who argue that the corpse should be endowed with personhood likewise attempt to extricate it from the matter of decaying flesh, practices for discarding waste and rendering it lucrative, and institutional processes for recycling cadaveric tissue into biomedical products, which all entangle the corpse and its parts in the materiality of the world. Entanglement, in other words, offers a different way of imagining how both wasted and recycled cadaveric tissue is tethered to matter, discourse and institutions.

In this framework, necro-waste cannot be considered purely as a by-product of organic life, just as the corpse cannot be categorized as either a thing or a person. The corpse should instead be viewed as emergent 'material-discursive' phenomena whereby discourse, whether legal or otherwise, is inextricable from the corpse's materiality and the multiple practices, humans and nonhumans involved. As noted earlier, Olson approaches necro-waste as a medium through which the corpse is *known*:

> Viewing the corpse as necro-waste sanctions new perspectives on the dead human body and on the actors, institutions, regulations, and material cultures within which human corpses are embedded. In short, it occasions new ways of knowing human corpses, as well as new ways of knowing ourselves, through the various norms and practices that govern the disposal of necro-waste. (Olson, 2016: 327)

Knowing the corpse is inextricable from the material practices involved in the social and legal worlds entangled in its production. It is thus impossible (and not productive) to consider necro-waste as an 'after the corpse' or 'after life' matter. If necro-waste is a different way of knowing the corpse, then feminist new materialism urges us to consider both *what* and *who* participates in this production of knowledge. This problematizes doctrinal perspectives of the corpse as either a thing or a person, and affirms that as cadaveric tissue is produced, used and traded, the embodiment of the corpse is both 'dead' and 'alive', swarming with vitalities. In applying a feminist new materialist approach to understanding how technologies produce necro-waste and recycle it in the production of medical treatments, devices, implants and pharmaceuticals, we suggest that both legal categories, social discourses and material boundaries between the corpse and the living become contested.

Conclusion

The legal status of the corpse and its parts is marked by a productive ambivalence. On the one hand, the law considers any parts removed from the body, whether that may be a viable organ or discarded tissue 'new' matter, different or separate from the corpse. However, at the same time, its materiality, even in the eyes of the law, remains entangled with the corpse. Knowledge of recycled cadaveric tissue is thereby mediated by understanding the corpse and the practices and norms that govern these entities, that is, how matter, discourses and institutions all play a role in transforming legal knowledge of the corpse. Law does not precede the corpse here, but rather emerges intra-actively with and through objects (and subjects). In so doing, the corpse is transformed into something else – whether that may be waste destined for the sewers or a biomedical product for human consumption – alongside law and discourse. The corpse then cannot be approached as a stable entity specifically bounded by legal frameworks. This has profound ontological significance for how we understand the corpse, its volatile but inextricable 'by-products', and indeed the body itself.

What we have proposed in this chapter is a re-reading of the intra-activity of recycled cadaveric tissue and its entanglements with human and nonhuman entities. This involves a fundamental rethinking of the corpse in law by insisting that we must 'stay with the trouble' (Haraway, 2016: 4) of affirming its multiple enactments with discourse and matter, rather than 'fix' its position as a person or a thing in legal worlds. Thus, when we speak of the matter of the corpse, we speak of *'substance in its intra-active becoming'* (Barad, 2007: 210, original emphasis). To stay with the trouble requires attending to the complex entanglements that make and unmake knowledge, that blur the boundaries between the living and the dead, and locate the material-discursive enactments of the corpse and necro-waste in and beyond legal epistemologies. This reconceptualization potentially can animate an improved regulation of the global trade in cadaveric tissue highlighted by the ICIJ.

This chapter has outlined how we can think differently about the entanglements of the corpse with law through a materialist examination of necro-waste. It becomes apparent by engaging with a feminist new materialist perspective that the corpse emerges intra-actively with legal institutions and is entangled in more-than-human worlds. Thus, as necro-waste reveals the entanglements of the corpse with matter, discourse and institutions, it challenges the conventional views of the corpse as a bounded and undivided person or a unitary or useful thing. This chapter thus asks the reader to take seriously the recycling of cadaveric tissue in our worlds – and not simply disregard it as wasteful knowledge – but also understand the limits of our capacity to understand the corpse, map its attachments to institutions and cultivate its legal epistemologies.

Acknowledgements

Our sincere thanks to Jesse D. Peterson, Philip R. Olson and Natashe Lemos-Dekker for their insightful comments on the chapter, and Emily Ross from Bristol University Press. Marc Trabsky's research for this chapter was funded by an Australian Research Council Discovery Early Career Researcher Award (DE220100064) and the chapter draws upon and takes portions from Chapter 4 of Marc Trabsky, *Death: New trajectories in law* (Routledge, 2023).

Notes

[1] Following *R v Stewart*, several cases, such as *R v Sharpe* (1856–1857) and *Williams v Williams* (1882), held that the executor of an estate had a non-proprietorial right of possession of a corpse until it is buried, however, it was unclear what duties pertained to this right.

[2] See, for example, *Bazley v Wesley Monash IVF Party Ltd* [2010]; *Edwards; Re Estate of Edwards* [2011]; *Re H, AE (No 2)* [2012].

[3] See *OrthoMetals*, https://orthometals.com/, a company operating in North America, Europe and Australasia that recycles metals that are removed before cremation because they should not be vaporized in the crematoria.

References

Barad, K. (2007) *Meeting the universe halfway: Quantum physics and the entanglement of matter and meaning*. Durham, NC: Duke University Press.

Bennett, J. (2009) *Vibrant matter: A political ecology of matter*. Durham, NC: Duke University Press.

Coole, D. and Frost, S. (2010) Introducing the new materialisms. In D. Coole and S. Frost (eds) *New materialisms: Ontology, agency and politics*. Durham, NC: Duke University Press, pp 1–43.

Davies, M. and Naffine, N. (2001) *Are persons property? Legal debates about property and personality*. London: Ashgate.

Frow, J. (2001) Invidious distinction: Waste, difference and classy stuff. *UTS Review*, 7(2): 21–31.

Gow, B. and Shiffman, J. (2017) The body trade: Cashing in on the donated dead. *Reuters*. https://www.reuters.com/investigates/special-report/usa-bodies-brokers (accessed 10 January 2022).

Haraway, D. (2016) *Staying with the trouble: Making kin in the Chthulucene*. Durham, NC: Duke University Press.

Hird, M.J. (2012) Knowing waste: Towards an inhuman epistemology. *Social Epistemology*, 26(3–4): 453–469.

The International Consortium of Investigative Journalists (2012) *Skin & bone: The shadowy trade in human body parts*. Washington DC: Center for Public Integrity. https://www.icij.org/investigations/tissue/ (accessed 10 January 2023).

Latour, B. (2002) Body, cyborgs and the politics of incarnation. In S.T. Sweeney and I. Hodder (eds) *The body (the Darwin College lectures)*. Cambridge: Cambridge University Press, pp 127–141.

McGuiness, S. and Brazier, M. (2008) Respecting the living means respecting the dead too. *Oxford Journal of Legal Studies*, 28(2): 29–316.

Olson, P.R. (2016) Knowing 'necro-waste'. *Social Epistemology: A Journal of Knowledge, Culture and Policy*, 30(3): 326–345.

Richardson, R. (2001) *Death dissection and the destitute*. Chicago: University of Chicago Press.

Sappol, M. (2004) *A traffic of dead bodies: Anatomy and embodied social identity in nineteenth-century America*. Princeton: Princeton University Press.

Stroud, E. (2018) Law and the dead body: Is a corpse a person or a thing? *Annual Review of Law and Social Science*, 14: 115–125.

Troyer, J. (2020) *Technologies of the human corpse*. Cambridge, MA and London: The MIT Press.

Willson, K., Lavrov, V., Keller, M., Maier, T. and Ryle, G. (2012) Human corpses harvested in multimillion-dollar trade. *The Sydney Morning Herald*, 17 July. https://www.smh.com.au/politics/federal/human-corpses-harvested-in-multimilliondollar-trade-20120717-2278v.html (accessed 10 January 2022).

Case list

Bazley v Wesley Monash IVF Party Ltd [2010] QSC 118.
Beard v Baulkham Hills Shire Council and Another (1986) 7 NSWLR 273.
Doodeward v Spence (1908) 6 CLR 406.
Edwards; Re Estate of Edwards [2011] NSWSC 478.
Gilbert v Buzzard (1820) 161 ER 1342.
Hayne's Case (1614) 77 ER 1389.
R v Kelly and Lindsay [1998] 3 All ER 741.
R v Sharpe (1856–1857) 169 ER 959.
R v Stewart (1840) 113 ER 1007.
Re H, AE (No 2) [2012] SASC 177.
Williams v Williams (1882) 20 Ch D 659.

12

The Dead Who Would Be Trees and Mushrooms

Hannah Gould, Tamara Kohn, Michael Arnold and Martin Gibbs

The *Capsula Mundi* biodegradable burial pods represent a vision of an ecological afterlife aesthetically wrapped. In soft tones, promotional photographs display three large ovum-shaped vessels, their surfaces progressively mottled with soil, lichen and minerals, while above, the delicate roots of young saplings stretch out to embrace the pods. These vessels are designed to hold a human corpse as it gradually decomposes, producing nutrients to support the growth of a tree. Cradling the corpse in a foetal pose, the womb-like pod invokes strong symbolism of fertility (see Westendorp and Gould, 2021), forging a material connection between death and the regeneration of life (Bloch and Parry, 1982). In so doing, *Capsula Mundi* evokes continuous cycles of renewal and rebirth, such that, as its website intimates: 'Life is forever.' Since its launch in 2003, *Capsula Mundi* has captured the imagination of news editors, social media users and artists worldwide. However, despite headlines rather naively proclaiming that the system will 'turn your body into a tree' (Erizanu, 2018), *Capsula Mundi* is currently only available as a container for ashes, functionally indistinguishable from the many biodegradable urns on the market. At the time of writing, the whole-body burial pod is described as 'still in a development phase … not ready for the market' (*Capsula Mundi*, nd).

Still, the promise of *Capsula Mundi* is clearly compelling. Images of the product periodically go viral on social media or are featured in news stories about 'eco-death'. When this happens, funeral companies who we work with across Australia are flooded with calls from people eager to secure this body disposal option for themselves. Workers are left with the difficult task of describing the inherent impracticalities of the *Capsula Mundi* vision: the challenge of moulding a corpse into the foetal position, the additional burial depth required, and the impact of volatile, decomposing flesh on new plant growth; all while trying to offer more pragmatic, if less aesthetic, options for eco-friendly deathcare. As *Capsula Mundi* so neatly demonstrates, the allure of a posthumous 'return to nature' or ecological afterlife belies the uncomfortable realities of the decomposing human corpse and, more broadly, humanity's relationship to the environment.

Environmentalism has driven some of the most widespread changes to mainstream Western deathcare over the last two decades. This broad movement includes efforts to lessen the impacts of conventional burial and cremation via, for example, mercury filtration. It also extends to new technologies for the treatment of the corpse, including natural burial, human composting and alkaline hydrolysis. Significantly, this movement has forged ahead despite a lack of clear accounting for the impact of 'greener' methods, or indeed, for the overall impact of the deathcare sector in comparison to other industries. But this movement is far more than a set of technical solutions to a scientific problem, it offers people a chance to affirm their values (Davies and Rumble, 2012: 3), to extend their identity posthumously (Stock and Dennis, 2021) or to express larger beliefs about one's place in the cosmos.

In particular, *Capsula Mundi* and other eco-death services anchor a set of new popular beliefs in an 'ecological afterlife' (Davies, 2005), whereby natural cycles of the growth, decay and regeneration of living things become a framework for making sense of human mortality. This contrasts Judaeo-Christian visions of an otherworldly or heavenly afterlife, as the human body decays and returns to earth, not to be resurrected, but to be reincorporated into a massive ecological network of living organisms. This mode of thinking thus emphasizes the union, rather than distinction, of humans and nature (Davies, 2005: 87). However, visions of an ecological afterlife are not singular, but plural.

In this chapter, we describe two emerging strands within Western vernacular spirituality, the dead who become 'trees' and the dead who become 'mushrooms'. Trees feature heavily across the spectrum of green death services. Some technologies promise to physically transform bodily decay into arboreal life, while others simply borrow the visual imagery of nature and generational legacy. More recently, fungi, mycelium and mushrooms have been incorporated into products designed to enhance or complement natural burial, including burial suits, coffins and pods. This chapter critically examines the metaphorical entailments of arboreal and mycelium afterlives as emerging forms of vernacular spirituality. We do so by drawing on interviews conducted between 2018 and 2021 with death technologists in Australia, the United Kingdom and United States, as well as analysis of their promotional materials and pitches at industry conferences, and analysis of the popular reception of new technological offering on news and social media. Both trees and mushrooms act as powerful ecological symbols, but in the contexts we examine, they offer up distinct configurations of the material and symbolic boundaries between human/nonhuman, corpse/nature, self/other. We ask, how is the human personhood or personal identity of the dead preserved, transformed or severed in the form of trees or fungi? What is the relationship between these trees or fungi and the community of the living? And what kind of afterlives are generated by the transformation of human life and decay into 'rhizomatic' or 'arborecent' (Deleuze and Guattari, 1980) life forms?

The dead who would become trees

Symbolic entanglements between trees and human mortality are rich and varied. In cemetery landscapes, trees have traditionally served to mark the boundaries of consecrated ground or to visually separate the cemetery from residential areas. Particular species, like yew or pine, are often associated with specific symbolism tied to mourning and remembrance. Trees are an even more pervasive symbol within natural burial grounds and green death organizations. This involves different levels of intimacy and kinds of semiotic relation between the dead and trees. Tree planting may be offered as a means of offsetting the environmental impact of one's life and death. For example, in addition to the arboreal monuments offered by Mornington Green, the company promises to plant 400 native trees in an offsite location for each dead. Their calculus suggests that this will produce 'double the amount of air you breathed in your lifetime', and thereby a net positive contribution to the environment (Mornington Green, 2022). Clayden and Dixon (2007) describe how natural burial sites in the UK are commonly imagined as 'memorial arboretum', where individual trees act as index for the deceased in place of traditional grave markings. Even more directly, some organizations like *Capsula Mundi* promise to transform the corpse into new arboreal life, thereby positioning trees as icons of the dead. Given the shifting range of associations between trees and death, for the purposes of this chapter, we focus on a kind of arboreal afterlife currently being offered in Melbourne, Australia: Mornington Green.

The botanical garden Mornington Green, run by company Living Legacy, actively cultivates an intimate physical and metaphorical relationship between the dead and trees. The garden spans 126,000 square metres of land reclaimed from a golf course, transformed into a highly manicured, carefully planned arboretum of contrasting species and foliage hues. Mornington Green exclusively offers for treated cremains (cremated remains) to be interred in 'Legacy Trees'. No whole-body burials take place on site, and it is not classified as a cemetery (which by Victorian law, can only be operated by State Trusts). Instead, cremains are first treated to address their high pH and then buried at the roots of an established sapling. The exact treatment process and then their 'infusion' into trees is the proprietary technology of Living Legacy, who have additionally licensed the product to a number of Australian cemeteries. As with many other new necro-technologies, as with *Capsula Mundi*, the technical details of this process, let alone independent, peer-reviewed scientific analysis, is not available.

On their website and in promotional materials, Mornington Green directly invites the living to 'Continue Your Legacy & Become A Tree'. This message fosters intimate personal identification with a particular tree, via which one might 'live on'. Notably, it is an invitation squarely addressed to people planning for their own deaths, rather than families arranging a memorial for a loved one. Between photographs of smiling silver-haired couples and second-person styles of address, Mornington Green asks customers to pre-select and even pre-plant their own Legacy Tree. In doing so, the service projects individual personalities posthumously. They offer a range of trees, both Australian natives and exotic European species, presented so as to anthropomorphize different species attributes. For example, the gingko is described as 'tenacious and hopeful', the redwood is 'wise, determined and strong', and the flame tree is 'charismatic and passionate'. The website even invites people to take a two-minute quiz to 'find out which tree matches your personality', based on lifestyle questions about one's ideal season, holiday destination and Sunday afternoon activity. Trees might also be selected for a seasonal pattern of flowering during a birthday or anniversary.

Through this close association between one's personal identity in life and the imagined character of a particular species, Legacy Trees provide a clearly identifiable, individuated and lasting trace of the dead within the landscape. The interment plot is reserved for the deceased in perpetuity and each tree is given a custom plaque with the deceased's name, dates of birth and death, and a few lines of text. On surveying the site recently, several of the inscriptions highlight a close identification with trees, such as: 'grow tall in our memory' and 'enjoy the sunshine'. Mornington Green thus upholds what Thomas W. Laqueur (2016) has called the doctrine of 'necro-nominalism' within Western death culture, that values the individuated identity of the deceased, particularly through practices of naming. Still, plaques and grave markers have proved controversial at natural burial grounds worldwide. In Australia, even when artificial markers are explicitly prohibited, families and visitors sometimes ignore directions and decorate graves (Gould et al, 2021). While some oppose grave markers because they disrupt natural landscapes and consume resources, others interpret them as evidence of the vital role of memorialization in families processing grief (see Balonier et al, 2019).

The arboreal afterlife facilitated at Mornington Green might be individual, but it is also deeply embedded in kinship networks. In total, Legacy Trees can hold up to eight additional 'family members' after the first interment, making it 'a real family tree' (Mornington Green, 2022).[1] As Davies and Rumble describe, trees manifestly grow beyond the lifespan of a single human, thus 'bridg[ing] the temporality of the fixed landscapes and the transient, fleeting landscape' (2012: 113). The Legacy Tree provides an anchor for visitation and ritual activities, with families encouraged to first plant the tree, and then, across generations, to regularly visit, to take a stroll around the gardens, have a family picnic beneath the tree, or even to let children climb and play in the boughs. Because Mornington Green only plants advanced trees (1–2 metres tall), the range of interactive possibilities between the living and the dead/tree are immediate. These idyllic visions very much affirm the distinctly upper-middle-class desires and White, nuclear family structures that characterize the Mornington Peninsula as an aspirational location within Australia for a holiday home or retirement 'sea-change'. Notably, the culture and infrastructure of the private golf club that Mornington Green repurposed are still in place: a 'Clubhouse' offers high tea on site, golf buggies roam the property, and events like 'Monet meets Chardonnay' (a monthly wine and painting session) frame the site as a desirable leisure destination, far beyond more traditional activities of grave visitation.

Arboreal afterlives are not always so idyllic. Where the health and growth of the tree can come to symbolize a good death and comfortable afterlife, the potential for disease and destruction to the tree might become a threat to the deceased. This is a fundamental problem of material religion, whereby the necessary mediation of transcendental forces into objects so as to make them knowable and sociable, also makes those forces vulnerable. It is a problem that extends beyond the ephemerality of organic memorials to cases of 'media decay', whereby new technologies that promise to help the dead live on forever are subject to technological obsolescence and organizational collapse (Nansen et al, 2021). Trees do not live forever, with the average lifespan of the species offered at Mornington Green about 30 years. The practical and symbolic solution proposed by Living Legacy to deal with these losses is to extend the lifespan of the tree – not just the human dead – through generations of life, death and rebirth. Seeds and cuttings are regularly taken from the Legacy Tree and cultivated for propagation offsite. As new plants are cultivated, the offshoots of both human and tree multiply.

Mornington Green also walks a difficult path in the green death space, by affirming the potential for unity between human remains and the natural environment, but also warning against the potential toxicity of untreated ashes. The green death movement generally favours whole-body shallow burial and embraces decomposition as a process for dispersing the nutrient capacity of the corpse into the surrounding environment. Indeed, the corpse is often framed as a precious 'gift' to nature (Davies and Rumble, 2012). Conversely, green death advocates tend to reject cremation as a waste of nutrient potential. For example, Mark Blackham of the New Zealand not-for-profit Natural Burials, describes how cremation 'turns your body into air pollution and barren ash' (nd: 1). For the Living Legacy team, however, cremated remains contain nutrient potential, if only it can be 'unlocked' (Mornington Green, nd). They claim that untreated cremains 'have the same pH as bleach and oven cleaner and are proven to cause lasting harm to soil and tree health' (Mornington Green, nd). In contrast, their patented solution is a 'perfected organic treatment that detoxifies and unlocks hidden nutrients', resulting in 'living molecules' that 'create micronutrients and healthy soil which can exchange energy with the tree' (Mornington Green, nd). This is a difficult needle to thread, but important rhetoric for Living Legacy's core value proposition, given both the popularity and relative affordability of both cremation and (untreated) ash scattering across Australia. Put simply, Living Legacy suggests that, if only through the right technical interventions, human remains can be harnessed to nourish nature, thereby extending an individual's personhood through to an arboreal afterlife.

The dead who would become mushrooms

The fungi kingdom has been a close companion to mammalian life from before the earliest threads of human evolution. Upon death, the body's temperature falls and blood circulation ceases, enabling decomposition to begin. A 'necrobiome' develops around a corpse in contact with the ground, containing bacteria, fungi, arthropods and other organisms. While microbes derived both from the soil and the corpse are largely responsible for decomposition, fungi may also contribute. Fungi become readily visible when fruiting, as mould and mildew or mushrooms, and post-putrefaction fungi is most visible on heavily decomposed cadavers. In contrast, mycelia are the root-like structures that extend underground. Decomposition is heavily dependent on the depositional environment, and most fungi are aerobic (requiring oxygen to survive). As a result, for more conventional burials, using sealed coffins, fungal growth is slowed or arrested.

While fungi play a relatively marginal role in human cadaver decomposition, they have a firm position in the broader cultural imagination as 'nature's decomposers' and 'recyclers'. A spate of bestselling nonfiction works over the last few years extol the virtues of the fungal kingdom (Pouliot, 2018; Sheldrake, 2021; Lim and Shu, 2022), while a *Scientific American* blog proclaims a forthcoming 'mycelium revolution' based on biofabrication (Bayer, 2019). Fungi are in all cases a powerful rhetorical device and motif for embracing decay. They straddle the worlds of the living and the dead by transforming decaying organic matter into nutrients for living plants to use. This rhetoric turns on the process of osmotrophy, whereby fungi decompose organic matter by excreting enzymes to break down the decaying material, and then absorb its nutrients, effectively externalizing a digestive system.

Fungi are also liminal actors, capable of transitioning humans to altered states of consciousness via hallucinations, or inducing death via poisoning, or even of bridging the worldly and otherworldly realms (as with popular myths of toadstool circles).

It is perhaps no surprise that fungi have been incorporated into experimental necro-technologies. Two designs, the Infinity Burial Suit and The Loop Living Cocoon, are notable examples of this trend. The Infinity Burial Suit was presented as a provocation by Jae Rhim Lee, an artist and entrepreneur who originally designed the work as part of her graduate studies at MIT, and later helped found the company Coeio. The company offered both a 'suit' and 'shroud' option for burial in an organic material that was embedded with mycelia. After a 2011 TED Talk by Lee went viral, interest in the disposal option exploded, later buoyed by reports that *90210*-star Luke Perry had chosen the suit as his preferred burial option (Kaur, 2019). However, the product faced criticism as to the scientific merits of its claims, including the implied imagery that a colony of mushrooms will grow from the shrouded corpse. Suits were once available for purchase within the United States, but Coeio appears to have ceased commercial operations by 2019. Early comments from Lee suggest that her work is driven less by commercial motives, noting that the suit was instead a 'symbol and tool' for a 'cultural shift in how we think about death and our relationship to the planet' (Coeio, 2019).

Dutch company Loop has found more immediate commercial success through its 2019 launch of The Loop Living Cocoon, developed by TU Delft researcher and entrepreneur Bob Hendrix. The Loop Living Cocoon is grown from mycelium, which is mixed with wet sawdust and then moulded into the boxy shape of a coffin during its course of growth over a week. A mycelium network can be minuscule or can grow to span many thousands of acres, sometimes expanding at a rate of half an inch per day. This material (composed of fibrous polymers such as chitin, cellulose and proteins) makes the coffins both strong and light. When interred in the ground, the coffin is purported to take 30–45 days to fully decompose. Hendrix also recommends that bodies are not embalmed and that no synthetic materials are placed in the coffin, so as to not disrupt decomposition. Wooden rods that serve as handles during transport are also removed before burial.

The marketing for Loop emphasizes the romance of a return to nature and ecological afterlife through generative natural lifecycles. Before interment, the base of each coffin is lined with a bed of moss sourced from a local farm, so as 'to give humans the experience of becoming part of the cycle of life' (Loop, 2022). This image of the dead lying in peaceful repose on a bed of lush moss, surrounded by verdant forests has garnered popular appeal. A sampling of social media comments on news reports (for example, Hitti, 2020) contain romantic projections of a green death: 'Imagine getting buried in a mushroom coffin filled with beautiful flowers and you wearing a flower crown on your head, that would be amazing' ('EmberMay', April 2021), and 'I want to be buried in this, with a dress made of flowers and moss. The ultimate cottage core death. 🍄💀🌸🌱' ('Maria b', May 2021). These comments, invoking Millennial, feminized aesthetics like 'cottage core', speak to a romanticized, almost fairy-tale image of death as a natural, even gentle, transition to another world.

Loop supports a vision of the afterlife death that is not only beautiful and natural, but also productive. The website directly asks consumers – 'Are you waste or compost?' There is a direct contrast drawn between conventional death, characterized as 'coffin – polluting process – waste – graveyard' and a promised generative equation of 'cocoon – natural process – compost – forest'. The addition of mycelium promises to optimize decomposition, by both accelerating the rate of decay and by detoxifying the body; The Living Cocoon 'contributes to the body's composting process after death and simultaneously removes toxic substances from the earth – creating richer conditions for new plants to grow'. The acceleration claim is supported by Loop's suggestion (2022) that a diffuse network of mycelia will construct pathways into the body, allowing bacteria to travel to otherwise inaccessible sites. Detoxification occurs as a result of mycelia helping corpses to 'enrich the soil instead of polluting it'. This relies on mycelia's capacity for mycroremediation, the process of expunging environmental pollutants via the release of digestive enzymes which break down chemicals like hydrocarbons and pesticides. Therefore, as with Living Legacy, Loop does not shy away from diagnosing the potential harms of the decomposing human corpse, as well as marketing its cure. And as with Living Legacy, the efficacy of claims to increased soil quality and biodiversity remain untested. Indeed, praise for mycroremediation is tempered by mycologists who declare it 'no simple fix' (Sheldrake, 2021).

Fungi offer a distinct kind of ecological afterlife, spread throughout a diffuse matrix. Mycelia form a subterranean structure that transports the nutrients of decomposing matter across a landscape, and this relation is reflected in the marketing of fungi-based necro-technologies. Loop describes how the decomposing body 'powers' a whole 'ecosystem', 'biome' or 'forest' (Loop, 2022) rather than a singularly located, individual tree. It is a more energetic and diffuse afterlife to arboreal imaginings. As anthropologists Elizabeth Hallam and Tamara Kohn describe, Coeio's fungi burial suit is rather aptly labelled 'infinite' because it facilitates a 'never-ending' relationship with the living organisms in the environment (2019: 4).

Deleuze and Guattari's work in *A thousand plateaus* (1980) highlights the metaphorical distinctions between these arborescent and rhizomatic structures. They suggest that the tree manifests an arrangement of relations which is both centralized and hierarchical. The tree is also firmly positioned in space, becoming more steadfast in that space through time, as branches extend upwards and roots grow down. The Legacy Tree provides a focal presence for ritual activity and fixes the deceased's memory in space and through time. It also signifies a hierarchy of human relations, with the deceased at its centre, immediate family emanating from the central trunk, and extended family and friends further distanced. On the other hand, rhizomic mycelia are structured horizontally rather than vertically. They have no commanding presence in the landscape and are largely invisible beyond fruiting fungi deposits. They have no single or lasting centre; mycelia abandon their centre as they grow. The intergenerational rhetoric that characterizes the arboreal afterlife pitched by Mornington Green appears entirely absent in the marketing of mycelium afterlives. Children and grandchildren are not pictured visiting the fungi gravesite and nor are future generations *en masse* described as the beneficiaries of eco-friendly burial practice.

Instead, a mycelium afterlife appears orientated towards supporting nonhuman life forms. Fungi are cast as necessary to healing the 'scar on this beautiful planet' that is human society, offering people absolution through death 'to become one with nature again' (Loop, 2022). Fungi are thus tasked with transforming the relationship between humans and nature from one of 'parasitism' to one of 'mutuality' (Loop, 2022). For necro-technologists seeking not just to decompose the body, but also to nurture the ecosystem through principles of collaboration and exchange, fungi are a rich resource. Wang (2006) estimates that 80 per cent of plant species have a mutualistic relationship with fungi, which provide plants with inorganic compounds and trace elements. These relations show biological ecosystems to be not entirely a product of patterns of breeding counterbalanced by predation and competition, but equally formed through mutualistic interactions. If there is a continuation of the dead offered by a mycelia afterlife, then it is a diffuse and depersonalized one.

Diverse ecological afterlives

Mounting concern for eco-friendly deathcare and the formation of ecological afterlives are only one strand of transformations currently occurring to Western death culture. Tony Walter's 2016 study of the UK, *The dead who become angels*, describes the emergence of a new strain of 'vernacular belief' in which the dead are popularly imagined as angels. He documents a significant shift in how the bereaved talk about the dead online, describing particularly dead children and infants as 'angels' or 'cherubs' who continue their earthly activities in heaven and look after living kin. This new imagining is a significant departure from how angels had previously figured in Christian theology, as nonhuman, supernatural entities. It further imbues the dead with new kinds of agency to intervene and guide family members, as well as a new 'final destination', as the dead linger on – at least for a time – in the earthly realms.

Unlike Walter's angels, the visions of the afterlife that we have described here are not chiefly or exclusively produced by the bereaved during memorialization practice. Walter suggests that angels go beyond any particular religious doctrine or subculture, to act as an emerging model or 'meme' of the afterlife that some mourners use or creatively extend. In the case of arboreal and mycelial afterlives, at this moment, this mimetic work is primarily undertaken by deathcare insiders and designers. And it is directly addressed towards people contemplating or planning for the end of their own lives. As our previous work demonstrates, those engaged in pre-planning their own funeral and disposition are more likely to adopt alternative and bespoke options for disposal and ritual (Allison et al, 2020). As the funeral sector is critiqued (sometimes justly) as singularly motivated by profiteering while deceiving customers, their role in a creative reimagining of vernacular belief is thus perhaps underemphasized. In her ethnography of the Japanese sector, Hikaru Suzuki (2000) articulates a different relational possibility, showing how industry and consumers are 'mutually dependent and ... responsible for supporting, representing and transforming cultural practices'. How these reconfigurations of the afterlife will then be taken up by the bereaved is a question still to emerge.

Even more so than guardian angels, trees and mushrooms signify a reorientation of vernacular visions of the afterlife from the transcendental to the earthly. Both extend the (after)life of the deceased through the crucible of nutrient transfer between the corpse and the surrounding natural environment. However, this liveliness is differently articulated, either as a personalized, singularly located arboreal presence, which can look over and interact with future generations, or as a more diffuse, energetic network, that fuses with and supports the natural world. Mycelial afterlives are perhaps the more radical proposition, as they appear to challenge core tenets of necronominalism, and a singular, locatable memorial. While environmental values represent a substantial shift in Western death culture, ecological afterlives cannot be collapsed into a single paradigm. The future direction of vernacular beliefs around death resides in the biological form and symbolic potentials of natural forms like trees, mushrooms and more.

Note

[1] *Capsula Mundi* goes even further in emphasizing this intergenerational engagement. Its website presents a scrolling montage of images: a young person hugging a tree superimposed with 'I love you, Grandma!', somebody touching bark superimposed with 'Hi, Dad!', and the bows of an evergreen with the phrase 'John, how you've grown!'

References

Allison, F., Gould, H., Arnold, M., Nansen, B., Gibbs, M. and Kohn, T. (2020) *The future cemetery survey 2020* [report]. https://deathtech.research.unimelb.edu.au (accessed 4 July 2023).

Balonier, A.-K., Parsons, E. and Patterson, A. (2019) The unnaturalness of natural burials: dispossessing the dispossessed. *Mortality*, 24(2): 212–230. DOI: 10.1080/13576275.2019.1585786

Bayer, E. (2019) The mycelium revolution is upon us. *Scientific American*, 1 July. https://blogs.scientificamerican.com/observations/the-mycelium-revolution-is-upon-us/ (accessed 4 July 2023).

Bloch, M. and Parry, J. (1982) *Death and the regeneration of life*. Cambridge: Cambridge University Press.

Capsula Mundi (nd) *Capsula Mundi*. Life Never Stops. https://www.capsulamundi.it/en/ (accessed 3 January 2022).

Clayden, A. and Dixon, K. (2007) Woodland burial: Memorial arboretum versus natural native woodland? *Mortality*, 12(3): 240–260.

Coeio (2019) Coeio Infinity Burial Suit. http://coeio.com/ (accessed January 2020).

Davies, D. (2005) *A brief history of death*. Malden: John Wiley & Sons.

Davies, D. and Rumble, H. (2012) *Natural burial*. London: Bloomsbury Publishing.

Deleuze, G. and Guattari, F. (1980) *A thousand plateaus*. Translated by B. Massumi. London and New York: Continuum.

Erizanu, P. (2018) The biodegradable burial pod that turns your body into a tree. *CNN*. https://edition.cnn.com/2017/05/03/world/eco-solutions-capsula-mundi/index.html (accessed 10 April 2022).

Gould, H., Arnold, M., Dupleix, T. and Kohn, T. (2021) 'Stood to rest': Reorientating necrogeographies for the 21st century. *Mortality*, 21 March. https://doi.org/10.1080/13576275.2021.1878120

Hallam, E. and Kohn, T. (2019) Life in death's residues. In T. Kohn, M. Gibbs, B. Nansen and L. van Ryn (eds) *Residues of death: Disposal refigured*. London: Routledge, pp 1–16. DOI: 10.4324/9780429456404

Hitti, N. (2020) Bob Hendrikx designs 'living coffin' from mushroom mycelium. *Dezeen*, 16 September. https://www.dezeen.com/2020/09/16/bob-hendrikx-living-cocoon-mycelium-coffin/ (accessed 4 July 2023).

Kaur, H. (2019) Luke Perry's daughter says he was buried in a mushroom suit. *CNN Entertainment*, 6 May. https://edition.cnn.com/2019/05/04/entertainment/luke-perry-mushroom-suit-trnd/index.html (accessed 4 July 2023).

Laqueur, T. (2016) *The work of the dead: A cultural history of mortal remains*. Princeton: Princeton University Press.

Lim, M. and Shu, Y. (2022) *The future is fungi: How fungi feed us, heal us, and save our world*. London: Thames & Hudson.

Loop (2022) Loop of Life. https://www.loop-of-life.com/product (accessed 25 October 2022).

Mornington Green (2022) Become a Tree. https://morningtongreen.com.au (accessed 1 May 2022).

Nansen, B., Gould, H., Arnold, M. and Gibbs, M. (2021) Media, mortality and necrotechnologies: Eulogies for dead media. *New Media & Society*, July. doi:10.1177/14614448211027959

Pouliot, A. (2018) *The allure of fungi*. Clayton South: CSIRO Publishing.

Sheldrake, M. (2021) *Entangled life: How fungi make our worlds, change our minds & shape our futures*. London: Random House.

Stock, P.V. and Dennis, M.K. (2021) Up in smoke or down with worms? Older adult environmentalist's discourse on disposal, dispersal, and (green) burial. *Mortality*, 28(1): 73–89.

Suzuki, H. (2000) *The price of death: The funeral industry in contemporary Japan*. Stanford: Stanford University Press.

Walter, T. (2016) The dead who become angels: Bereavement and vernacular religion. *OMEGA: Journal of Death and Dying*, 73(1): 3–28.

Wang, B. (2006) Phylogenetic distribution and evolution of mycorrhizas in land plants. *Mycorrhiza*, 16(5): 299–363.

Westendorp, M. and Gould, H. (2021) Re-Feminizing Death: Gender, Spirituality and Death Care in the Anthropocene. *Religions*, 12(8): 667.

13

Beyond the Norms

Jesse D. Peterson, Natashe Lemos Dekker and Philip R. Olson

Relational death

No one, and nothing, dies alone. That is perhaps the most comprehensive theme that gathers all the chapters in this volume. We do not mean to deny the social and affective realities of loneliness or solitude that sometimes attend death. Instead, we wish to emphasize that each of the 12 chapters in this volume draw attention to the inevitable socio-ecological relationalities involved in dying, death and deathcare. Beyond the truism that death makes kindred of us all, the chapters collected here reveal complex interconnections among human and nonhuman creatures, environments, geographies, temporalities, narratives and scales of being. The relationalities explored in this volume are variously material, affective and discursive; they extend across differing scales of space and time, and across dependencies, disruptions, renewals, losses and absences. Still, death's complex relationality does not lack structure. Indeed, though death may sometimes appear to be the dissolution or disorganization of life's resoluteness and orderliness, what the chapters contained in this volume reveal is that dying and death, too, harbour orderly relationalities of being and becoming, knowing and making, in which various networks of actors collaborate, contend and toil towards states and activities that confound received norms regarding dying, death, living and life.

Haraway's compost heap – the 'wormy pile' in which possibility is madly made over (2016) – is not a venue for impotent chaos. It is a generative, mind-boggling, hope-ridden meaning maker. It may be said that the chapters in this volume form a generative compost heap as well, to the extent that they chip, shred and layer the different categories, norms, subjects and objects they cover. By breaking down these component parts, this volume's contributors form fertile grounds from which to think through and approach death and dying in new and unexpected ways. For instance, they highlight the relevance of disparate literatures that draw on scientific, materialist, environmental and ecological, and affective perspectives that challenge our thinking of death as a solely human affair. They compost the materiality of dying and dead bodies – whether they be humans, microbes, seas, legal documents, death banners, seals, television characters – with the cultural values, meanings and discourses that surround conceptions of them. They also exhibit different ways for conceptualizing death beyond the traditional human subject and beyond death as a singular event.

As a result, such treatments on death craft nutritive questions. How can we make the lives or deaths of nonhumans, other-than-humans, more-than-humans come to matter? What does the death of communities, cultures, civilizations or species mean and for whom do they become significant? How and for whom, including nonhumans and nonhuman phenomena, is death profitable? Or, even, what constitutes gentleness and flourishing environments for the dead? To pursue these questions involves increasing attention to the relationalities among more-than-human bodies, their purposes and meanings, and who takes care of them.

More-than-human bodies

First, reconfigurations of matter and meaning emerge from analyses and practices that decompose and recompose across fungible states of being. Consider, for example, Peterson's onto-epistemological unveiling of many possible versions of a dying Baltic Sea, each bound to a different set of value-laden claims about the sea's water (Chapter 4). Chopping, shredding and layering the Baltic Sea's many characteristics through an analysis of the sea's water reveals new possibilities for thinking about the sea's viabilities and mortalities. Moreover, by extending the categories of living and dying to a range of entities that could include whole bodies of water, Peterson stirs up new ways of thinking about some classic questions. If, as Lofland famously acknowledges in *The craft of dying* (2019), dying is 'a way of "being" in the modern world' (27), then what does it mean for a waterbody – or a part of the earth or sky – to 'be dying'? And how do entities like these get admitted to the category of the dying? According to Lofland, human beings' admission to (and inhabitation of) that category is constructed through complex social, cultural, biological, technoscientific and personal choices and processes. The same appears to hold true for waterbodies and other organisms, as Zanzu (Chapter 3) also makes clear in her chapter. The lives of microbial communities, whose numbers seem infinite and replaceable, are not afforded the possibility to die or go extinct, which then leaves these communities susceptible to programmed cellular death through gene manipulation. Undergirded by technoscientific and naturalistic logics, microbial death becomes inconsequential to the purposes by which humans wish to instrumentalize their lives to deal with human produced toxins. By expanding death studies' scope of interest to include nonhuman and even non-organismic entities, the chapters in this volume help us to begin thinking more promiscuously about the choices and processes that 'make-dying'.

Moreover, situating the human corpse within ecological and material relations provides similar opportunities. Biomedicine and bioengineering have opened the door to the interchangeability of human and nonhuman organs, as evidenced by the 2022 transplantation of a genetically modified pig heart into the body of Maryland patient David Bennett. Although Bennett died two months after receiving the transplant, his autopsy revealed no sign of organ rejection. Through organ and tissue donation and transplantation, the material components of a dead body move between different organisms and blur the boundaries between the living and the dead by transferring life-giving material from the dead to the living. When conceptualized as reusable, reconfigurable matter, the human corpse lends itself to enrollment in the logics of fungibility, exchange and indefinite reconfiguration that also underlie both capitalism and information science. As Trabsky and Flore point out (Chapter 11), this replaceability leads to corporeal exchanges that trouble existing legal frameworks that demarcate public responsibility towards the human dead as persons or things. Understood through, for instance, feminist new materialism or as 'immanently fragmented, relational, and entangled', the dead human body defies 'the conventional views of the corpse as a bounded and undivided person or a unitary and useful thing' (Chapter 12). At the furthest extreme of material analysis and fungibility, all material entities become reducible to temporary assemblages of common building blocks: star-forged atoms that pass through solution and dissolution over and over again.

Purposes and meanings

Exploring these different kinds of relations that human (and nonhuman) bodies gain access to in death suggests alternative possibilities by which the dead become meaningful or valuable to the living. In respect to dignity, Olson (Chapter 2) struggles precisely with the challenge of reconciling long-standing interests in the individual/personal meanings of the dead human body with emerging interests in the collective materiality of death. Similarly, Holleran (Chapter 7) suggests that traditional and contemporary ways for communal burial may create affective and appropriate responses to collective suffering resulting from widespread epidemics or war but also to the future loss of a loved one. Whether such reconciliations can take place through a rethinking of deathcare policy (as Olson suggests), or whether any possible reconciliation of the dead body's 'personhood', mere-thingness and collective connectivity to others who have died requires (also) deeper metaphysical, epistemological or ethical reconstructions remains an open question.

Somewhat counterintuitively, a materialism of this sort may underwrite claims to identity across future material incarnations, as Olson, Holleran and Gould et al point out in their respective discussions of the discourse and physical processes involved in the construction of 'ecological afterlives' (Chapter 12) through emerging disposition technologies. Transformed into trees or fungi by way of emerging disposition technologies and the labours of microorganisms, the material energies (or nutrient potentials) of human bodies are reanimated as new forms of life. But by what conception of identity (material, spiritual, psychological, social) can a human person *be* or *become* a different organism or entity, or *be again* after death? Is ontological identity across the boundary of death – to the extent such a boundary can be identified – any more or less miraculous than the ontological identity of a caterpillar and the butterfly it has become? At one extreme, some metaphysicians working on the philosophy of death have argued *not only* that a living body is something ontologically different from that body's corpse, *but even* that corpses do not strictly exist because their combined particles do not amount to any*thing* at all[1].) At another extreme we find commitment to the idea that personal identity is not restricted to any specific form of material (re)incarnation; the self-same personal identity is multiply realizable across a potentially infinite variety of material instantiations. In-between, the body takes central stage as a social and material form that invokes a confrontation with death and notions of disgust, as well as a range of practices to maintain attachment and integrity while transitioning between life and death.

As Abou Farman points out in *On not dying* (2020), transhumanists who embrace an informatic understanding of the identity personhood=brain contend that deanimated persons may one day regain consciousness as machine-animated data. The materialism that links transhumanists with those who aspire to some kind of 'arboreal [or fungal] afterlife' (Chapter 12) share a view of the person or self as a fungible, material potency, the agency or active principle of which can survive the demise of its organismic origin in the form of a *Homo sapien*. Such views, as Gould et al point out, depend upon faith in the labour of others to ensure the continued survival of the self across the boundary of death. For the preservation of tree and plant life may require tending across multiple generations (of trees *and* people), just as the preservation of 'deanimated' persons in cryovats requires the continuous energy, labour and maintenance of (potentially) multiple generations of caretakers.

Such instantiations of the self beyond death also exhibit various symbolic promises of continuation. As Gould et al point out, trees and fungi promise different kinds of afterlives. Additionally, as Michael-Fox highlights in her analysis of the television drama, *Les Revenants*, the dead who come back challenge how their past lives were remembered and valued. Her analysis complicates what the lives of the dead mean and how they impact the living, offering grounds for critical conceptions about the meanings of life and death as they extend through space and time. Understanding what promises the living extend to the dead, through material objects, other beings and narrative, becomes a critical place from which to understand the meaning that death takes on for the living and the dying.

Additionally, the contributions in this volume highlight how death and the dead may mean different things to other beings. Hoerst, Zanzu and Peterson all raise concerns related to nonhuman phenomenology where it concerns the death of nonhumans, and Olson, Gould et al and Holleran think ecologically about the corpse. As other beings get recognized as historical actors, we cannot but see them as also biopolitical agents. Though intentionality has long been at discussion in these debates (see Latour, 1992), speculating alternative perspectives that might emanate from these beings gives new dimensions to the meanings of life and death, for what is it like for lungworms, seas, atoms, species or planets to be and to be dying?

Norms and care

Third, complex relationalities of community, care and labour (often involving technologies, nonhuman organisms, symbols, language, places and rituals) bind the living and the dead. Care clearly does not end with death but is fundamental to the transformation of connections among the living as well as between the living and the dead. As the chapters in this volume have shown, care relations are essential to how the deceased may or may not be remembered and underpin the practices of how and where the body is disposed. Care, in this sense, can be seen as a commitment to achieving a good death. Notions of a good death motivate practices, interactions and narratives to provide meaning to death. Yet, what makes death good is highly volatile. A single death can be experienced and perceived from many different standpoints, raising the question, for whom or what is this death 'good' (Howarth, 2007; van der Pijl, 2016)? This is illustrated by Sicilia's chapter (Chapter 8) on the deathcare for spirit mediums, whose separation from the living serves a spiritual 'good' yet is detrimental to the bereavement experiences of relatives.

As the chapters by Bredenbröker (Chapter 6) and Yépez and Johnson (Chapter 5) demonstrate, the material form of death is a decisive factor in the construction of a good death, showing the potentiality of materials to confirm and challenge normative claims of the 'good'. Memorial banners on prominent display can have the power to turn the perception of a death by centring on the deceased and their position in society. Plastics used to prevent COVID-19 contagion, conversely, have been perceived to prevent desired contact between the living and the dead, obstructing relations of care. As materials become tied to notions of dignity and value, deaths can become valued differently through material mediations and representations.

In this way, the relation between the living and the dead are further infused with particular sets of values and mediated by particular means of communication and exchange: be they banners (Chapter 6), rumours (Chapter 5) or images (Chapter 7). The chapters variously show what the body may become in the sense of how it is remembered, the place it takes in emerging social relations, the material forms it takes, and the new positionings it assumes and relations it engages in. The socio-material form of death, then, is a site in which norms around living, dying and death are exposed – and a site in which the construction of lives and deaths of unequal value takes place, as both humans and nonhumans whose deaths do not conform to this normativity may become excluded and relegated to the margins.

Inequalities permeate the complex relationalities and communities of the living, dying and dead. For example, whereas Lofland identifies doctors as the ultimate authorities about when and whether 'dying has begun' (2019: 29), it remains unclear *who* can make authoritative determinations about the dying status of 'natural' entities, or *how* such determinations are to be made. As Schnegg et al make clear in their study of the dead body's reality within forensic experience (Chapter 1), certain ontologies are produced and enforced by specific sets of norms, technologies, practices and professional identities. Yet even in these 'settled' spaces, where '[s]ome versions of the body are definitely more valuable, powerful, and real than others' (Chapter 1), unresolved questions still linger regarding the social, political, epistemic and ontological implications of claims to expertise. Hoerst (Chapter 9) shows how such questions permeate the adjudication of whether a seal's life is worth saving. She demonstrates how veterinarians, public officials, society, seals and lungworms all lay claims in the process of determining which seals receive treatment, which get euthanized and which get set free. Through appeals to the 'inevitability' of death, such human interventions in the deaths of others become naturalized to the point where such determinations become 'invisible'.

Revealing these determinations, however, is critical to ensure deaths, particularly those deemed of lesser value, come to matter. These issues await the concerted attention of scholars engaged in technology studies, anthropology, death studies, environmental studies, science and technology policy, and various scientific fields. And as new relationships between human, nonhuman and technological actors emerge in response to anxieties about the global climate crisis, environmental degradation, species deaths and global pandemics, we can expect that emerging modes of care and labour may offer novel forms of 'ontological security' (Giddens, 1984) to allay those anxieties – that is, forms of material identity and agency must extend beyond the boundaries of human embodiment or self-awareness because threats to ontological security do not only challenge the stability, continuity and identity of human lives, but *earthly life itself*.

Note

[1] See Olson (2013) for further discussion.

References

Farman, A. (2020) *On not dying: Secular immortality in the age of technoscience.* Minneapolis: University of Minnesota Press.

Giddens, A. (1984) *The constitution of society: Outline of the theory of structuration.* Berkeley: University of California Press.

Haraway, D. (2016) Tentacular thinking: Anthropocene, Capitalocene, Chthulucene. *E-Flux*, 75. https://www.e-flux.com/journal/75/67125/tentacular-thinking-anthropocene-capitalocene-chthulucene/ (accessed 4 March 2022).

Howarth, G. (2007) *Death and dying: A sociological introduction.* Cambridge: Polity Press.

Latour, B. (1992) Where are the missing masses? The sociology of a few mundane artifacts. *Shaping Technology/Building Society: Studies in Sociotechnical Change*, 1: 225–258.

Lofland, L. (2019) *The craft of dying: The modern face of death, 40th anniversary edition.* Cambridge, MA: MIT Press.

Olson, E. (2013) The person and the corpse. In B. Bradley, F. Feldman and J. Johansson (eds) *The Oxford handbook of philosophy of death*. Oxford: Oxford University Press, pp 80–96.

van der Pijl, Y. (2016) Death in the family revisited: Ritual expression and controversy in a Creole transnational mortuary sphere. *Ethnography* 17(2): 147–167.

Index

References to figures appear in *italic* type.

2020 4S/EASST conference panel 2

A

'actor-enacteds' 132
Africa, cultural importance of death in 85
African American people, trafficking of remains of 156
African Burial Ground, New York 104
Agar, Jon 28
agency
   human agency and climate change 145
   nonhuman animals 133
AIDS crisis, and mass burials 101, 102–103
albert 145
Alcaligenes 43
   see also microbes, use of in bioremediation
algal blooms 58, 59–60
'alive/dead' dichotomy, *Les Revenants* television series 7, 147–149, 152
alkaline hydrolysis 27, 32, 35, 36, 37, 160–161, 169
American Civil War 105
Anatomy Act 1832 (UK) 156–157
ancestors, in Ghana 87, 90, 96
angels, imagining the dead as 8, 176–177
Angwa area, Zimbabwe *see* Zimbabwe
Anthropocene, the, and large-scale death 5, 27–29
anthropogenic change 3, 4
Apple products, exploitative working practices 145
arboreal afterlives 8, 172–173
   see also Capsula Mundi burial pods; Mornington Green, Australia; 'trees', dead who become
artisanal cheese production, and microbes 48, 49
ashes 107–108
   see also cremains
Australia
   Aboriginal people 107

COVID-19 pandemic 101, 104–105
   Mornington Green 170–172, 176
autopsies *see* forensic pathology, and postmortem imaging

B

bad death, transformation of in Ghana 88–91, *89*, *92*
Baltic Sea, 'dead' or 'dying' imaginaries of 5–6, 54–55, 181
   diagnoses 57–60, *58*, *59*
   environmental imaginaries of waterbodies 61–63
   gains and losses from 63–65
   physical attributes 55–57
   treatment 60
Baltic Sea Science Centre 55
Barad, Karen 61, 143–144, 152, 157, 163, 165
Barnett, Joshua 28, 35
Baudrillard, J. 145
Beard v Baulkham Hills Shire Council and Another (1986) 159
Bennett, Jane 163
'biological capital' 50
biopolitics 7
   seal conservation 131–134
biopower 133
bioremediation, use of microbes in 5, 43–46, 51, 181–182
   forced microbe death in the remediation process 44, 45–46, 48
   microbial death in the experimental stage 46–48
   'remedial microbe', the 44, 48–51
Blackham, Mark 172–173
Blackstone, William 158
Bobi, George 91, 93, *93*, *94*
'body viewing', Zimbabwe 115–117
bones *see* human bones
Boomer generation 109

Borger, J. 106
bounded individualism 29, 33, 38, 39
Box project 60
'brackish' water, Baltic Sea 56
Bradshaw 37
Brazier, M. 160
Brempong, Bright Akosua 91, *92*
Brown, Bill 121–122
bubonic plague 103
Butler, Judith 102, 144, 148

C

cadaveric human tissue market 156–157, 158, 163, 165
  see also necro-waste
cadavers see corpses
California, natural organic reduction 35, 109
Campillo, Robert 147
capitalism, work/leisure divisions 145–146
Capsula Mundi burial pods 37–38
carbon cycle, and corpses 36–38
'Carbon Cycle Ceremony', Recompose 36
care practices 6–7, 184–185
  seal conservation 132–134
carrying capacity, seal population, Wadden Sea 131, 132, 134, 139, 140
Catholic church 32, 36, 108
cemeteries
  churchyard cemeteries 103
  as mass burial sites 104–105
  municipal cemeteries 103–104
  potters' fields 100, 102
Chicago heatwave, 1995 106
Christian funerary practices, Ghana 85, 87–88, *88*, 96
churchyard cemeteries 103
Clayden, A. 170
climate change 27, 28, 145
Coeio 174, 175
Collectif les Morts de la Rue, Paris 102–103
collective burial 182
  COVID-19 pandemic 6–7, 100–102, 103, 106–107, 110
  public burial sites 102–103
  traditions of interment of ashes or bones 107–108
  see also mass burial
collective death 5
  as a source of environmental degradation 29, 32
Colorado, natural organic reduction 37, 109
commingling of human remains 5, 28, 31–32
  DeathLAB's research *30*, 30–31
  human and nonhuman 35–38
  Recompose (Urban Death Project/UDP) natural organic reduction system 32–35, *33*, *34*, 36, 37
Connerton, P. 117
Coole, D. 163

corpses 6, 182, 184
  cadaveric human tissue market 156–157, 158, 163, 165
  and the carbon cycle 36–38
  COVID-19 pandemic and 'contagious' bodies, Mexico and Ecuador 6, 71–82
  'dignified treatment' of, and the COVID-19 pandemic in Mexico and Ecuador 73
  images of body storage 105–107
  legal epistemologies of 7, 157–160, 165
  necro-legal entanglements 162–165
  necro-waste 7–8, 157, 158, 160–162, 165–166
  'no property' rule 158, 159
  putrefaction and death disgust, Zimbabwe 115, 119–125
  trafficking of indigenous peoples' and African Americans' remains 156
  Western modernity's perceptions of 75
corruption, and the COVID-19 pandemic 72, 79, 80, 81
Coverley, M. 150
COVID-19 pandemic 2
  biopower of states 75–76
  collective burial 6–7, 100–102, 103, 106–107, 110
  'contagious' bodies treatment, Mexico and Ecuador 6, 71–82
  and large-scale death 27, 31
cremains 107–108
  Mornington Green, Australia 170–171
  potential toxicity of 172–173
cremation 27, 160, 170–171
crime, television as a factor in 146
CT scans see forensic pathology, and postmortem imaging
Cummins, E. 36
Cupriavidus metallidurans 43
  see also microbes, use of in bioremediation

D

Das, V. 81
Davies, D. 172
Davies, M. 158
'death positive' movement 108
death studies 2–3, 4, 8
DeathLAB (Columbia University Graduate School of Architecture, Planning and Preservation) *30*, 30–31
Debarati, P. 45–46
Defoe, Daniel 103
Deleuze, G. 175–176
Derrida, J. 150, 151
Despret, V. 116
diffractive analysis 143–144
'dispotif' of forensic examinations 14, 15
Dixon, K. 170
doctors, and the COVID-19 pandemic 78–79

INDEX

Domingo, Kathleen 36
Doodeward v Spence (1908) 159
Douglas, Mary 74–75
'Dying at the margins: A critical exploration of material-discursive perspectives to death and dying' workshop, Stockholm 1

E

East Asia, communal interment of ashes 108
eaten, human fear of being 35–36
ecological afterlife 7, 8, 169, 183
Ecuador, COVID-19 pandemic and 'contagious' bodies treatment 6, 71–82
El Paso, Mexico 106–107
embalming 160–162
Eng, D.L. 151
Environmental Humanities for a Concerned Europe network 1
environmentally-friendly disposition technologies 27, 28, 29, 38, 168–170, 176–177
  see also alkaline hydrolysis; green burial; 'mushrooms', dead who become; natural organic reduction; 'trees', dead who become
Ethiopia 31
eutrophic conditions in waterbodies *see* nutrient pollution, Baltic Sea
Ewe communities, Ghana *see* Ghana, funeral banners
extinction studies 3

F

Fades, The, television series 147
Fajardo, C. 46–47, 49
Farman, Abou 183
feminist new materialism 4, 8, 162–163, 165–166, 182
Firmicutes 43
  see also microbes, use of in bioremediation
First World War 105
Fisher, M. 150
flame cremation 32
Fontein, J. 115, 117, 122
Forbes, Edward 56
forensic pathology, and postmortem imaging 4–5, 13–15, 23–24, 185
  ethnographic study 15–17, *16*, *17*
  contesting of imagery 22–23
  contradiction between imaging and autopsy 14–15, 21–22
  discordant versions of the body between imaging and autopsy 19–21
  imaging tools as a tool to guide the autopsy 17, *18*, 19
Foucault, M. 132–133
Franco-Prussian War 105
Freedberg, David 93
freeze-drying technology 37

Freud, S. 151
Frost, S. 163
funeral banners, Ghana 6, 83–85, *84*, 96–97, 97, 184–185
  afterlives of 93–95, *95*, *96*
  death and funerary practices 85–86, *86*
  as new ancestral representations 87–88, *88*
  social lives of 91, *92*, 93, *93*
  transformation of bad death 88–91, *89*
fungi *see* 'mushrooms', dead who become

G

Gadamer, H.-G. 38
Galapagos Islands 133
Gamble, C.N. 149
Gell, Alfred 91
geoengineering, Baltic Sea 60
Ghana, funeral banners 6, 83–85, *84*, 96–97, *97*
  afterlives of 93–95, *95*, *96*
  death and funerary practices 85–86, *86*
  as new ancestral representations 87–88, *88*
  social lives of 91, *92*, 93, *93*
  transformation of bad death 88–91, *89*, *92*
Gilbert v Buzzard (1820) 159
Giroux, H. 146
Glitch television series 147
Gobert, Fabrice 146
good death 184
  Ghana 88–91, *89*, 96
Goody, Jack 85
Granjou, Céline 47, 49, 50
grave robbing 156, 158
green burial 27, 35, 36–37, 38, 162, 169
Green Burial Council 36
Green Cremation 37
grief 6, 171
  'continuing bonds' theory 151
  and the COVID-19 pandemic in Mexico and Ecuador 72, 74, 80
  'moving on' from 150–152
  and television 148
Grill, M. 60
Grondelski, J.M. 108
Guattari, F. 175–176
Gupta, P. 121

H

hakatomo 6–7, 108, 110
Hallam, Elizabeth 117, 175
Haraway, Donna 29, 38, 50, 51, 82, 165, 180
Harries, J. 122
Hart Island cemetery, Bronx, New York 31, 101–102
hauntology 144, 150
Hay, J. 145
Haynes Case 158
heavy metal pollution *see* bioremediation, use of microbes in

Helmreich, Stefan 44
Henare, A. 122
Hendrix, Bob 174
Hennigan, W.J. 31
Hird, Myra 50, 162
Hockey, J. 117
Hodgetts, Timothy 134
Hollbraad, M. 122
Holmes, O.W. 105
Huddleston, G. 143
human bodies *see* corpses
human bones, spirit mediums in Zimbabwe 114–115, 125
human composting 6–7, 110, 169
  see also natural organic reduction
human exceptionalism 29, 35, 36, 38, 39
Hunt, Melinda 101
'hydrosocial hybrids' 62

I

ICIJ (International Consortium of Investigative Journalists) 156, 157, 162, 165
immunological gestures, and the COVID-19 pandemic 74–79
impurity, and the COVID-19 pandemic 75
In the Flesh television series 147
indigenous peoples, trafficking of remains of 156
industrial pollution
  Baltic Sea 55, 62
  see also bioremediation, use of microbes in
Infinity Burial Suit 174, 175
institutional violence, and the COVID-19 pandemic 78, 80
International Consortium of Investigative Journalists (ICIJ) 156, 157, 162, 165
Iron Coffin Case (1820) 158, 159

J

Japan, communal burial societies 108

K

Kanyemba, Zimbabwe *see* Zimbabwe
Kazanjian, D. 151
Kelly, Philip 28
Kirkby, V. 151
Klass, D. 151
Klinenberg, Eric 106
Kohn, Tamara 175
Krmpotich, C. 115
KTH Environmental Humanities Laboratory 1
Küchler, S. 95

L

Lacquer, Thomas 38, 103, 171
Lambek, M. 116–117
Lan, D. 125

large-scale death 5, 27–29
  commingling of human remains 28, *30*, 30–40, *33*, *34*
Latin America, and the COVID-19 pandemic 71, 74, 77, 81
Latour, Bruno 28–29, 31, 162
Lee, Jae Rhim 174
Les Revenants television series 7, 143, 144, 145, 146–147, 183–184
  alive/dead dichotomy 7, 147–149, 152
  now-then dichotomy 7, 149–152
Linton, Jamie 62, 64
Living Legacy 170, 171, 173
  see also Mornington Green, Australia
Lofland, L. 181, 185
Loop Living Cocoon 174–175, 176
lungworms, and seals 7, 131–132, 185
  parasitical collaboration 135–138
  Project B 131, 132, 134–140
  science and ethics 138–140

M

Mahendra, Shaily 44–45
malanggan, Papua New Guinea 95
Malley, Patty Ann 33
margins, the 71, 81
Martin, Emily 82
mass burial 6, 31
  in cemeteries 104–105
  see also collective burial
material semiotics 132
Mauss, Marcel 86
May, William 35–36
McGinn, C. 121
McGuiness, S. 160
media images and coverage of mass death/burial 101, 102, 105–107, 110
'medianatures' 146, 152
melancholia 151
mercury 161, 169
Merleau-Ponty, Noémi 47
methylation 43
Mexico, COVID-19 pandemic and 'contagious' bodies treatment 6, 71–82
Meyer, Birgitte 87
microbes, use of in bioremediation 5, 43–46, 51, 181–182
  capitalist exploitation of 50
  forced microbe death in the remediation process 44, 45–46, 48
  microbial death in the experimental stage 46–48
  'remedial microbe', the 44, 48–51
'microbial turn' 5, 44, 48, 51
'microbiocapital' 50
microbiopolitics 5, 49
Millennial generation 109
'molecular politics' 51
more-than-human bodies 181–182

INDEX

morgues, temporary, in the COVID-19 pandemic 102, 106–107, 110
Mornington Green, Australia 170–172, 176
mourning
 'body viewing', Zimbabwe 115–117
 and closure 117
 and the COVID-19 pandemic in Mexico and Ecuador 72, 73, 74, 80, 81–82
 'moving on' from 150–152
MRI scans *see* forensic pathology, and postmortem imaging
municipal cemeteries 103–104
'mushrooms', dead who become 8, 169, 173–174, 175, 176, 183
 Infinity Burial Suit 174, 175
 Loop Living Cocoon 174–175, 176
mycelium
 mycelial afterlives 8, 173–175, 176, 177
 see also 'mushrooms', dead who become

N

Naffine, N. 158
National Oceanic and Atmospheric Association (NOAA) 36
Natural Burials, New Zealand 173
natural organic reduction 27, 28, 35, 36, 38, 110
 Recompose (Urban Death Project/UDP) 32–35, *33*, *34*, 36, 37, 108–109
 see also human composting
'nature-inspired technologies' 45
 see also bioremediation, use of microbes in
necro-waste 7–8, 157, 158, 160–162
 see also cadaveric human tissue market
neoliberalism 146
Netherlands, seal conservation *see* seals, and lungworms
Neumann, Erich 35–36
New York City
 collective burial and the COVID-19 pandemic 100–101
 DeathLAB's research *30*, 30–31
New York, natural organic reduction 109
Nickman, S.L. 151
NOAA (National Oceanic and Atmospheric Association) 36
now-then dichotomy, *Les Revenants* television series 7, 149–152
nutrient pollution, Baltic Sea 57–60, *58*, *59*

O

obituary posters, Ghana 84, *86*
Ocean Health Index 54
Old Jewish Cemetery, Prague 103
oligotrophic conditions in waterbodies *see* nutrient pollution, Baltic Sea
Olson, Philip 161, 162, 164
Oostvaardersplassen 134

organ transplantation 157, 160, 161, 182
Östersjöcentrum 55

P

Palm Island, Australia 107
Papua New Guinea 95
Parikka, J. 146
Paris, public burials 102
Parker, John 85
paupers' graves 102–103
Paxson, Heather 44, 48–49
Peki, Ghana *see* Ghana, funeral banners
Penfold-Mounce, R. 146, 147
Perry, Luke 174
Phillips, Catherine 47, 49, 50
plague pits 103
planned obsolescence 145
Plumwood, Val 35
PMCT (postmortem computed tomography) *see* forensic pathology, and postmortem imaging
Poole, D. 81
Posel, D. 121
postmortem magnetic resonance imaging *see* forensic pathology, and postmortem imaging
postmortems *see* forensic pathology
potters' field burials 100, 102
pragmatism 14, 24n2
private healthcare, and the COVID-19 pandemic 80
Promessa 37
Pseudomonas aeruginosa 43
 see also microbes, use of in bioremediation
Pseudomonas maltophilia 43
 see also microbes, use of in bioremediation
public healthcare, and the COVID-19 pandemic 80
public policy, and deathcare practices 39
putrefaction and death disgust, Zimbabwe 115, 119–125

Q

queer death studies 3
queer studies 4
Qum, Iran 106

R

R v Kelly and Lindsay (1998) 159
R v Stewart (1840) 158–159
Recompose (Urban Death Project/UDP)
 natural organic reduction system 32–35, *33*, *34*, 36, 37, 108–109
refrigerated trucks, and the COVID-19 pandemic 102, 107, 110
relational death 180–181
Resurrection television series 147
Return Home 109–110
Robben, A.C.G.M. 117

Rocha, S.D. 143
Ross, R. 108
Rowe, M.M. 108
RTI Surgical 157
Rumble, H. 172

S

salinity, of the Baltic Sea 56–57
scale 28–29
science and technology studies 163
Scientific Advisory Committee, Netherlands 134–135
Scranton, Roy 27–28
seals, and lungworms 7, 131–132, 185
  parasitical collaboration 135–138
  Project B 131, 132, 134–140
  science and ethics 138–140
Shaw, K. 150
Sherman, David 75
Silverman, P.R. 151
soil pollution *see* bioremediation, use of microbes in
Spade, Katrina 32, 33–34, 108, 109
Spanish flu, 1918–1920 103
Sphingomonas 43
  see also microbes, use of in bioremediation
Spieth, Joseph 88, 90
spirit mediums, funerary practices in Zimbabwe 6, 7, 114–115, 117–125, 184
squirrels 133, 134
St. James's Burial Ground, London 104
Steinmetz, George 100
Strang, Veronica 62
Stroud, Ellen 121, 160
Suzuki, Hikaru 177
Sweden, public burials 102
Switzerland, forensic pathology *see* forensic pathology, and postmortem imaging

T

television, and death 7, 143–146
  see also Les Revenants television series
'temporal loop' trope 149–150
'then/now' dichotomy, *Les Revenants* television series 7, 149–152
'Thing theory' 121–122
Torres Strait Islanders 107
traditional funerary practices, Ghana 85, 87–88, *88*, 96
transhumanism 183

'trees', dead who become 8, 169–170, 175–176, 183
  Capsula Mundi burial pods 37–38, 168–169, 170
  Mornington Green, Australia 170–172, 176
trench burial 103–104, 110
  COVID-19 pandemic 102
  Hart Island, New York 101
  Qum, Iran 106
Tsing, Anna 133–134

U

Ukraine 31, 156
uncanny return trope 149–150
United States EPA (Environmental Protection Agency) 45

V

von Bujdoss, Justin 31

W

Walter, Tony 27, 28, 176–177
Wang, B. 176
war, media coverage and imagery of dead bodies 105
Washington state, natural organic reduction 34–35, 109
waste management, large-scale death as 29
Wastell, S. 122
waterbodies
  discourses of 'death of' 54–55
  environmental imaginaries of 61–63
  see also Baltic Sea, 'dead' or 'dying' imaginaries of
Wheatley, H. 146
work/leisure divisions 145–146

Y

Yarborough, Morgan 36
Yehuda, Ben 73

Z

Zillén, L. 56
Zimbabwe
  death disgust 115, 119–125
  funerary practices for spirit mediums 6, 7, 114–115, 117–125
  mourning practices and body viewing 115–117